The Morality Wars

The Morality Wars

The Ongoing Debate Over the Origin of Human Goodness

Edited by
Louise Mabille
Henk Stoker

LEXINGTON BOOKS/FORTRESS ACADEMIC
Lanham • Boulder • New York • London

Published by Lexington Books/Fortress Academic
Lexington Books is an imprint of The Rowman & Littlefield Publishing Group, Inc.
4501 Forbes Boulevard, Suite 200, Lanham, Maryland 20706
www.rowman.com

6 Tinworth Street, London SE11 5AL, United Kingdom

Copyright © 2021 by The Rowman & Littlefield Publishing Group, Inc.

All rights reserved. No part of this book may be reproduced in any form or by any electronic or mechanical means, including information storage and retrieval systems, without written permission from the publisher, except by a reviewer who may quote passages in a review.

British Library Cataloguing in Publication Information Available

Library of Congress Cataloging-in-Publication Data

Names: Mabille, Louise, editor. | Stoker, Henk, 1960- editor.
Title: The morality wars : the ongoing debate over the origin of human goodness / edited by Louise Mabille and Henk Stoker.
Description: Lanham : Lexington Books/Fortress Academic, [2021] | Includes bibliographical references and index. | Summary: "In this book, contributors who are atheists, believers, and anything in between debate the origins and nature of morality and the human impulse for good"— Provided by publisher.
Identifiers: LCCN 2021011769 (print) | LCCN 2021011770 (ebook) | ISBN 9781978710863 (cloth) | ISBN 9781978710870 (epub) | ISBN 9781978710887 (pbk)
Subjects: LCSH: Ethics.
Classification: LCC BJ21 .M5955 2021 (print) | LCC BJ21 (ebook) | DDC 170—dc23
LC record available at https://lccn.loc.gov/2021011769
LC ebook record available at https://lccn.loc.gov/2021011770

Contents

The Morality Wars: A Discussion on Why We Are Good   1
Louise Mabille

Part I: The Naturalists   7

1. A Science of Good and Evil   9
   Sam Harris
2. The Origins of Morality in the Human Psyche   17
   Bert Olivier
3. Morality as Delusion   33
   Michael Ruse
4. Return to the Enlightenment   55
   Susan Neiman

Part II: The Ambivalents   71

5. No Science of Morality   73
   Steven Weinberg
6. Misunderstanding Moral Psychology   77
   Jonathan Haidt
7. The Use and Abuse of Naturalism for Morality   91
   Louise Mabille

Part III: The Theists   111

8. My God-Given Conscience   113
   Henk Stoker

9 Theism as Meta-Ethical Foundation for Morality *William Lane Craig*	133
10 Morality as Based on Natural Law *Richard Howe*	147
11 Ethics Needs God *Paul Copan*	163
12 Biologizing Ethics and the Destruction of Morality *John Lennox*	177
Index	195
About the Editors and Contributors	199

The Morality Wars

A Discussion on Why We Are Good

Louise Mabille

For perhaps the first time in history, it appears easier to be moral than to say what morality is. The good life, it seems, is rather like Samuel Johnson's description of poetry: "We all know what it is, but it is surprisingly difficult to *say* what it is."[1] This is why we have decided to have a conversation on the meaning and origin of moral goodness. While the age-old conflict between the Christian faith and its scientific offspring often finds itself on the debating stage—our contributors Sam Harris, Michael Ruse, William Lane Craig, Richard Howe, Paul Copan, and John Lennox are well-known debaters—many aspects of morality fall by the wayside in public exchanges about science and religion that are formulated for nonacademic audiences. There are also important aspects that seldom get an airing and important, underacknowledged differences even between those who in principle share the category of "atheist" or "believer." What is more, although the debate between faith and evolution is more important than ever, exchanges on the topic should also include thinkers who attack the very terms according to which the debate is being conducted, such as Darwin's fellow hermeneuticians of suspicion, Nietzsche, Marx, and Freud. In this volume, you will discover that for all its apparent simplicity, the question of morality is far from as clear as we would like to pretend. In fact, to adopt Andrew Brown's famous phrase, used to describe the battle between the followers of Dawkins and Gould over the essence of Darwinism, nothing short of a cultural war has raged over the past few decades over the origins and nature of what we call the good life.

In order to make things clearer, we have decided to divide the book into three sections. First, we hear from the naturalists, atheists who hold that morality can be accounted for through a purely materialistic framework, usually by means of evolutionary theory. The contributors in this section are firmly opposed to any kind of theistic solution. But not everybody sees things in such stark terms: there are scientists as well as philosophers who are uneasy about the route intellectuals like the New Atheists have taken, even if some of them are atheists themselves. The thinkers in the next section therefore include theists as well as atheists, and their contributions show that the conversation about morality also needs to include factors that go beyond the debate on God's existence alone. Finally, there are the theists themselves. The thinkers in the third section are firm and sincere believers in God, who have all spent significant time on the question of the origin of morality. All of them have thoroughly engaged the atheist position, yet each makes their case from a different perspective, ranging from phenomenological reflection on the human conscience to the implications of the notion of having an objective or shared morality to Thomistic natural law and the consequences of biologizing the question of morality.

At first, the notion of a war over morality appears to be completely unnecessary, if not self-contradictory. Even if one can no longer wholeheartedly agree with Francis Fukuyama's original eschatological optimism that the end of the Cold War signified the dawn of a new era and the arrival of the happy humanist paradise that history has promised all along, one aspect of his original idea still widely accepted is the steady decrease in tolerance for all forms of violence and suffering. We can still easily share Fukuyama's amazement at Mme. de Sevigne's nonchalant description in 1675 of an old Parisian fiddler broken and quartered, "with his four limbs exposed at the four corners of the city,"[2] for stealing some paper. Today, capital punishment has almost disappeared entirely in the West, and there is a growing skepticism toward punishment in general. Wars, although still being fought, must be sold carefully to an increasingly cynical citizenry (or hidden from them), and significant sections of the public sphere show an unprecedented intolerance of anything that smacks of cruelty, harshness, or discrimination.

For many, this is the good news for which we have been waiting. Not only is the moral law easy to define, it is equally easy to follow. Schopenhauer certainly thought so. Here is Nietzsche on his teacher's great insight:

> Let us listen to the almost admirable innocence with which even Schopenhauer describes his own project, and then we can draw our conclusions as to how scientific a "science" could be when its ultimate masters are still talking like children or old women. "The principle," he says, "the fundamental claim, on whose content all ethicists actually agree: harm no one, but rather help everyone as much as you can—this is actually the claim that all moralists attempt to ground ... the actual foundation of ethics that people have sought for millennia, just as they have looked for the philosophers' stone."[3]

Schopenhauer's notion today forms the backbone of the moral claims made by several prominent latter-day atheists, albeit reformulated in the vocabulary of evolutionary biology, neuroscience, and philosophy of consciousness. Our first contributor, Sam Harris, certainly claims to have found the philosophers' stone when it comes to the moral good. What is more, this indubitable certitude about the good life appears to be fully supported by the natural sciences. Harris invites a comparison with Dorothy from *The Wizard of Oz*: we have had what we need to be good all along—it is only the irrational attachment to religious sentiments that holds humanity back from achieving the good life. Yet, as the respective responses of fellow atheists Michael Ruse, Steven Weinberg, and Jonathan Haidt show, things are not that simple: we have only just begun our conversation.

We have said that it is time to bring in the forgotten thinkers. Freud is of course far from forgotten: psychoanalysis continues to thrive and, after Jacques Lacan's reinterpretation in terms of semiology, has experienced a new lease on life and made its presence felt in literature departments as well. The path toward skepticism does not automatically lead from or through scientific naturalism: today one may be even more likely to find committed atheists in the humanities than in natural science faculties. Bert Olivier shows that the ideal of moral autonomy is the result of a complex psychological process, ranging from classic Freudian repression and the demands of the superego to the mediation of desire through language. Olivier articulates the Enlightenment ideal of achieving rational autonomy without reference to any form of deity. Ultimately, it is possible to view this psychoanalytical account as an extension of the naturalistic account given by the Darwinists: where conversations on morality are concerned, Freud may be described as Darwin 2.0.

Michael Ruse, too, believes that Darwin has forever changed the way morality is practiced. However, he is also quite well-versed in the major ethical theories of the rest of the philosophical canon (unusual for a philosopher of science who specializes in evolutionary biology: he pioneered the use of the concept of orthogenesis—the notion that evolution has a mechanism of its own that carries organisms along certain tracks) and relates Darwin to the Judeo-Christian moral tradition; Socrates, Kant, and Hume; and that old favorite the is-ought problem, which you will also find in John Lennox's defense of the sanctity of life. Importantly, he gives us a thoughtful, if perhaps slightly startling account of the role of evolution in the development of moral consensus without turning the question into a blatant confrontation with religion.

Susan Neiman, author of *Evil in Modern Thought*,[4] gives us a thorough overview of the emergence of the Enlightenment as a moral ideal and why the Enlightenment project is worth reconsidering. Coming from a Jewish background, she nevertheless eschews a theological foundation for morality.

In her view, in an increasingly globalist situation, we have no choice but to try to recover the original Enlightenment metanarrative. As a result, she defends a version of rational moral autonomy similar to Olivier's but using more of Kant's original vocabulary instead of psychoanalysis.

Thus far, we have fairly straightforward naturalistic accounts of the origins of morality, and the minds that have given us these accounts number among the best in their respective fields. But now we come to the troublemakers. You may have wondered, after the down-to-earth explanations we have been given thus far, why we need to have the conversation at all? If the facts supplied thus far are so easily verifiable and what they imply so incontestable, why are there such enormous differences in opinion between groups—and even on the individual level—about what constitutes the good life? Sure, there are enormous areas of overlap, but having those does not provide us with solid, indubitable foundations. At best we have what Kant in his third critique called the *sensus communis*, or "the universal assent or agreement of others to an individual's judgments of taste,"[5] or something along the lines of Jürgen Habermas's ethics of communication. But as anybody who has ever been part of a family feud will be able to tell you, bridging communication gaps is easier said than done. Some of our participants who hold opposing viewpoints, such as Harris and Craig, and Howe and Ruse, have debated each other, but the most stimulating differences can sometimes occur between thinkers who share similar views. Thus we have the Nobel Prize–winning scientist Steven Weinberg, who, although sharing the same naturalistic outlook as Harris, differs radically in his approach to science and the ethical domain. For one, he casts doubt upon the ease with which science can negotiate morality. Although he shares Harris's aversion to misogyny, particularly Sharia law, he draws on a number of different sources, such as Hume, to reach his conclusion. And, breaking the Darwinist trend to refer to T. E. Huxley, he draws on Aldous Huxley instead.

Jonathan Haidt, author of, among others, *The Happiness Hypothesis*,[6] takes a position similar to Weinberg's. He shows that the conversation between science and religion as it has hitherto been conducted exhibits some serious flaws. It is precisely Haidt who is in fact loyal to the implications of Darwinism: he is fully aware that the presence of religious faith is one of the most constant and persistent factors in the development of human society, and that it is deeply intertwined with who we are, not something alien and parasitical to an originary rational nature.

Drawing on Nietzsche's genealogical method, Louise Mabille demonstrates that science and faith are far from the polar opposites popularly supposed, and that the soteriological motif—the notion that we have been alienated from an original paradise through the introduction of an alien pollutant—is to be found throughout New Atheist literature. This raises the question whether it is even possible to have a purely atheistic grounding for morality and whether God is not, in the end, unavoidable.

In the third section, Henk Stoker introduces the theists. Following a phenomenological approach, he grounds morality in a form of intuitive authority; that is, along with Descartes, Locke, and to some extent Kant, he views morality as innate. For him, the "moral instinct" is more than just "natural" or even historical. It points toward a definite divine origin and links the bearers of this instinct with its Creator.

William Lane Craig's position, ironically, is in a sense not that distant from Neiman's. Although he is well known for his defense of the Christian faith, he may also be described as a humanist: a Christian humanist who holds that classic humanist values such as universal human dignity and the freedom of the individual are compatible with essential Christian teachings. Like Neiman, Craig is a realist, believing it possible for humans to use reason in order to arrive at an independent and objective truth. For Craig, the correct application of reason leads to belief in objective moral values and, by implication, God.

There are several ways to ground morality in God, but most of them tend to fall either under divine command theories, according to which morality is ultimately the direct result of suprahuman involvement, or natural law (*ius naturale*, *lex naturalis*), which holds that certain rights are inherent, by virtue of human nature endowed by God, or at any rate a transcendent source, and can be understood universally through human reason. Divine command theories tend to be more theoretical and abstract, and they tend to be traceable to Platonic idealism. Natural law theories tend to be Aristotelian and slightly more worldly (not materialistic!) in nature. They are usually a natural fit with virtue ethics and appear to be popular with Catholic ethicists (Thomas of Aquinas is the theory's most important post-Aristotelian representative). Here, however, natural law theory is represented by Richard Howe, a well-respected Reformed thinker.

Paul Copan challenges the idea that atheism should be the default position. Instead, he shows that theism is the much more reasonable foundation for dignity that we as modern people ascribe to the value of each individual life.

The question of morality is not only an academic exercise but concerns the value of human life itself. We conclude this venture into the morality wars with John Lennox, who shows us the dangers of veering into bioethics and attempting to defend the value of life on the basis of a utilitarian logic alone.

It seems as if the morality wars are far from over. But here at least is one civilized conversation. By going through these essays, you will encounter old arguments and new ones, arguments you have heard before, and ideas reformulated in a radically new way.

Wherever you stand in the morality wars, you are likely to agree at least with Socrates that it is examining life that makes it worth living. Here is an excellent opportunity to join the age-old conversation on the good life. Consider the variety of viewpoints, and decide for yourself what goodness really is. In a world where honest discussion is increasingly replaced by the contrived moralism of political correctness and postcapitalist convenience, it is a privilege that should never be taken for granted.

NOTES

1. James Boswell, *The Life of Samuel Johnson* (Frankfurt am Main, Germany: Outlook Verlag, 2019), 508.
2. Francis Fukuyama, *The End of History and the Last Man* (New York: The Free Press, 1992), 261. The original citation occurs in Alexis de Tocqueville's *Democracy in America*, 2 vols. (New York: Vintage Books, 1945), II:174–175.
3. Friedrich Nietzsche, *Beyond Good and Evil*, edited by Rolf-Peter Hostman and Judith Norman, translated by Judith Norman (Cambridge: Cambridge University Press, 2002), 76. Also see Arthur Schopenhauer, *The Two Fundamental Problems of Ethics*, edited by Christopher Janaway (Cambridge: Cambridge University Press, 2009), xiii.
4. Susan Neiman, *Evil in Modern Thought: An Alternative History of Philosophy* (Princeton, N.J.: Princeton University Press, 2002).
5. Immanuel Kant, *The Critique of Judgment*, translated, with an introduction by Werner S. Pluhar and foreword by Mary J. Gregor (Indianapolis: Hackett Publishing Company, 1987), 159, § 40. For Jürgen Habermas's notion on communicative ethics, see, among others, his *Theory of Communicative Action, Volume One: Reason and the Rationalization of Society* translated by Thomas A. McCarthy (Boston, Mass.: Beacon Press, 1981).
6. Jonathan Haidt, *The Happiness Hypothesis: Finding Modern Truth in Ancient Wisdom* (New York: Basic Books, 2006).

REFERENCES

Boswell, James. *The Life of Samuel Johnson*. Frankfurt am Main, Germany: Outlook Verlag, 2019.
Fukuyama, Francis. *The End of History and the Last Man*. New York: The Free Press, 1992.
Habermas, Jürgen. *Theory of Communicative Action, Volume One: Reason and the Rationalization of Society*. Translated by Thomas A. McCarthy. Boston, Mass.: Beacon Press, 1981.
Haidt, Jonathan. *The Happiness Hypothesis: Finding Modern Truth in Ancient Wisdom*. New York: Basic Books, 2006.
Kant, Immanuel. *The Critique of Judgment*. Translated, with an introduction by Werner S. Pluhar and foreword by Mary J. Gregor. Indianapolis: Hackett Publishing Company, 1987.
Neiman, Susan. *Evil in Modern Thought: An Alternative History of Philosophy*. Princeton, N.J.: Princeton University Press, 2002.
Nietzsche, Friedrich. *Beyond Good and Evil*. Edited by Rolf-Peter Hostman and Judith Norman. Translated by Judith Norman. Cambridge: Cambridge University Press, 2002.
Schopenhauer, Arthur. *The Two Fundamental Problems of Ethics*. Edited by Christopher Janaway. Cambridge: Cambridge University Press, 2009.

Part I

The Naturalists

Chapter One

A Science of Good and Evil

Sam Harris

We begin our conversation with a figure well known from international bestseller lists, the author and activist Sam Harris. As one of the "Four Horsemen" of the modern atheist movement—the group that also includes Richard Dawkins, Daniel Dennett, and the late Christopher Hitchens—Sam Harris is known for, among others, The End of Faith *(2004) and* The Moral Landscape *(2011). The argument presented here may be regarded as a condensed version of the latter. To a significant extent, Harris presents his account of morality as commonsensical: at first blush, to define the good life as the "well-being of conscious creatures" seems completely reasonable. It is therefore perhaps not entirely surprising to detect a hint of impatience in Harris's text.*

However, Harris's explanation of morality is ultimately a version of utilitarianism, and it is no accident that his most basic delineation of morality matches the Wikipedia definition of utilitarianism almost verbatim: "Utilitarianism is an ethical theory that states that the best action is the one that maximizes utility. 'Utility' can be defined in various ways, usually in terms of the well-being of sentient entities." Although it is possible to find utilitarian traces in almost every thinker in the history of philosophy, it was only formally used as a foundation for ethics in the works of Jeremy Bentham (1747–1832) and John Stuart Mill (1806–1873). Bentham, a social reformer as well as moral philosopher, is best known for his axiom that "it is the greatest happiness of the greatest number that is the measure of right and wrong." Since then, utilitarianism has been reformulated in a more sophisticated fashion, distinguishing, for example, between act utilitarianism and rule-based versions. At the heart of utilitarian theories lies the problem of pain and pleasure. Bentham writes:

> *Nature has placed mankind under the governance of two sovereign masters, pain and pleasure. It is for them alone to point out what we ought to do, as well as to determine what we shall do. On the one hand—the standard of right and wrong, on the other the chain of causes and effects, are fastened to their throne. They govern us in all we do, in all we say, in all we think: every effort we can make to throw off our subjection—will serve but to demonstrate and confirm it. In words a man may pretend to abjure their empire: but in reality, he will remain subject to it all the while.*[1]

Mill also wrote on scientific methodology and how it pertained to matters of truth and reason. Taking it a bit further, Harris believes that science should not only be involved in how we determine the origins of morality, but that questions of good and evil (closely associated with pain and pleasure) are ultimately questions of brain states. As such, science can tell us what happiness is, why it matters, and how to achieve it.

—The Editors

The people of Albania have a venerable tradition of vendetta called "Kanun": if a man commits a murder, his victim's family can kill any one of his male relatives in reprisal. If a boy has the misfortune of being the son or brother of a murderer, he must spend his days and nights in hiding, forgoing a proper education, adequate health care, and the pleasures of a normal life. Untold numbers of Albanian men and boys live as prisoners of their homes even now. Can we say that the Albanians are morally wrong to have structured their society in this way? Is their tradition of blood feud a form of evil? Are their values inferior to our own?

Most people imagine that science cannot pose, much less answer, questions of this sort. How could we ever say, as a matter of scientific fact, that one way of life is better, or more moral, than another? Whose definition of "better" or "moral" would we use? Scientists generally believe that answers to questions of human value will fall perpetually beyond our reach—not because human subjectivity is too difficult to study, or the brain too complex, but because there is no intellectual justification for speaking about right and wrong, or good and evil, in universal terms. While many scientists now study the evolution of morality, as well as its underlying neurobiology, the purpose of their research is merely to describe how human beings think and behave. No one expects science to tell us how we should think and behave. Controversies about human values are controversies about which science officially has no opinion.

This has made science appear divorced, in principle, from the most important questions of human life. While most educated people will concede that the scientific method has delivered centuries of fresh embarrassment to religion on matters of fact, it is now an article of almost unquestioned certainty, both inside and outside scientific circles, that science has nothing to say about what constitutes a good life. Religious thinkers in all faiths, and on both ends of the political spectrum, are united on precisely this point: the defense one most often hears for belief in God is not that there is compelling evidence for His existence, but that faith in Him is the only reliable source of meaning and moral guidance. Mutually incompatible religious traditions now take refuge behind the same non sequitur.

As I argue in *The Moral Landscape*, questions about values—about meaning, morality, and life's larger purpose—are really questions about the well-being of conscious creatures. Given that the experience of conscious creatures is the product of natural laws, meaning, morality, and human values must translate into facts that can be scientifically understood. And if there are important cultural differences in how people flourish—if, for instance, there are incompatible but equivalent ways to raise happy, intelligent, and creative children—these differences are also facts that must depend upon the organization of the human brain. In principle, therefore, we can account for the ways in which culture defines us within the context of neuroscience and psychology. The more we understand ourselves at the level of the brain, the more we will see that there are right and wrong answers to questions of human values.

I once spoke at an academic conference on these themes, arguing that when we have a more complete understanding of human well-being, ranging from its underlying neurophysiology to the political systems and economic policies that best safeguard it, we will be able to make strong claims about which cultural practices are good for humanity and which aren't. I then made what I thought would be a quite incontestable assertion: we already have good reason to believe that certain cultures are less suited to maximizing well-being than others. I cited the ruthless misogyny and religious bamboozlement of the Taliban as an example of a worldview that seems less than perfectly conducive to human flourishing.

As it turns out, to denigrate the Taliban at a scientific meeting is to court controversy. At the conclusion of my talk, I fell into debate with another invited speaker, who seemed, at first glance, to be very well positioned to reason effectively about the implications of science for our understanding of morality. In fact, she has since been appointed to the President's Commission for the Study of Bioethical Issues and is now one of only thirteen people who "advise the President on bioethical issues arising from advances in biomedicine and related areas of science and technology."[2] Here is a snippet of our conversation, recalled from memory:

> She: What makes you think that science will ever be able to say that forcing women to wear burqas is wrong?

Me: Because I think that right and wrong are a matter of increasing or decreasing well-being—and it is obvious that forcing half the population to live in cloth bags, and beating or killing them if they refuse, is not a good strategy for maximizing human well-being.

She: But that's only your opinion.

Me: Okay . . . let's make it even simpler. What if we found a culture that ritually blinded every third child by literally plucking out his or her eyes at birth? Would you then agree that we had found a culture that was needlessly diminishing human well-being?

She: It would depend on why they were doing it.

Me [slowly returning my eyebrows from the back of my head]: Let's say they were doing it on the basis of religious superstition. In their scripture, God says, "Every third must walk in darkness."

Such opinions are not uncommon in the Ivory Tower. I was talking to a woman (it's hard not to feel that her gender makes her views all the more disconcerting) who had just delivered an entirely lucid lecture on the moral implications of advances in neuroscience. She was concerned that our intelligence services might one day use neuroimaging technology for the purposes of lie detection, which she considered a likely violation of cognitive liberty. She was especially exercised over rumors that our government might have exposed captured terrorists to aerosols containing the hormone oxytocin in an effort to make them more cooperative. Though she did not say it, I suspect that she would even have opposed subjecting these prisoners to the smell of freshly baked bread, which has been shown to have a similar effect. While listening to her talk, as yet unaware of her liberal views on compulsory veiling and ritual enucleation, I thought her slightly overcautious but a basically sane and eloquent authority on the premature use of neuroscience in our courts. I confess that once we did speak, and I peered into the terrible gulf that separated us on these issues, I found that I could not utter another word to her. In fact, our conversation ended with my blindly enacting two neurological clichés: my jaw quite literally dropped open, and I spun on my heels before walking away.

As someone who often speaks about morality in a scientific context, I regularly encounter highly educated, secular, and otherwise well-intentioned people who pause thoughtfully, and sometimes interminably, before condemning practices like compulsory veiling, genital excision, bride burning, forced marriage, and the other cheerful products of alternative "morality" found elsewhere in the world. While much of the debate about the relationship between human values and human knowledge must be had in academic terms, I hope it is clear that this is not merely an academic debate. There are girls getting their faces burned off with acid at this moment for daring to learn to read, for not consenting to marry men they have never met, or even for the "crime" of getting raped. The amazing thing is that many Western intellectuals do not realize what abject failures of compassion are enabled by their "tolerance" for, and "contextual understanding" of, moral difference.

If we were to discover a new tribe in the Amazon tomorrow, there is not a scientist alive who would assume a priori that these people must enjoy optimal physical health and material prosperity. Rather, we would ask questions about this tribe's average life span, daily calorie intake, the percentage of women dying in childbirth, the prevalence of infectious disease, the presence of material culture, and so forth. Such questions would have answers, and they would likely reveal that life in the Stone Age entails a few compromises. And yet news that these jolly people enjoy sacrificing their firstborn children to imaginary gods would prompt many (even most) anthropologists to say that this tribe was in possession of an alternate moral code, every bit as valid and impervious to refutation as our own. However, the moment one draws the link between morality and well-being, one sees that this is tantamount to saying that the members of this tribe must be as fulfilled, psychologically and socially, as any people in human history. The disparity between how we think about physical health and mental/societal health reveals a bizarre double standard: one that is predicated on our not knowing—or, rather, on our pretending not to know—anything at all about human well-being.

Imagine that there are only two people living on earth: we can call them "Adam" and "Eve." Clearly, we can ask how these two people might maximize their well-being. Are there wrong answers to this question? Of course. (Wrong answer #1: they could smash each other in the face with a large rock.) And while there are ways for their personal interests to be in conflict, it seems uncontroversial to say that a man and woman alone on this planet would be better off if they recognized their common interests—like getting food, building shelter, and defending themselves against larger predators. If Adam and Eve were industrious enough, they might realize the benefits of creating technology, art, medicine; exploring the world; and begetting future generations of humanity. Are there good and bad paths to take across this landscape of possibilities? Of course. In fact, there are, by definition, paths that lead to the worst misery and to the greatest fulfillment possible for these two people—given the structure of their brains, the immediate facts of their environment, and the laws of Nature. The underlying facts here are the facts of physics, chemistry, and biology as they bear on the experience of the only two people in existence.

Even if there are a thousand different ways for these two people to thrive, there will be many ways for them not to thrive—and the differences between luxuriating on a peak of human happiness and languishing in a valley of internecine horror will translate into facts that can be scientifically understood. Why would the difference between right and wrong answers suddenly disappear once we add 7.8 billion more people to this experiment?

Granted, genuine ethical difficulties arise when we ask questions like, "How much should I care about other people's children? How much should I be willing to sacrifice, or demand that my own children sacrifice, in order to help other people in need?" We are not, by nature, impartial—and much of our moral reasoning must be applied to situations in which there is tension between our concern for ourselves, or for those closest to us, and our sense that it would be better to be more committed to helping others. And yet "better" must still refer, in this context, to positive changes in the experience of sentient creatures.

And yet many smart people will still insist that we cannot speak about moral truth, or anchor morality to a deeper concern for well-being, because concepts like "morality" and "well-being" must be defined with reference to specific goals and other criteria—and nothing prevents people from disagreeing about these definitions. And here we glimpse another double standard rigging the game against any universal conception of morality: Most people take scientific consensus to mean that scientific truths exist, and they consider controversy among scientists to be merely a sign that science is a work-in-progress and that further insights await us. But many of these same people believe that moral controversy proves that there can be no such thing as moral truth, while moral consensus shows only that human beings often harbor the same biases (like not wanting to live in continuous, excruciating pain). This makes absolutely no sense. And truth is deeper than consensus, in any case. It has been 150 years, and we still cannot convince the majority of Americans that human beings evolved from nonhuman ancestors. Does this suggest that there may be no such thing as biological truth?

Many people worry that there is something unscientific about making value judgments. But this split between facts and values is an illusion. Science has always been in the values business. Good science is not the result of scientists abstaining from making value judgments; good science is the result of scientists making their best effort to value principles of reasoning that link their beliefs to reality, through reliable chains of evidence and argument. The very idea of "objective" knowledge (that is, knowledge acquired through careful observation and honest reasoning) has values built into it, as every effort we make to discuss facts depends upon principles that we must first value (e.g., logical consistency, reliance on evidence, parsimony, etc.). This is how norms of rational thought are made effective. As far as our understanding of the world is concerned, there are no facts without values.

Just as there is nothing irrational about valuing human health and seeking to understand it (this is the science of medicine), there is nothing irrational about valuing human well-being more generally and seeking to understand it.

There is no problem in presupposing that the worst possible misery for everyone is bad and worth avoiding or that normative morality consists, at an absolute minimum, in acting so as to avoid it. To say that the worst possible misery for everyone is "bad" is, on my account, like saying that an argument that contradicts itself is "illogical." And anyone who would ask, "But is the worst possible misery for everyone actually bad?" has hit philosophical bedrock, with the shovel of a stupid question.

The skeptical demand for radical justification—Why value well-being? Why value health? Why value evidence? Why value logic?—can be directed at any branch of science, or to reason generally. Certain "oughts" are built right into the foundations of human thought. We need not apologize for pulling ourselves up by our bootstraps in this way. It is far better than pulling ourselves down by them.

A science of morality, predicated on the value of well-being, would be on no weaker footing than physics, chemistry, medicine, or any other branch of science that must rely on similar, axiomatic assumptions. By analogy to the rest of science, I have argued that the value of avoiding the worst possible misery for everyone can be presupposed; and upon this axiom, we can build a science of morality that can then determine myriad other human values. How much should humanity in the twenty-first century value compassion, for instance? And how should this value be balanced against other competing priorities, like bureaucratic efficiency? These are hard questions, but a completed science of human flourishing would tell us exactly how and to what degree compassion conduces to the well-being of individuals and societies.

Will we ever have a completed science of human flourishing? Probably not. But whether morality becomes a proper branch of science is not really the point. Is economics a true science yet? Judging from the past few years, it wouldn't seem so. And perhaps a deep understanding of economics will always elude us. But does anyone doubt that there are better and worse ways to structure an economy? Would any educated person consider it a form of bigotry to criticize another society's response to a banking crisis? Imagine how terrifying it would be if great numbers of smart people became convinced that all efforts to prevent a global financial catastrophe must be either equally valid or equally nonsensical in principle. And yet this is precisely where most intellectuals stand on the most important questions in human life.

If our well-being depends upon the interaction between events in our brains and events in the world, as it surely does, then there will be better and worse ways to secure it. Some cultures will tend to produce lives that are more worth living than others; some political persuasions will be more enlightened than others; and some worldviews will be mistaken in ways that cause needless human misery. Whether or not we ever understand meaning, morality, and values in practice, I am arguing that there must be something to know about them in principle. And I am convinced that merely admitting this will change the way we think about the frontiers of science and about the role of science in society. It will also transform the way we think about human happiness and the public good.

The question of how human beings should live in the twenty-first century has many competing answers—and most of them are surely wrong. Only a rational understanding of human well-being will allow billions of us to coexist peacefully, converging on the same social, political, economic, and environmental goals. A science of human flourishing may seem a long way off, but to achieve it, we must first acknowledge that the intellectual terrain actually exists.

NOTE

1. Jeremy Bentham, *Introduction to the Principles of Morals and Legislation* (Oxford: W. Pickering, 1823), 1.
2. https://bioethicsarchive.georgetown.edu/pcsbi/about.html.

REFERENCES

Harris, S. *Letter To A Christian Nation*. New York: Transworld, 2011.
———. *The Moral Landscape*. New York: Transworld, 2011.

Chapter Two

The Origins of Morality in the Human Psyche

Bert Olivier

Keeping our promise to place our Darwinians in conversation with the fellow skeptics they seldom engage, here we have Bert Olivier arguing that morality can be described in purely naturalistic terms. Like Sam Harris, he believes that our sense of the good is the result of a complex natural process. But whereas many skeptics look outward, he goes inward. For them, knowledge about the good—to some extent knowledge as such—is a question of empirical observation, the stuff of hard science.

For Olivier, it is more a question of inner reflection. Much of the material reflected on can be derived from empirical information, but the conclusions are often reached on the psychologist's couch. He sees morality as the result of a complex psychological struggle, beginning with Freud's classic notion of repression. According to Freud, the demands of the superego—a representation of society, or the group—lead to the repression of the id (the disorganized collective of instincts that is present from birth and reacts according to the pleasure principle). The ego is formed through the mediation between the demands of the superego and the needs of the id. Classic Freudian theory sees morality as forming through the violent act of originary repression of the (biological) drives through which the autonomous ego emerges. It is a very famous theory, made part of our common consciousness through a wide variety of narratives, ranging from popular psychology to crime fiction.

However, psychoanalysis has moved on since the days of the famous couch. Olivier adds the ideas of the poststructuralist Freudian Jacques Lacan, who held that "the unconscious is structured like a language."[1] *This meant that, unlike Freud, Lacan did not see the unconscious as an unstructured reservoir of primitive urges separate from the conscious, linguistic ego but as a sophisticated structured complex already full of ideas. One implication of the notion that the subconscious is structured like a language is that the self or subject is denied an originary reference point or point of return to which a therapist can guide a patient following an event of trauma.*

Olivier's conclusion, despite using a radically different language to Sam Harris and Michael Ruse, is rather similar to theirs: morality is not something to which we aspire, nor does it need a source from the outside, such as Holy Scripture, in terms of which the good life may be justified. Precisely because the subconscious is structured like a language, upon entering the world, we are already part and parcel of a preexisting moral vocabulary. Furthermore, it is precisely the universal character of the linguistic network that provides the universality of morality (the moral law) and makes it possible for individuals to develop an ego capable of moral self-legislation and autonomous, authentic moral actions.

—*The Editors*

The question concerning the ground of the human capacity for moral choice has been answered in many ways, from those of theism grounding it in divine creation and illumination, through transcendental philosophy's deontological argument, to the utilitarian or consequentialist claim that morality is the result of experience: the actions that yield the best social results are those that shape our moral choice. Here I would like to elaborate on the psychoanalytic claim that moral choice is rooted in the human subject's split nature—more specifically, moral behavior or action presupposes the constitutive event of the formation of the unconscious by the originary act of repression in every subject's life—an act that coincides with the infant subject being faced with social prohibition of some kind.

FREUD, REPRESSION, AND MORALITY

It is well known that Sigmund Freud, the "inventor" of psychoanalysis as a human science and clinical practice, built this discipline on the insight that human beings are constitutively characterized by a certain psychic duality—that between consciousness and the unconscious—and that recognition of this enables one to approach psychic disturbances by means of the so-called talking cure.[2] As early as *The Interpretation of Dreams* of 1900, Freud draws a comparison between Sophocles' tragedy, *Oedipus Rex*, and psychoanalysis by arguing that the pattern of unwittingly (unconsciously, that is) killing the father and desiring the mother, encountered in the ancient Greek drama, is a pattern repeated in every generation (on the part of boy children specifically).[3] The following remark contains, in a nutshell, Freud's insight that there is an indissoluble bond between repression (that is, relegating to the unconscious) of certain desires, on the one hand, and morality, on the other. Referring to Oedipus, he says:

> Here is one in whom these primaeval wishes of our childhood have been fulfilled, and we shrink back from him with the whole force of the repression by which those wishes have since that time been held down within us. While the poet, as he unravels the past, brings to light the guilt of Oedipus, he is at the same time compelling us to recognize our own inner minds, in which those same impulses, though suppressed, are still to be found. . . . Like Oedipus, we live in ignorance of these wishes, repugnant to morality, which have been forced upon us by Nature, and after their revelation we may all of us well seek to close our eyes to the scenes of our childhood.[4]

The connection between repressed (that is, unconscious) wishes and morality is clearly indicated here, in an early work. In a much later work—*Totem and Taboo* of 1919, where Freud traces the connection between the psychic lives of primitive societies and (modern) neurotics—this is reaffirmed. Referring to the aftermath of the mythical parricide carried out by a band of brothers, rebelling against the primitive father's jealous possession of all the women in the group, which gave rise to the prohibition of two things simultaneously (in this way constituting totemic and eventually monotheistic society as we know it), namely murder and incest, Freud writes:

> What the father's presence had formerly prevented they themselves now prohibited in the psychic situation of "subsequent obedience" which we know so well from psychoanalysis. They undid their deed by declaring that the killing of the father substitute, the totem, was not allowed, and renounced the fruits of their deed by denying themselves the liberated women. Thus they created the two fundamental taboos of totemism out of the *sense of guilt of the son*, and for this very reason these had to correspond with the two repressed wishes of the Oedipus complex [killing the father and possessing the mother]. Whoever disobeyed became guilty of the two only crimes which troubled primitive society.[5]

Here, again, we witness Freud's resolute claim that morality and the repression of primitive desires to the realm of the unconscious are indissolubly linked. Nor should this surprise anyone, for Freud knew the history of philosophy well, including the thought of Immanuel Kant, which is pertinent to the present theme, given the fact that, where repression is concerned, it invariably relates to the repression of desire in some or other form, whether it is the originary "desire for the mother" or desire for something else that is prohibited. The important point here is that in his second *Critique (of Practical Reason)*, Kant displays profound insight into the constitution of the moral insofar as he makes it clear that morality—or practical judgment—is predicated on desire; to be sure, not desire that proceeds from some or other object as potential source of gratification, but what Kant terms reason as a "true *higher* power of desire," which ultimately obeys the universal moral law, instead of the "inclinations" toward sensory (*hedonism*) or, for that matter, intellectual gratification (*eudemonism* of the Epicurean kind).[6] After all, judging in favor of Kant's "categorical imperative" would make no sense at all unless it occurs on the basis of desire for something, albeit here desire of a distinctly practical, rational kind.

But while Kant establishes a connection between this "higher rational desire" and morality or ethical choice, he does not provide a "genealogy of morality," as it were, which Freud does present in psychoanalytic terms. It should be noted, however, that it is different from Nietzsche's genealogical account of morality, despite a resemblance insofar as Nietzsche, too, accounts for (moral) guilt or "bad conscience" by tracing it back to societal inhibition of the instincts, with the paradoxical result, that "*conscience*" becomes the "dominant instinct."[7] One might dwell on Nietzsche's work in this regard or on Martin Heidegger's account of human beings as *Dasein*,[8] whose fundamental ontological structure is *care* (and not reason, as the tradition would have it)—something that resonates conspicuously with "desire" as construed by Freud—but here I would like to concentrate on the contribution of Jacques Lacan, where the question at hand is addressed in a particularly nuanced manner.

LACAN AND THE ABYSSAL FOUNDATION OF MORALITY

Freud's French "heir" to psychoanalysis, Jacques Lacan, elaborated on the groundwork that Freud had laid regarding the connection between morality (the ethical) and repression, or the unconscious, by stressing the indispensable role played by language—or the symbolic register of subjectivity—in the constitution of the human subject. This should surprise no one; from an early date, psychoanalysis was dubbed the "talking cure" (following one of Freud and his colleague Josef Breuer's early "psychoanalytical" patients, Bertha Pappenheim[9]), emphasizing the crucial function of language in psychoanalytic therapy. Why is language, or the symbolic, so crucial? Bowie puts it in a nutshell where he remarks that:

> Lacan's difference from Freud is nowhere more evident than in his talk of "the Symbolic". This category was important to Lacan precisely because it was versatile and inclusive and referred in a single gesture to an entire range of separate signifying practices. It linked, in what promised to be a coherent and durable fashion, the world of unconscious mental process to that of speech, and both of them to the larger worlds of social and kinship structure. "The Symbolic," for Lacan in the mid-fifties, is a supra-personal structural order.[10]

From the above it should be apparent that Lacan read Freud through the lenses of Saussurean structural linguistics, which regards language as a system of differences with no positive terms, and Lévi-Strauss's cultural-anthropological elaboration of it, which emphasizes the symbolic as a cultural system.[11] Nowhere is Lacan's debt to these thinkers more evident than in his paper, "The Function and Field of Speech and Language in Psychoanalysis,"[12] where Lacan deftly disposes of (particularly ego-) psychology's quest for certainty on the part of the analysand or patient.[13] Instead, he proceeds to show that what is needed on the part of the analysand is to have her or his certainties destroyed, including that of having a distinct "identity"—which is no more than an illusion flowing from a "misrecognition" of one's mirror-image as "oneself" at the level of what Lacan calls the "imaginary" register (as distinct from the "symbolic" and the "real").[14] The point of disabusing the analysand (here representing the human subject as such) of her or his certainties is to drive the point home that what has always been experienced as his or her "desire" really belongs to an imaginary construct[15] and that his or her speech has therefore in a certain sense been "empty." According to Lee, "It has been emptied of the subject by being filled with his alienating *moi* identity"[16] (where the *moi* or "me" is located at the level of the imaginary, in contrast to the *je* or "I"—the subject position of the symbolic, or the "subject of the speaking"[17]).

To make sense of this, it is only necessary to think of popular culture celebrity icons with whom people identify, such as Prince Harry and Meghan Markle: the more people identify with them, the less able they are to construct their "own" personal narrative. In other words, in the course of analysis, the analysand discovers, frustratingly, that there is a gulf separating him or her from what was previously thought of as his or her "identity" but is now uncovered as something imaginary and alienating. Lacan puts it as follows:

> He [the analysand] ends up by recognizing that this being [his or hers] has never been anything more than his construct in the imaginary and that this construct disappoints all his certainties. . . . For in this labour which he undertakes to reconstruct *for another*, he rediscovers the fundamental alienation that made him construct it *like another*, and which has always destined it to be taken from him *by another*.[18]

What is the significance of the above for the provenance of ethical choice on the part of human beings? The "gap" between the two subject positions (*moi* and *je*) is an index of the decisive role of *repression*, as demonstrated by the fact that, unlike the imaginary *moi* (me, ego), the *je* ("I") of the symbolic, which designates the position *from which* one speaks, cannot be addressed directly, lest it simply be transformed into an objectified *moi*—paradoxically by the *je* (which remains repressed) in the instant when the attempt is made to focus on it. In other words, strange as it may seem, the *je* or "I" *who speaks* remains mercurially impossible to pin down, or "unconscious."

This explains why Lacan, like Freud[19] before him, claims that the status of the unconscious is "ethical." After all, the significance of the discontinuity or gap between the *moi* and the subject as *je* (from the "perspective" of which any discourse "about" the *moi* is conducted)—a gap that, as already observed, represents the function of repression—clarifies Lacan's cryptic reversal of Descartes's paradigmatically "modern" maxim, "*Cogito ergo sum*" ("I think, therefore I am"), namely "I think where I am not, therefore I am where I do not think," or—in expanded form—"I am not wherever I am the plaything of my thought; I think of what I am where I do not think to think."[20] The subject as *je* or "I" is located where it exceeds the domain of conscious deliberation and control, that is, at the level of the unconscious. It is therefore emphatically *not* the same as the rational ego or *moi* of the Cartesian tradition, with its (illusory) attributes of autonomy and self-transparency. It also clarifies Lacan's contention, alluded to above, that the status of the unconscious is ethical, which is another way of saying that it is the locus of the subject's desire in an ethical sense—what we truly want is hidden from us via repression. Moreover, lest the impression be created that this desire is nothing more than the subject's arbitrary quest for individual fulfilment of the kind that Kant denied moral import—and here the role of the unconscious regarding the moral or ethical manifests itself—this is by no means an arbitrary "desire" on the subject's part. This becomes apparent when one considers that Lacan thinks of the unconscious as being "structured like a language" and as the "discourse of the Other," with the upshot that the latter discourse represents the social system in its entirety, including the moral values and norms that structure social life.[21]

There is another consideration that suggests the ethical import of the unconscious. By foregrounding the indispensable role of language as discourse here, Lacan is pointing to the way of transmuting the "empty" speech of the subject as *moi* into the "full" speech of the "psychoanalytically realised subject."[22] One is struck by the irony that "empty" speech corresponds with the (spurious) "fullness" of the ego, while "full" speech corresponds with the "lack" or mercurial mobility of the subject as *je* or "I." What is needed, therefore, is a "symbolic interpretation" of what occurs in the course of psychoanalytic "free association" (aimed at neutralizing putatively "rational" attempts by the analysand to control his or her discourse), a process that enables the subject to reconstruct an "intelligible narrative" or life story.[23] In other words, the "narrative" of the analysand, as it emerges in the course of the dialogue between her or him and the psychoanalyst (no matter how minimal the latter's participation in it), is a product of this dialogue, where the analyst's art consists in timely (and well-timed) interventions in the speech of the subject with the purpose of utilizing manifestations of repression, such as discursive slips, gaps, negations, hesitations, or signs of aggression, to give the associative discourse a specific interpretation, direction, punctuation, or emphasis. This procedure is predicated on Lacan's contention that there is a "third term" (the unconscious) at work in the analytical situation: "The unconscious is that part of the concrete discourse, in so far as it is transindividual, that is not at the disposal of the subject in re-establishing the continuity of his conscious discourse."[24] How does this make the emergence of "full speech" possible? For Lacan, the unconscious is that "chapter" of the subject's history that has been "censored"—it is a "marked by a blank" but can be "rediscovered" through the interpretive "cooperation" between the analyst and the free-associative discourse of the subject, despite resistance on her or his part.[25] The "language" of the unconscious manifests itself in the subject's memories of her or his childhood, their bodily symptoms, and in the very specific, "idiosyncratic diction or verbal expressions he or she uses."[26] Keeping in mind Lacan's knowledge of structural linguistics and of structuralist cultural anthropology, it is evident that this is the avenue that led to his startling insight that "the unconscious is structured in the most radical way like a language."[27] This resonates with his assertion that the unconscious "is the discourse of the other" (or "Other," considering its transindividual status), which follows from the (for Lacan) clinically demonstrable claim that the subject's "full speech" is a function of the interaction between the subject's discourse, the analyst's discourse, and the "third term" or "discourse" of the unconscious as manifested in parapraxes or slips of the tongue, memories, and so on.[28]

How is it possible for the unconscious to be the "discourse of the other/Other"? Because language, with cultural values, behavioral, norms and taboos embedded in it, pre-exists the individual subject's entry into it. Highlighting the meaning of what it is to be a human "subject," this implies that one becomes "subject to" the laws of society (and of the moral law in the Kantian sense) through one's entry into the symbolic realm and through the constitutive function of the latter regarding the structure of the unconscious. In brief: the unconscious, as "discourse of the other/Other," constitutes the "abyssal foundation" of the subject's moral and ethical sense. This claim requires further elaboration.

THE UNCONSCIOUS AS SOURCE OF MORALITY AND ETHICAL VALUES

Despite the earlier allusion to Lacan's theoretical path from Freud through the work of Saussure and Lévi-Strauss, to arrive at the insight that societal values are embedded in the unconscious as discourse of the other/Other, the question still lingers on what grounds it may be asserted that the unconscious, which is "structured like a language," is also the repository of ethical norms. Why does Lacan, following Freud, state explicitly that the status of the unconscious is "ethical"? He makes this observation in the context of a discussion of a passage in Freud's *The Interpretation of Dreams* where a father dreams that his dead son, whose corpse is lying in the room adjacent to his own, is asking the father whether he cannot see that he (the son) is on fire—something that Lacan interprets as signifying the father's feeling of guilt at an unconscious level (indicative of this by its appearance in a dream, which marks the realm of appearance of repressed materials). Where guilt manifests itself, the question of moral culpability enters, as Kant also indicated[29] —guilt marks the (negative) manifestation of the moral law; hence Lacan's perspicacious insight into the link between guilt, the unconscious, and the ethical/moral. The positioning of the subject (*je*) as narrator of her/his life-story within the symbolic register, which—as "discourse of the Other"—bears the ethical norms of society, has clarified this issue in what has been discussed so far.

But it is not only the two registers, namely the imaginary (instantiated by the mirror stage as ego-register) and the symbolic, that constitute and therefore affect the subject. The register of the "real"—that which resists symbolization and is irretrievably "left behind" when the subject enters language (although it continues having an impact on the subject's life—is equally important, especially because it involves the subject's "desire." "Desire" is, for Lacan, the *gap* that separates "need" from its linguistically articulated demand[30] —such as when a child asks a parent to buy her a doll. The upshot is that, no matter how hard the parent tries to satisfy the child's demand, the need can never be met, insofar as the demand covers up what it is a disguised expression of, namely a desire for a removal or filling of the child's (constitutively human) "lack" or "want" of being by way of *recognition* by the other (in this case the parent). The important point is that every subject's "desire" in this Lacanian sense (deriving from Plato's account of *eros* in *The Symposium*) is hidden from him or her by repression or, in cases of being so repugnant to the subject that it does not even enter the unconscious, "foreclosed," relegated to the "real," which manifests itself symptomatically on the subject's body, for instance as hallucination. This occurs insofar as their unique desire conflicts in some way or other with the *moral* demands of society—otherwise it would not be repressed or foreclosed—and hence it functions negatively as an index of conventional morality (which is not the same as moral or ethical values which are endowed with universal validity, such as the incest taboo and the proscription of murder, referred to earlier in Freud's work).[31] Žižek adduces an exemplary instance from Freud's clinical practice of such a hidden desire (that conflicts with the moral norms of society) on the part of a woman whose repressed (if not foreclosed) desire for a lover whom she had given up for the sake of satisfying conventional expectations in marriage showed itself symptomatically in the course of therapy.[32] I shall briefly return to the question of the "real" below.

Returning to the argument concerning the encompassing "background language" that constitutes the unconscious as transindividual repository of social values, it makes sense that the values that circulate in a society at any given time are not equal to one another—invariably there is some founding principle or "anchoring point(s)" for organizing the system of values that structures cultural practices. Indeed, such an organizing principle(s) is identified out by Lacan. Referring to the structure of language as "signifying chain," he states: "There is in effect no signifying chain that does not have, as if attached to the punctuation of each of its units, a whole articulation of relevant contexts suspended 'vertically,' as it were, from that point."[33] This "vertical" axis involves the relation between language as a metonymical chain of signifiers (where each signifier bears the trace of all others that it is *not*) and the network of signifieds (conceptual meanings) with which it is ineluctably connected (even if, according to Lacan's poststructuralist revision of Saussure, every signified is again, in turn, a signifier referring to other signifieds). As Lee puts it, the linear chain of signifiers that manifests itself in the subject's discourse is "tied down" by the operation of metaphor, where metaphor functions as the replacement of "repressed" signifiers by others but also indexes the stabilizing or "anchoring" meanings (signifieds) of the subject's signifying discourse, which fulfill a crucial axiological function.[34] For example, in the current global political arena, certain world leaders—such as Recep Tayyip Erdogan, Kim Jong-un, Xi Jinping, and Vladimir Putin—have been identified as embodying "strong leaders," or the so-called strongman who represents a threat to democratic values. This "strongman" figure is a metaphor for the "ruler" or emperor that ultimately goes back to the autocratic monarch of centuries ago, who (like Alexander the Great of the fourth century BC, Frederick the Great of Prussia in the eighteenth century, or Louis XIV of France, the "Sun King," in the seventeenth and eighteenth centuries) had absolute power over their subjects. Arguably such figures are themselves metaphors for a figure that is much older than the absolute monarch, namely the powerful "father figure" of ancient communities and families,[35] which resonates with the "father" in some contemporary households, of course.

Although these discursive "anchoring points" are themselves "unsaid" insofar as they may not appear overtly in a particular discourse, they nevertheless "ground" or organize the other signifiers in a systematic axiological (and therefore ethical) manner. For instance, in contemporary society, it is arguably the case that we still live in a largely patriarchal culture, despite the apparent social changes in favor of women's emancipation that have occurred over the past hundred years. In other words, society today is still structured by and "anchored" in the "name of the father"[36] as pervasively grounding, authoritative (albeit chiefly occulted) signifier that imparts to all other signifiers their axiological "place" in the cultural system. The fact that the "name of the father" is the repressed signifier that still occupies the position of central authority in contemporary culture explains the description of the patriarchal order as "phallogocentric"; that is, it is centered by the phallic *logos* or word. It must be added, however, that this does not mean that its centrality cannot and has not been challenged. It has in fact been challenged consistently and persistently by many thinkers, especially, for obvious reasons, feminist ones such as Luce Irigaray, Julia Kristeva, and others. Besides, as Michel Foucault has argued, the operation of a dominant discourse (such as patriarchy) opens the way for a counterdiscourse (like feminism) to oppose it.[37]

In light of the above, the source of ethical and moral values should not be a mystery, nor should one have to look for it in some transcendent, divine realm. It is to be encountered in the censored "chapters" of the analysand's discourse, that is, in the unconscious, which is usually obscured precisely because of its ethical charge and which, for that reason—as perceptible in the example from Freud, of the father dreaming that his dead son is on fire—is suffused with signs of guilt, even where this is negatively signified or expressed. Such a "negative" expression of guilt could take the form of a *denial* of responsibility for certain states of affairs or of too vehement a *refusal* to discuss certain topics with the psychoanalyst.

Arguably, in Lacan's work, there is something even more fundamental than the "name of the father" as pervasively grounding, albeit repressed, signifier that organizes the "discourse of the Other" as unconscious linguistic-cultural system along (patriarchal) axiological, ethical, or moral lines. More central than this, the signifier referred to as "the phallus" (which functions symbolically and therefore must be carefully distinguished from Freud's concept of the penis in his theory of castration) seems to fulfil this grounding function.[38]

In effect, the phallus is the ultimate *point de capiton*, the signifier that fixes the meaning of the signifying chains of every subject's discourse, by virtue of its being "veiled" or repressed. The phallus is present beneath every signifier as the signifier that has been repressed, and as such every signifier in effect is a metaphor substituting for the phallus. As such a signifier, the phallus is not anything that any man or woman could possibly "have" (hence, it must not be confused with the penis). Precisely because no one can *have* the phallus, it becomes that which all want to *be*. The phallus then serves to signify as well that fullness of being, that complete identity, the lack of which is the fact of our ineluctable want-of-being.

It follows from the above that, if the "name of the father" is the signifier that, according to Lacan,[39] instantiates a "symbolic function" linked to the "figure of the law" with its universalistic conceptual and ethical implications, it (the "name of the father") marks the human subject's separation, through language, from the (unattainable) "fullness of being" represented by the phallus (as being located at the level of the "real"). It therefore seems conceivable that another figure—possibly "the name of the mother" or "the human being in general"—could take the place of the founding axiological-moral figure of the "father" as representative of the moral "law."

In fact, if this search for the provenance of morality is taken to a more "primordial" level—that of the register of the "real," as suggested by the notion of the "phallus"—it is illuminating to note that, in one of Lacan's two early papers on "family complexes" (written for volume 8 of the *Encyclopédie F rancaise* of 1938), one encounters a feminine counterpart of the phallus, namely the "maternal imago," which seems to have an anchoring function even more basic than its symbolic patriarchal counterpart, the "name of the father." Briefly, what Lacan outlined in the first of these two papers— "The Complex as a Concrete Factor of Family Psychology"—amounts to the fundamental structural or formal constituents of subjectivity. He distinguishes here among three so-called imagoes that, as fundamental family-structures, organize the behavior of individuals.[40] Each of these imagoes— the maternal, the fraternal, and the paternal—is the unconscious embodiment of a family complex that "reproduces a certain reality of the environment." The relevance of this—particularly of the first of these imagoes—for the question of moral behavior consists in the manner that these unconscious imaginary representations (to be found in family relations) shape lasting human responses to their environment in the form of their actions. The significance of the "maternal imago" (its imaginary appellation, although it functions at the level of the "real") consists in its connection with the child's "weaning complex" and therefore its representation of the child's "congenital deficiency," signaled by its dependence on the mother's breast as source of satisfaction for its bodily needs.[41]

It is not difficult to grasp the structuring function of this "maternal imago" as being ultimately responsible for all those (fundamentally ideological) quests for a *plenum* or fulfilment of some kind, whether religious, "philosophical" (that is, metaphysical), or political. After all, it marks the interminable *lack* on the part of the (Lacanian) subject in the face of whatever totality or fulfilment it desires, behind which the image of the maternal breast, reminiscent of its function in the "real" (before the infant enters the imaginary), lies in wait. In Lacan's words,

> If it were necessary to define the most abstract form where it is refound, we might characterize it thus: a perfect assimilation of the totality of being. Under this formulation with a slightly philosophical aspect, we can recognize these nostalgias of humanity: the metaphysical mirage of universal harmony, the mystical abyss of affective fusion, the social utopia of a totalitarian guardian-

ship, and every outburst of the obsession with a paradise lost before birth or of the most obscure aspiration toward death.[42]

But if the maternal imago marks the source, in the "real," of the illusory sources of ideological, metaphysical, or religious *jouissance* (ultimate enjoyment or fulfilment), it makes sense to perceive in it the ground of moral or ethical values as well, which stand in the service of such commitments, after all, although (importantly) at a universalistic niveau, such values can transcend exclusivist ideologies. It seems to me that, as such, the "maternal imago" correlates with the "phallus" as symbol of unattainable fullness, and that the repression, or perhaps rather foreclosure, of the phallus is simultaneously the repression/foreclosure of the "maternal imago" as marker of a lost, but nostalgically albeit unconsciously, desired plenum that motivates human ethical or moral behavior. Consider that the cultural system of ethical values is *indirectly* accessible to us—and to the psychoanalyst—at the level of the unconscious as "discourse of the Other." It is therefore noteworthy that, as Lacan indicates,[43] it is the repression/foreclosure of the phallus as signifier by the subject, followed by its (the subject's) passing through the mirror stage, and eventually its entry into language that fundamentally functions to constitute the unconscious as "discourse of the Other." Recall that the phallus denotes the lost, "real" fullness of being that the subject incrementally loses through its separation from the mother's body, in turn represented by the "maternal imago" at the level of the "real."

CONCLUSION

In the light of what has been recounted and argued here, the psychoanalyst has access (albeit indirectly) to a medium, or discourse, that serves as a touchstone for the relation of the subject as analysand to the moral or ethical values in terms of which a culture functions, even if—as noted—these values are not impervious to critique. Most notably, for reasons advanced here, this discourse provides an indispensable means to resist the ubiquitous pitfalls of relativistic moral stances that tend to render one helpless in an era of multiculturalism.[44] One might say that the unconscious, as "structured like a language," constitutes the cultural system in its axiological "distribution," against the backdrop of which various identifiable "conventional moralities" may be identified that deviate from (or pervert) the normative implications of the system as such. "Conventional" morality does not simply coincide with the ethical-axiological articulation of the unconscious. Even the "conventional morality" of patriarchy (which has arguably outlived its acceptability), according to which the father is the authority figure and is often regarded as being "free to do as he likes," is not compatible with a more benign patriarchal system where a father's actions have to be measured against the norms prescribed by the "name of the father," which include kindness and consideration of women and children. "Conventional morality" here would be a perversion of the moral system inscribed in the unconscious, as indeed would that of apartheid or of Nazi-Germany of the Third Reich. Normatively speaking, the unconscious, to the extent that it is structured as explained above and to the degree that (through psychoanalytically astute interpretation of the way) it manifests itself "negatively" in the analysand's discourse, could therefore function as a basis of critique regarding so-called conventional morality.

In the final analysis, therefore, as has been argued with reference to psychoanalytic theory in this chapter, there is no need to look further than the evidence adduced by psychoanalytic practice—as encountered in the work of Freud and Lacan—of the unconscious, as repository of repressed wishes, being the wellspring of moral values and actions. In short, humans are moral, ethical beings not because of some divine plan or design, but because of cultural practices of prohibition that proscribe certain actions and "desires," which are subsequently repressed into the unconscious, from where (as embedded in the "discourse of the Other") they exercise ethical or moral "force," either negatively through guilt or affirmatively through desire. The best-known examples of these are probably the prohibition of incest and of murder, which are universally condemned by people of all nations.

NOTES

1. See in this regard Jacques Lacan, "Function and Field of Speech and Language in Psychoanalysis," in *Ecrits: A Selection* (New York: W. W. Norton, 1977), 57–58.
2. Sigmund Freud, "Studies on Hysteria," in *Freud: Complete Works*, 1–269 (Ivan Smith e-book, 2011), 29–30, 37, 39.
3. Sigmund Freud, *The Interpretation of Dreams*, in *Freud: Complete Works*, 507–1048 (Ivan Smith e-book, 2011), 741.
4. Freud, *The Interpretation of Dreams*, 741.
5. Sigmund Freud, *Totem and Taboo : Resemblances between the Psychic Lives of Savages and Neurotics*, translated by A. A. Brill (New York: Moffat, Yard and Company, 1919), 239.
6. Immanuel Kant, *Critique of Practical Reason*, translated by W. S. Pluhar (Indianapolis: Hackett, 2002), 37.
7. Friedrich Nietzsche, *On the Genealogy of Morality*, translated by Carol Diethe (Cambridge: Cambridge University Press, 2007), 37.
8. Martin Heidegger, *Being and Time*, translated by J. Macquarrie and E. Robinson (Oxford: Blackwell, 1978), 225–241.
9. Sigmund Freud, *The Origin and Development of Psychoanalysis*, translated by H. Chase, in *A General Selection From The Works of Sigmund Freud*, edited by J. Rickman (New York: Doubleday Anchor, 1957), 5; Lacan, "The Function and Field," 46.
10. Malcolm Bowie, *Lacan* (London: Fontana Press, 1991), 57–58.
11. Dylan Evans, *An Introductory Dictionary of Lacanian Psychoanalysis* (London: Routledge 1996), 99–100; Bowie, *Lacan*, 58–59; Jonathan Lee, *Jacques Lacan* (Amherst: University of Massachusetts Press, 1990), 62.
12. Lacan, "The Function and Field."
13. Lee, *Jacques Lacan*, 42–43.

14. Lacan, "The Function and Field," 41–42.
15. Lacan, "The Function and Field," 42.
16. Lee, *Jacques Lacan*, 40.
17. Lee, *Jacques Lacan*, 40–41.
18. Lacan, "The Function and Field," 42; see also Lee, *Jacques Lacan*, 39.
19. Freud, *The Origin and Development*, 12–15.
20. Jacques Lacan, "The Agency of the Letter in the Unconscious or Reason Since Freud," in *Écrits: A Selection*, translated by A. Sheridan (New York: W. W. Norton, 1977), 166.
21. Lacan, "The Function and Field," 55.
22. Lacan, "The Function and Field," 46.
23. Lee, *Jacques Lacan*, 41–42.
24. Lacan, "The Function and Field," 44.
25. Lacan, "The Function and Field," 50.
26. Lacan "The Function and Field," 50; see also Lee, *Jacques Lacan*, 44.
27. Jacques Lacan, "The Direction of the Treatment and the Principles of Its Power," in *Écrits: A selection*, translated by A. Sheridan (New York: W.W. Norton, 1977), 234; Lee, *Jacques Lacan*, 46.
28. Lacan, "The Agency of the Letter," 148; Lee, *Jacques Lacan*, 46.
29. Joan Copjec, "Introduction: Evil in the Finite Time of the World," in *Radical Evil*, edited by J. Copjec (London: Verso, 1996), vii–xxviii.
30. Lacan, "The Direction of the Treatment," 263.
31. Julia Kristeva, *Powers of Horror: An Essay on Abjection*, translated by L. S. Roudiez (New York: Columbia University Press, 1982), 58, 63, 66.
32. Slavoj Žižek, "'The thing that thinks': The Kantian Background of the *Noir* Subject," in *Shades of Noir—A reader*, edited by J. Copec (London: Verso, 1993), 199–206.
33. Lacan, "The Agency of the Letter," 154.
34. Lee, *Jacques Lacan*, 61–62.
35. Freud, *Totem and Taboo*.
36. Lacan, "The Function and Field," 67; Jacques Lacan, "On a Question Preliminary to Any Possible Treatment of Psychosis," in *Écrits: A Selection*, translated by A. Sheridan (New York: W. W. Norton, 1977), 199.
37. Lee, *Jacques Lacan*, 84.
38. Lee, *Jacques Lacan*, 66–67.
39. Lacan, "The Function and Field," 67.
40. Lee, *Jacques Lacan*, 14.
41. Lee, *Jacques Lacan*, 14.
42. Lee, *Jacques Lacan*, 14.
43. Jacques Lacan, "The Signification of the Phallus," in *Écrits: A Selection*, translated A. Sheridan (New York: W. W. Norton, 1977), 288.
44. Slavoj Žižek, *Living in the End Times* (London: Verso, 2010), 43–53.

REFERENCES

Andelman, D. A. "The Global Move from Democracy to Autocracy." CNN World, June 25, 2018. https://edition.cnn.com/2018/06/24/opinions/trump-end-to-democracy-opinion-andelman/index.html.
Bowie, M. *Lacan*. London: Fontana Press, 1991.
Copjec, J. "Introduction: Evil in the Finite Time of the World." In *Radical Evil*, edited by J. Copjec, vii–xxviii. London: Verso, 1996.
Evans, D. *An Introductory Dictionary of Lacanian Psychoanalysis*. London: Routledge, 1996.
Foucault, M. "Politics and Reason." In *Michel Foucault: Politics, Philosophy, Culture. Interviews and Other Writings 1977–1984*, edited by L. D. Kritzman, 57–85. New York: Routledge, 1990.

Freud, S. *The Interpretation of Dreams*. In *Freud: Complete Works*, 507–1048. Ivan Smith e-book, 2011. https://www.topoi.net/wp-content/uploads/2012/12/Freud-Complete-Works.unlocked.pdf (downloaded July 7, 2014).

———. *The Origin and Development of Psychoanalysis*. Translated by H. W. Chase. In *A General Selection from the Works of Sigmund Freud*, edited by J. Rickman, 3–36. New York: Doubleday Anchor, 1957.

———. *Studies on Hysteria*. In *Freud: Complete Works*, 1–269. Ivan Smith e-book, 2011. https://www.topoi.net/wp-content/uploads/2012/12/Freud-Complete-Works.unlocked.pdf (downloaded July 7, 2014).

———. *Totem and Taboo: Resemblances between the Psychic Lives of Savages and Neurotics*. Translated by A. A. Brill. New York: Moffat, Yard and Company, 1919.

Heidegger, M. *Being and Time*. Translated by J. Macquarrie and E. Robinson. Oxford: Blackwell, 1978.

Irigaray, L. *Speculum of the Other Woman*. Translated by G. C. Gill. New York: Cornell University Press, 1994.

Kant, I. *Critique of Practical Reason*. Translated by W. S. Pluhar. Indianapolis: Hackett, 2002.

Kristeva, J. *The Portable Kristeva*. Edited by K. Oliver. New York: Columbia University Press, 1982.

———. *Powers of Horror: An Essay on Abjection*. Translated by L. S. Roudiez. New York: Columbia University Press, 1982.

Lacan, J. "The Agency of the Letter in the Unconscious or Reason since Freud." In *Écrits: A Selection*, translated by A. Sheridan, 146–178. New York: W. W. Norton, 1977.

———. "The Direction of the Treatment and the Principles of Its Power." In *Écrits: A Selection*, translated by A. Sheridan, 226–280. New York: W. W. Norton, 1977.

———. "The Function and Field of Speech and Language in Psychoanalysis." In *Écrits: A Selection*, translated by A. Sheridan, 114–145. New York: W. W. Norton, 1977.

———. "On a Question Preliminary to Any Possible Treatment of Psychosis." In *Écrits: A Selection*, translated by A. Sheridan, 179–225. New York: W. W. Norton, 1977.

———. "The Signification of the Phallus." In *Écrits: A Selection*, translated by A. Sheridan, 281–291. New York: W. W. Norton, 1977.

Lee, J. *Jacques Lacan*. Amherst: University of Massachusetts Press, 1990.

Nietzsche, F. *On the Genealogy of Morality*. Translated by Carol Diethe. Cambridge: Cambridge University Press, 2007.

Žižek, S. *Living in the End Times*. London: Verso, 2010.

———. "'The thing that thinks': The Kantian Background of the Noir Subject." In *Shades of Noir—A Reader*, edited by J. Copjec, 199–226. London: Verso, 1993.

Chapter Three

Morality as Delusion

Michael Ruse

Of all the thinkers grounding their views on morality in Darwinian natural selection, Michael Ruse is perhaps the most consistent. It is also this very consistency that leads to a rather unexpected conclusion.

While he shares a formal atheist position with Sam Harris and Bert Olivier, he is willing to concede that it is not impossible to reconcile the Christian faith with evolutionary theory.[1] *That said, he is an ardent defender of Darwinian theory, and like figures such as Harris, Peter Singer, and Richard Dawkins, he sees significant evidence for the role of kin selection and reciprocal altruism in the development of morality. He was called as a witness for the plaintiff in the 1981 test case* McLean v. Arkansas *regarding the state law permitting the teaching of creation science in the Arkansas school system. He has also debated William Dembski on intelligent design on more than one occasion. However, it would be fair to describe Ruse as more committed to science (and reason) than atheism in particular: he has said on occasion that the New Atheists "do the side of science a grave disservice" and even called the endeavor of the Four Horsemen "a bloody disaster."*

Having authored more than sixty books on topics related to Darwin, natural selection, and evolutionary theory, Ruse may be regarded as one of the foremost authorities in this field. He is no stranger to controversy either. Aside from engaging anti-Darwinians in conversation, he has also challenged orthodox views within biology itself. He is known for having championed the notion of orthogenesis, the view that evolution has a kind of momentum of its own that carries organisms along certain tracks. This view is seen by some as too teleological, even too Aristotelian.

It should be clear to the reader that Ruse's views on morality are thoroughly considered and properly informed by both philosophy and science. Unlike Sam Harris (and like Steven Weinberg), he does not dismiss the is/ought distinction—Hume's famous distinction between what is and prescriptive moral statements about what ought to be. Rather unexpectedly for a thinker of the analytical school, there is even a distinct Nietzschean touch to his evolutionary vocabulary. What is more, as Darwinian as he is, his conclusion about morality signifies a radical departure from the comfortable humanism that characterizes his more ardently atheistic colleagues.

—The Editors

The most incredible fact ever discovered about human beings is that our ancestors were the products of a long, slow, gradual process of evolution, fired by a causal mechanism known as "natural selection."[2] In recent years, students of human evolution, so-called paleoanthropologists, have brought home to us with great force just how incredible a fact this is.[3] The earth is about four and a half billion years old. Life first appeared on earth at least three and a half billion years ago. Mammals, the class to which humans belong, first appeared in primitive form some two hundred million years ago, but it was not until the death of the dinosaurs that the age of mammals was able to get under way, about sixty million years ago. Our ancestors, australopithecines, broke from the apes a mere six million years ago. This means that we share virtually all of our evolution with the animal world, particularly the higher apes, the chimpanzees, and the gorillas.[4] Moreover, this fact still remains with us. Biologically speaking, we are closer relatives of the chimpanzees than chimpanzees are of gorillas. Although through self-importance and ignorance, humans are in fact classified quite separately, under normal circumstances we would be members of the same genus as chimpanzees and gorillas. This is how close we are to the animal world.[5]

And yet, the average member of the philosophical community ignores these startling facts. It is not too much of an exaggeration to say that as far as the average philosopher is concerned, it makes little difference whether we are modified monkeys or created some six thousand years ago on the final day of Creation, miraculously, by a supernatural being, as is supposed by today's so-called scientific creationists.[6] I do not, of course, imply that the average philosopher is not an evolutionist but rather that evolution is taken to be totally irrelevant to the basic inquiries of the philosopher, both in the realm of epistemology and in the realm of ethics. Hillary Putnam tells us that Wittgenstein, one of the most influential philosophers of the twentieth century, had doubts about the truth of evolution.[7]

It is this pre-nineteenth-century attitude toward the major problems of philosophy that I intend to challenge in this paper. Specifically, I intend to concentrate on the problems of moral philosophy and ethics and to argue that you simply *must* take evolutionary ideas seriously if you are to have hope of an adequate approach to morality. I shall argue that our knowledge of evolution, and of the mechanism by which it came about, throws light on the foundations of ethics, that is to say that it is pertinent to meta-ethical questions. Furthermore, I argue that evolution tells us something about the nature of the specific ethical principles to which human beings are committed, that is, evolution tells us something about substantival ethical questions. It is now more than a century since Charles Darwin first published the modern theory of evolution through natural selection in his *Origin of Species* (1859). The time has surely come for moral philosophers to start taking Darwin's message seriously.

TRADITIONAL EVOLUTIONARY ETHICS

Already, philosophical readers will be feeling somewhat depressed because the history of attempts to show evolution relevant to philosophy, particularly to moral philosophy, hardly inspires confidence.[8] On the one hand, so-called evolutionary ethics have tended to be little more than thinly veiled apologia for reactionary social positions.[9] All too often, it is argued that the key to evolution is some form of bloody struggle for existence, leading to the survival of the fittest. Consequently, an ethic based on the evolutionary process supposedly must emulate and indeed encourage the struggle. Thus, it is concluded that one ought to allow all kinds of conflict, personal and social, welcoming the success of the few winners.

This so-called philosophy is often labeled "Social Darwinism," although it owes at least as much in its genesis to the nineteenth-century thinker Herbert Spencer as it does to Charles Darwin. It reached its ridiculous extreme in the mind of John D. Rockefeller, the founder of Standard Oil, who solemnly assured a Sunday school class that the law of big business is the law of nature: it was right and proper that Standard Oil push all its competitors to the wall because this is what evolution demands. Thankfully, most philosophers, and indeed most right-thinking folk, conclude rapidly that this kind of evolutionary moralizing is about as far from true morality as it is possible to get. Morality means helping the weak and defenseless, not stamping on them, literally and metaphorically.[10] On the other hand, with reason, evolutionary ethics has been condemned by philosophers for committing very serious logical errors. As David Hume pointed out in the eighteenth century, there is a drastic difference between claims about matters of fact and claims about morality.[11] To put it in modern terms, there is a difference between "is" statements and "ought" statements. Thus, if, for instance, I say that I hate killing, that is one thing. In particular, it is a factual claim about my emotions. However, if I say that killing is wrong, that is quite another thing. That is a statement about an apparently objective matter of moral fact. It has nothing to do directly with my feelings. What Hume pointed out is that you cannot properly go straight from factual statements, from "is" statements, to value statements, that is, to "ought" statements. To do so is to violate what has properly become known as Hume's Law. In this century, Hume's Law was revived strongly by the writings of G. E. Moore, when he argued that it is a fallacy to try to define the good in terms of natural, that is to say factual, properties. Moore's description of such incorrect moves was that they commit the "naturalistic fallacy."[12]

Critics argue, with good reason, that all attempts at evolutionary ethics violate Hume's Law. What happens is that people try to deduce the way that things ought to be from the way that things are. They point to the fact that there is an ongoing struggle for existence occurring in nature. Even between humans, this struggle supposedly occurs. Thus, it is concluded that this is the way that things ought to be. Hence, humans have an obligation to allow a struggle to proceed without letup or hindrance. And we should cherish as morally worthwhile the ultimate products of evolution, namely human beings. But, unfortunately, as critics point out, this is to go from fact to value. Such a move is without warrant. Why should the process and product of evolution in themselves be morally good? To argue this way is to make unjustified inferences. Fallacies are being committed. In short, there can be no warrant for an evolutionary ethics.[13]

Let me say right at once that I am aware of and sensitive to such criticisms as these. I believe nevertheless that one can formulate a sound evolutionary ethics: an ethics that is, on the one hand, not a thinly disguised excuse for fascist ideology and that is, on the other hand, quite innocent of fallacious moves from "is" to "ought." Indeed, what I shall argue is that Hume and Moore and followers were quite right in drawing attention to the distinction between fact and value, and that a true evolutionary ethics not only acknowledges this fact but makes use of it. Thus, whatever the faults of a revised evolutionary ethics, they are not the traditional ones.

THE EVOLUTION OF MORALITY

To start making my case, let me begin by discussing contemporary thinking about the evolution of morality. This will show that the idea of evolution necessarily implying a literal bloody struggle for existence is simply bad biology. When this part of the discussion is over, it will be possible for us to turn to questions about the status of moral claims and put to rest fears that any evolutionarily inspired moral philosophy must necessarily commit serious logical blunders.

As has been said, humans evolved through the process of natural selection. Natural selection is a consequence of several clearly defined and well-established facts about the organic world.[14] In particular, more organisms are constantly being born than can possibly survive and reproduce. This leads to what is known, technically, as a "struggle for existence." However, it must be emphasized right at the start that this struggle does not necessarily involve bloody hand-to-hand combat between organisms. A struggle could as well involve a difference in relative rates of reproduction or some other nonviolent process. Because there is a population pressure brought about by limitations in space and size, not all organisms that are born can possibly survive and reproduce. It is the claim of the evolutionist that the ensuing differential reproduction is a function, not merely of chance factors, but also of the distinctive characters that organisms themselves have.

Some organisms will survive and reproduce because of their peculiar characteristics. These characteristics are known as "adaptations." Following Charles Darwin, it is argued that, given enough time, the ongoing process of different reproduction of distinctive organisms adds up to an evolutionary effect. This is known as "natural selection." The important point to note here is not simply that organisms evolve, but they evolve with characteristics that aid their possessors in the ongoing struggle for reproduction. Thus we have the adaptations of hands and ears and eyes and so forth. Darwinism (that is to say, Darwin's theory of evolution) provides a natural explanation for these characteristics, which in pre-evolutionary times were taken as paradigmatic evidence for God's creative design. Do note, however, that the "raw stuff" of evolution—the peculiarities of organisms that eventually add up to full-blown adaptations—is not teleologically put in place, as pre-Darwinian theists supposed. Darwinians believe that new variations appear constantly but that their nature is "random." They do not appear according to the needs of organisms. Selection has to make do with what it gets and thus must cobble together an answer somehow. For this reason, the course of evolution is fundamentally nonprogressive.[15] Humans came about through natural selection, thereby showing adaptations.[16] However, at this point, we must recognize what this means, particularly in modern terms. Humans have taken the path of sociality. In this, they are unlike most mammals, where males tend to live separately from females and where there is often a separation between the generations. Humans live together in packs or bands, like dogs and baboons. There are advantages to doing this, particularly if you do not have strong weapons of attack or defense.[17] (Fairly obviously, sociality and the lack of strong weapons were things that coevolved.) But if you are to live communally, then you must have various social facilitating mechanisms to allow you to live with your fellows. Otherwise, you will simply have ongoing battles and fights within the group, as well as between groups. Modem evolutionists claim that the social relations that have evolved between humans are a direct function of natural selection. There are two major mechanisms that are presumed to have brought about such cooperative-type living. The first is known as "kin selection." In evolution, what counts is passing on your units of heredity, the so-called genes. But fairly obviously what you pass on are not the actual genes of your body. Rather, you pass on copies. This means that in theory, and indeed it turns out in practice, there is no reason why you should not reproduce, as it were, by proxy. Your close relatives, like siblings, share some of the copies of the genes that you have. Therefore, inasmuch as close relatives reproduce, you reproduce yourself vicariously. Kin selection is the mechanism that captures this reproduction at a distance. Inasmuch as one human helps another, that helper indirectly helps its own reproduction. Hence, cooperation serves one's own individual reproductive interests.

The second mechanism that is presumed to have brought about sociality is so-called reciprocal altruism. This is a mechanism that can even bring about cooperation between nonrelatives. Basically, it is all a matter of enlightened self-interest. If I help you, then you will be more ready to help me in return. And the amount of effort it costs me to help you is probably going to be much compensated by the return help that I will get. If, for instance, I help you when I am fit and healthy, it will cost me little. But then perhaps at some point, say, when I am sick, your return help, which costs you little, will be of immeasurable value to me. Through the mechanism of reciprocal altruism, help can spread through a group. Obviously, it is not necessary for immediate help to be received or even expected for reciprocal altruism to occur. It could well be, and indeed probably is, that one individual pours its help into the pool, which is then drawn upon by others as needed, rather like an insurance policy. I must point out here, to quell any possible doubts, that there is strong evidence both for kin selection and for reciprocal altruism through the animal world. These are not figments of some biologist's frenzied imagination. These are well-established models. Furthermore, there is growing evidence that such mechanisms were extremely important in human evolution. Therefore, I do want to emphasize at this point that I am not wildly speculating about how evolution might have brought about morality. I am talking now about a level of fairly well-established fact. But, with good reason, you might object that, although this points to the evolution of cooperation between humans, this tells us nothing about true morality.[18] True morality demands giving because it is right, not because one hopes for reward. Indeed, generally hope of reward is taken to be inconsistent with a true moral sense. This is all true, but the claim of today's evolutionists, particularly of those who concern themselves with the evolution of social behavior (so-called sociobiologists), is that the way that cooperation has evolved between humans does indeed involve a true moral sense.[19] We could, as it were, calculate, every time we give help or receive help, what would be in our best biological interests. I help you; but, as I do, I mentally note down the amount of help I have received from you, the probability of receiving help from you, and so on and so forth, very much as though I were an insurance actuary. The trouble with this is that such a process is highly inefficient. Every time I interact with you or with another human being, I have to stop and think about what the payoff is for me. This requires time and, moreover, requires a fairly complex mathematical ability. Presumably, for something like this to work, my brain is going to have to be very much more powerful than it is at the moment.

The alternative strategy, one which modern evolutionists believe to have occurred, is to shortcut the calculation process by supposing that there is some objective set of standards that we all ought to obey. Then, when I help you, I help you not because I have calculated the payoff for me but because I think it is right for me to help you.

Conversely, when you help me, you help me and I expect help, not because of payoffs, but because we think that it is right. In other words, what is claimed by sociobiologists is that morality has evolved as a kind of social facilitating mechanism, which will enable all of us to play the social game. In a way, therefore, objective morality is a kind of collective illusion that we all believe in, in order to function socially together. If we did not have such a belief in objective morality, then no one would help anyone else, and our social structure would collapse. "Do this because it is right" has an effect on you that "Do this because I want you to" could never have.

How is this all supposed to come about? It could be that humans have completely blank minds at birth, *tabula rasa*, which then, as it were, get filled up with moral thinking. However, there are good evolutionary reasons to suppose that this is not so.[20] Rather, what is believed now is that the human mind at birth is already biased in certain predisposed ways. These biases are known technically as "epigenetic rules." They have been developed most thoroughly by the sociobiologists.[21]

According to modern theory, what happens is that the human mind, as it grows, develops in certain preset ways so that it is disposed to think along certain channels. In the realm of epistemology, for instance, we have a predisposition to think in certain logical and mathematical ways. We are inclined to believe that 2+2=4 rather than 5. And the reason why we have this inclination, an inclination brought about by an epigenetic rule, is quite simple. Those of our would-be ancestors who believed that 2+2=4 tended to survive and reproduce a lot more efficiently than those of our would-be ancestors who believed that 2+2=5. Similarly, we are predisposed to think about certain things in a causal fashion. Those of our would-be ancestors who were predisposed to believe that fire causes burning tended to outreproduce those of our would-be ancestors who happily, at least at first, drew no connections between the fire and the consequent pain brought about by the burning.

In the realm of moral behavior, one of the best-worked-out epigenetic rules is that which lies behind incest barriers.[22] Virtually every human society has barriers, often made explicit as taboos, against sibling intercourse.

Brothers and sisters simply may not, or rather should not, sleep together, at least not during their reproductive years. (I'm sure that many siblings have experienced some sort of preadolescent sex play.) There are very good biological reasons why humans are biased against sibling intercourse. Such close inbreeding has horrific biological effects. Children of siblings stand a very high chance of having genetic ailments of one sort or another. Consequently, there is and has been strong selective pressure against such sexual relationships.

Sociobiologists argue that the human mind is biased or influenced against such relationships by one or more epigenetic rules. We have revulsion at the thought of sibling incestual relationships, and we elevate them into explicit moral prohibitions. More generally, it is argued by sociobiologists that kin selection and reciprocal altruism, and possibly other like mechanisms, have brought about sociality and cooperation between humans.[23] This cooperation is caused proximately by epigenetic rules, which themselves have their roots in natural selection, brought about by the struggle for existence. Thus, the epigenetic rules incline us to think that we ought to behave morally toward our fellow humans, particularly those in our pack or society. Morality, therefore, rests ultimately on the innate biases of the human mind, these biases being an adaptive function of the evolutionary process. This is all there is to the evolution of morality.

Let me not overexaggerate. This is all there is to the biological story of the evolution of human morality. No one, least of all an evolutionary biologist, wants to deny that the human cultural dimension takes off and leads to effects that do not tie in directly to biological advantage. This cultural divergence and evolution are responsible for the differences between moral codes that one notes from country to country. However, it is the claim of the biological evolutionist, the modern-day Darwinian, that underlying any cultural differences, there is a common foundation of biological influence. This influence is brought about by the epigenetic rules that are themselves rooted in the evolutionary process, no less than our human hands and eyes and other anatomical adaptive features.

Let me emphasize that, thus far, my discussion has been at the empirical level. Everything that I have said is part of the modern scientific theory of evolution. I do not pretend that it is all absolutely correct in every detail. Indeed, we are pushing at the frontiers of science. Moreover, there are well-known arguments about the ultimately unprovable status of any scientific claim.[24] But what I do argue is that what has been presented so far is to be taken as science and not as ethereal armchair philosophizing. It is the basic background against which any philosophical discussion must be cast.

But what kind of philosophical discussion is appropriate here? Are we any further down the line with the kinds of inquiries that concern philosophers? Or is what we have covered thus far no doubt interesting but irrelevant to our main inquiry? Many philosophers would argue that it is as irrelevant as it is interesting.[25]

This is the conclusion I want to dispute strongly now. I shall argue in this section that what we have learned has profound implications for the status of ethics. In particular, I want to argue that, meta-ethically, one ought, as a Darwinian evolutionist, adopt a positive of "ethical skepticism." By this, I mean (as is typically meant) not that there is no such thing as ethics but, rather, there is no such thing as an objective foundation to ethics.

In fact, I would argue this conclusion about the lack of objective foundation to ethics ought to be apparent to you already.[26] As we have seen, what the evolutionist claims is that morality exists as a collective illusion, in order to facilitate cooperation among humans. It is an adaptation, brought about by natural selection, to help us survive and reproduce that much better. It has no further or ultimate end. It is as much a chimera as the voices that the schizophrenic "hears" or the messages that come from beyond at the spiritualist's séance. What makes ethics different from the schizophrenic's voices and the spiritualist's messages is that it is an illusion shared by us all. Hence, linguistically, one can properly point out that ethics is not that which we mean by "illusion," if illusion applies to something possessed only by an aberrant few. The whole point of ethics is that everybody, or at least almost everybody, shares in the belief that there is some sort of objective compulsive morality. But it does not exist all the same.

When I say ethics does not exist, of course it exists for us, but it does not exist as some kind of objective phenomenon irrespective of human beings. Let me put matters this way: perhaps when no one is around in the forest, a tree falls and makes a noise. However, if no one is around in the forest, then there is no moral obligation to tell people to get out of the way!

You might be tempted to agree with my premises but deny my conclusions. You might feel inclined to agree with me that our ethical sense or capacity, or whatever you want to call it, is indeed a product of evolution through natural selection—that that which makes us moral beings is as much part of our biology as is that which makes us seeing or even thinking beings. However, you might then go on to argue that, just as the fact that we see through evolutionarily acquired abilities does not deny the objectivity of material objects, so the fact that we become aware of ethics through evolutionarily acquired capacities does not deny the reality and independent objectivity of morality. (I myself argued precisely this![27])

Unfortunately, this argument does not stand up if you look at the full implications of Darwinian evolutionary theory. Let us grant for the sake of this discussion that there is, in fact, a real material world and that we humans can obtain some knowledge of it or at least some reasonable approximation to such knowledge. This means that we are accepting the approximate truth of Darwinian evolutionary theory. (If you are prepared to grant this much and argue that our knowledge of the external world is subject to a fairly radical skepticism, then, for obvious reasons, the claims that I am making about ethics follow even more readily than otherwise.)

The point that we must now go on to accept, as Darwinians, is that ethics could have been quite other than it is. Therefore, there is absolutely no necessity to ethics, a quality that an independent objective ethics is always thought to have. (Remember how Immanuel Kant, for instance, stresses the synthetic a priori nature of ethical claims.) What the Darwinian is committed to believing is that the way that we think ethically is a purely contingent fact, which could have been quite other had we not evolved from savannah-dwelling primates some six or seven million years ago. Indeed, there is absolutely no reason why, for instance, our ethical code should not have included a moral prescription toward cannibalism or feces eating or infanticide or any one of a number of other practices that, as it so contingently happens, we find not merely repulsive but positively immoral. The reason why this is so is that there are already organisms existing today—higher organisms existing today—that practice one or all of these—to us—revolting activities. Had we, for instance, evolved from cave dwellers or some such thing, then it is quite possible that we would feel a moral compulsion to eat our children or to dine on the feces of our fellows.

What these rather horrible examples show is that that which we take to be moral is a purely contingent facet of our evolution. Had things gone another way, which Darwinism insists that they might have done, then we would have a completely different moral code. This is a point that cannot be overemphasized. As noted earlier, the absolute essence of modern evolutionary theory is that there is no progression up toward some fixed point, remarkably like humans. This is a remnant of pre-Darwinian Christian thought, most specifically the old "chain of being" hypothesis.[28] It has no place whatsoever in the modern evolutionary world. Evolution goes with the most adaptively advantageous at the time and is thus totally random from a long-term perspective. Ethics, in short, is contingent. It is a happenstance facet of our primate nature and, as such, can have no eternal underpinning. This denies it the special status that it is always accorded by those who argue for an objective ethics, with a reality in some way independent of, or transcending, human existence. But still you might persist, arguing that even though it so contingently happens to be our nature that we recognize such moral imperatives as "love your neighbor," this is hardly to deny the existence of some kind of eternal objective reality to such a moral claim as "love your neighbor." Perhaps it is part of our evolutionary nature that we believe such moral dictates. But this is not to deny that it is also (and more importantly) God's desire that we love our neighbor or that something akin to a Platonic world of eternal forms demands that we love our neighbor or some other such thing that gives an extrahuman foundation to moral codes.

Unfortunately, however, you are now stuck with the consequence that objective morality is redundant. Consider two possible universes: one with objective morality and the other with no such morality. And suppose them to be identical otherwise and of such a nature that human beings evolve. (In speaking of Darwinian evolution as being random, I am not denying that it is causal. Nor am I pretending that, were the world exactly as it was in the beginning, it would not produce organisms just as they have evolved.) What you have then is two sets of humans, one in each imaginary universe. Both of them believe exactly the same things: both of them have the same moral code. Both of them, for instance, believe that a binding ethical dictate is "love your neighbor." The only difference is that, in the one universe, the human beliefs correspond to objective reality and, in the other universe, there is no such objective morality for the beliefs to correspond to. What this all means, obviously, is that the objective morality is totally redundant. The universe without the objective morality functions just as well as the universe with it. But surely, this is a contradiction, at least as the notion of objective morality is commonly understood. If there's one thing an objective morality cannot be, it is redundant. If it is God's will that we should love our neighbor, it cannot be immaterial to us humans that it is indeed God's will that we should love our neighbor. This is what makes it right and proper for us to love our neighbor. What I argue, therefore, is that even if one supposes an objective morality, it is going to be redundant, given a Darwinian background, and that this is a reductio ad absurdum of the very notion of objective morality. If you are a Darwinian evolutionist, then you must be an ethical skeptic.

I would argue indeed that, given Darwinism, the situation is even worse for objective morality than that of redundancy. Given the randomness of Darwinian evolution and the fact that we could well have evolved into rational beings that think it morally obligatory to eat our fellows, then it could well be that we all share a collective delusion about eating our fellows, even though objective morality would have us love our fellows.[29] In other words, given Darwinism, it is quite possible that we all believe one thing morally, although it is the rule of objective morality that we should believe something else quite different. In fact, as you might imagine, there is absolutely no reason why we in our present state should have actually arrived at objective morality.

Perhaps indeed it is God's will that we should eat our fellows, but we poor deluded fools think otherwise. The point that must be reiterated again and again is that Darwinian evolution has no place for progress.[30] We are where we are because of random factors and the opportunistic effects of natural selection. It simply cannot be that we have evolved, as it were, toward an end that makes us aware of the way that we really ought to behave. The only sense that can be given to "ought" by a Darwinian evolutionist is a contingent sense, which is purely a function of our present social state. There is no correspondence to anything over and beyond us.

We have seen how a Darwinian must answer the basic questions of metaethics. When queried about the ultimate foundations of morality, the Darwinian evolutionist must argue that there are no such ultimate foundations. But I do want to emphasize that this does not mean that the Darwinian is totally amoral. Indeed, as was pointed out earlier, the whole point about Darwinian evolution is that one can explain the evolution of morality. One is not explaining away morality. What one is doing, at most, is explaining away the supposed objective foundation to morality. But what, then, is the morality of a Darwinian, you may ask. This is a fair question, and it is that which I shall attempt to answer in this section. The easiest way to answer the question is to play off Darwinism against already-established traditional answers to the ultimate bases of moral behavior. Let me pick out three well-known ones for purposes of discussion. The first is a kind of idealistic ethic, which is based on a combination of the view of Socrates in the first book of Plato's *Republic* and the views of Jesus in the Sermon on the Mount. The second position is one roughly associated with the name of Immanuel Kant. It is a view that puts an emphasis on the individual as opposed to the group. Remember that Kant's supreme ethical norm, the Categorical Imperative, had, as one of its major forms, the exhortation to "treat others as ends in themselves, and not merely as means."[31] A modern version of Kantianism is that of John Rawls, who expects us to treat everyone fairly.[32] The third well-known philosophical position specifying a basic ethical philosophy is utilitarianism. This is the view that demands that actions be judged in accordance with the happiness they cause and against the side consequences of unhappiness. Inasmuch as an action tends to promote happiness as opposed to unhappiness, it is to be judged good. As a corollary: the more happiness, the better.[33]

The Darwinian position certainly captures some of the basic tenets of the idealistic approach to morality. The whole force of the mechanisms of kin selection and reciprocal altruism is that we will have epigenetic rules demanding of us that we help others and that, moreover, we do this because we think that it is right to help others.

Nevertheless, if you push this idealism to an extreme, demanding with Jesus that you give not merely seven times but seven times seventy times, and even more—in other words, if you demand that you go on giving virtually without end, and that this should continue whether or not one gets any response—then I suspect that the evolutionist at some point will cry "stop." There has to be some sort of return, or at least a prospect of return, for the mechanisms of evolution to function adequately.[34]

In short, the evolutionary approach to ethics suggests that our moral capacities only go thus far, and if the people that we interact with give no response or return whatsoever, then we will shut off our feeling of moral obligation. We will regard such people as beyond the moral realm in some way—"pathological" or some such thing. Furthermore, my suspicion is that given the difference between kin selection and reciprocal altruism, as a Darwinian, you expect to find morality extending further if you are dealing with relatives rather than nonrelatives. The evolutionist expects people to have a stronger feeling of moral obligation toward their own children than toward strangers. This, it seems to me, is incompatible with the way in which both Socrates and Jesus are usually read. I would add, however, that this incompatibility may be a modern reading because Socrates did not extend his views on morality to non-Athenians or to slaves, and there is some doubt about how far Jesus intended his views in the Sermon on the Mount to extend to non-Jews. (Remember, it was only after Jesus's death that Christianity was broadened to the Gentile world.)

You may object that this is a serious limitation to morality as understood by the Darwinian. However, I would respond that it is merely a realistic appraisal of our moral feelings anyway. Most people certainly behave as though they have a far stronger obligation to their own children than to the children of others. Moreover, I suspect that most people would back this up if challenged and feel morally nauseated by someone who was spending all his/her money on the children of strangers while his/her own family did without. There would be a feeling that such a person was trying to buy his/her way into the kingdom of heaven at his/her family's expense and that this was simply wrong. (Remember Dickens's savage attack on such people in *Bleak House*.)

Moreover, the evolutionist would argue that when we look at people's feelings of morality, generally, it is pretty clear that whatever we may say on a Sunday about the need to love everyone indifferently, in fact, few, if any of us, really believe this. We really believe that we should help those who are prepared to help us. Certainly, we should go that extra way with other people, but ultimately morality requires some sort of response. If no response is forthcoming, then (as noted) we tend to strike off people as moral agents, arguing that they are sick or monsters or some such thing. Or, effectively, we do the same thing. We take them out of society, by imprisoning or executing them. Note, however, that we usually demand response (or inflict punishment) not in the name of self-calculation—"I help you, now you should help me"—but in the name of morality—"You have a moral obligation to help me, just as I had such an obligation to help you." What about Mother Teresa? Does she not confound your approach toward idealism?

She gave unstintingly, without thought or hope of return. Well, the evolutionist is certainly not going to be bothered by one or two counterexamples. Natural selection, unlike a Christian God, never guarantees perfection or total harmony. At best, what one looks for is a rough and ready working, from an adaptive point of view. The fact that one or two people behave in maladaptive ways, in the name of idealistic morality, hardly disproves Darwinism. Moreover, perhaps somewhat cynically but not necessarily unfairly, the Darwinian would suspect that many so-called saints are in fact looking for rewards, if not in this world, then in the next. In other words, saints believe that there is some sort of payoff in the broad scheme of things. If they do not, why does the church have to keep harping on the heresy of doing good for the wrong reasons?

The Kantian view of substantive morality, particularly as offered in some of its more modern manifestations, for instance, by John Rawls in his theory of justice, fits very readily with an evolutionary backing. In fact, the Kantian emphasis on the individual seems almost like reciprocal altruism in action. What this biological mechanism leads to are epigenetic rules demanding that we help others and that we individuals in turn have the right to expect help. In other words, it makes us think that everybody is entitled to some share of the pot and that this sharing should be done in the name of fairness because, if this is thus performed, then we ourselves will benefit along with the rest.

This sounds very close to the Kantian Categorical Imperative, as well as the claims of like philosophers. It is interesting to note, in fact, that John Rawls does at one point speculate that the kind of neo-Kantian philosophy that he expounds, where the emphasis is on justice as fairness, might have an evolutionary background.[35] Rawls does not follow this up in any great detail, but I would suggest that he should, as should we.

A utilitarian approach to ethics likewise strikes a happy response from biology. There are good biological reasons why a good meal or sexual intercourse or the love of our children makes us happy. But note that the Darwinian is not simply saying that we want happiness. That is no moral dictate at all. What the Darwinian says is that we want happiness for ourselves because happiness is generally associated with those things that are biologically good for us—the causal connection being that biology promotes a sense of happiness about those things that we ought to have, biologically speaking. The Darwinian then goes on to say that we are most likely to maximize those things that make us happy if we share the sentiment that we ought to promote the happiness of others. If we believe in this—that we ought to promote the maximum happiness—then this will rebound to our benefit, more than if we simply set out selfishly to promote our own happiness. Thus, the Darwinian is not simply arguing that we ought to look after ourselves but that we ought to promote the general happiness. This, of course, is the basic proposition of the utilitarian. I would not want to say that the Darwinian would go right down the line with every utilitarian. For instance, I could well imagine that situation, biologically speaking, where it might be better to do something that is not a very pleasurable thing to do. For instance, if you had some disease that you knew was going to make you progressively unhappier, the biological urge to live might nevertheless outweigh the apparent minimizing of unhappiness by committing suicide.³⁶ But subject to qualifications like these, which I suspect many utilitarians would admit and argue for anyway, the Darwinian evolutionist seems to embrace quite readily something like the Greatest Happiness Principle.

I argue, therefore, in conclusion, that although the evolutionist will subscribe to an ethics that will be somewhat more circumscribed than one would get from an idealistic position, the Darwinian evolutionist would feel happy in arguing for moral philosophies along the lines of those sketched by the Kantians and by the utilitarians. We have epigenetic rules that lead us to think that such courses of action as endorsed by Kantians and utilitarians are those that we ought to promote. You might, perhaps, complain that this is all a little bit too catholic. After all, there are differences between Kantians and utilitarians. The Kantian puts an emphasis on the individual, whereas utilitarians tend to put an emphasis on the value of the group.³⁷ Traditionally, also, there is a difference between Kantians and utilitarians in that whereas the former find value in the intention and the act, the latter tend to judge morality in terms of consequences: did your actions maximize happiness? Surely, the Darwinian ought to decide between one position or the other.

However, in response, I would point out that, in fact, usually Kantian and utilitarian and others who subscribe to variant or alternative moral philosophies do not differ that greatly about the right course of action. Most of the time, the Kantian and the utilitarian would agree that certain things are right and that certain things are wrong. Raping small children, for instance, is unambiguously wrong, both because it violates the Categorical Imperative and because it violates the Greatest Happiness Principle. Conversely, helping a widow in distress is something that is good both for the Kantian and for the utilitarian. It should not be forgotten that the job of moral philosophers is to pick out counterexamples and awkward instances. That philosophers are very good at doing this does not deny the fact that, most of the time, what one ought to do is fairly unambiguously obvious and that all of the major moral philosophies cohere. Thus, that the Darwinian would feel happy with both Kantianism and utilitarianism is not to say that Darwinism has no moral force at all. It is rather to say that, in the 90 or more percent of times when Kantian and utilitarian would agree on the right course of action, the Darwinian would likewise agree.

But what about the points where there are disagreements? Well, perhaps when there are genuine differences in moral insight, this is simply a point where evolution lets us down. Should you sacrifice the individual for the group? Should you value the well-intentioned bungler over the efficient cynic? Perhaps there is no ultimate answer. I keep emphasizing the fact that evolution is a rough and ready process and does not guarantee perfection.³⁸ Certainly, evolution does not guarantee that there must always be an answer to every moral problem. This is the strong implication of such an empirical approach as I am advocating in this paper. If there were an objective ethics, then presumably there would always be an ultimately right answer. God could not, for instance, leave us hanging about what we ought to do (or prefer) in some particular case—although, possibly, we might never realize fully what we ought to do because of our personal limitations. But if you take the naturalistic approach to ethics that I am advocating, then perhaps sometimes there simply are cases where there is no morally right or wrong answer. Fortunately, these are relatively rare, and so, from a biological point of view, they can be tolerated. I would argue, however, that this inability to yield answers to all moral queries is not a weakness of the Darwinian approach to ethics. It is rather a fact, just as it is a fact that quantum mechanics no longer subscribes to conventional notions of causality. This is no weakness in quantum mechanics. It is, if anything, a strength in that it acknowledges the way that the world really is.

OBJECTIONS

I do not expect that such a radically naturalistic philosophy as I promote in this discussion will find ready acceptance among philosophers. There will, no doubt, be many objections. I cannot hope to answer all of them in this discussion, but let me address three that will almost certainly be made.

First, there will be the objection that what I am talking of is not true morality at all but rather some cynical, self-directed set of emotions that portray humans as calculating, hypocritical, amoral, computer-like robots.[39] It will be argued that an approach that explicitly starts with the biological advantages to be accrued from cooperating can have little or nothing to do with the disinterested goodness that is at the heart of all true morality.

In response to this objection, let me simply say that if you think it has force, then either you have not followed what I have said or I have failed to make myself clear. The whole point is that we are talking of the evolution of genuine morality. Humans believe that there is some objective disinterested code of ethics that they should obey. That is what morality is all about. What the evolutionary explanation does is show that this is illusory, in the sense that there is no such referent to morality. But the explanation certainly does not deny that when we use moral claims, we mean something very different from that which we mean when we use factual claims.

The evolutionist, more than anyone, agrees that humans do not calculate self-interest when they cooperate. Morality is a more efficient way of achieving self-interest than conscious calculation. The fact that the evolutionist argues that there is a causal underpinning to morality no more denies the genuine nature of moral sentiments than, for instance, would it deny the genuineness of Mother Teresa's altruism, were one to point out that her behavior had its origins in, say, a very strict upbringing. Mother Teresa was a fine moral person, whatever her background. However, surely, no educator would want to argue that her background, or the background of anyone else, is totally irrelevant to his/her present behavior, including his/her present moral behavior. For this reason, I would deny the surely-to-be-made charge that, protestations aside, the evolutionary ethicist (as defended in this discussion) is violating Hume's law or committing the naturalistic fallacy.

One is not attempting to deduce ought-statements from is-statements. A value claim, an ought-statement, means something quite different from an is-statement, a factual claim. What one is doing is using factual claims, is-statements, to explain away the supposed objective referent of value claims, ought-statements. In a way, therefore, what one can say is not that the evolutionary ethicist is denying the is/ought distinction or trying to bridge the is/ought distinction. Rather, to use a sporting metaphor, the evolutionist is doing an end run around the is/ought distinction. He or she is agreeing that the is/ought distinction is important, in the sense of meaning, but he/she denies that this implies that one cannot explain morality in terms of factual claims. There are no formal fallacies being committed in this brand of evolutionary ethics. No one is trying to deduce that which we ought to do from the way that things are. Rather, the evolution of the moral capacity is being revealed, and once this revelation has occurred, then it is argued that we can draw important philosophical implications about that which the capacity supposedly deals with.

The second objection is that since the evolutionary approach makes morality dependent upon human beings, then all becomes relative. If I feel like doing one thing, I can, and if you feel like doing another thing, you can, and there is ultimately no way of deciding between us. Thus, supposedly, morality collapses into a morass of different wishes and desires. This again, however, is to misunderstand radically the force of the evolutionary argument. The evolutionist claims not simply that we have certain desires but that we have moral inclinations, brought about (via the epigenetic rules) by natural selection. I do not simply hate killing; I think that killing is wrong. Likewise, you think that killing is wrong. And I think you ought not kill, just as you think I ought not kill. The point is that we humans are all members of the same biological species, with the same evolutionary past. Morality may be relative to the human species, or to species like us, but within the species, morality is a shared phenomenon. Indeed, the whole point about morality is that it will not work unless it is shared. If only a few of us held the illusion of morality, then we would be suckers to be wiped out in the course of evolution by natural selection very rapidly.[40]

Thus, it can be seen that any relativism is of a kind that leaves morality untouched. The evolutionist indeed affirms the universality of moral sentiments within our species. What he or she does is deny their ultimate objectivity, but this is quite another thing. We all know that there are certain rules of baseball that you cannot, or at least should not, break. If you do break them, you will be penalized and ultimately thrown out of the game. Obviously, no one pretends that baseball is other than a human invention. Morality is not in this sense an invention. It is something that has been conferred on us by our past. However, it is just as human as baseball. It too has its rules that you must not break. Otherwise, you too will be penalized or thrown out of the game.

The third objection is perhaps not so much an objection but more a query. How is it that philosophers can have been so blind to the true nature of morality as the evolutionist claims? Does this mean that 2,500 years of philosophizing about morality is virtually worthless, little more than an academic exercise in moral logic-chopping? The answer to this query is that, in a sense, one would expect much moral philosophizing that occurred before Darwin to be redundant or radically incomplete. The evolutionist—and here I would include myself—is quite serious when he or she argues that the coming of evolutionary theory must necessarily make a radical difference to our conceptions of ourselves, calling for fundamental reevaluations.

Thus, in a way, I welcome a break with the past, feeling that it strengthens the case that I am making rather than weakening it. However, having said this, I do not pretend that no one before the publication of Darwin's *Origin* had any inkling of the way in which morality occurs or functions. To assume this would be presumptuous indeed. In fact, one vigorous well-known approach to moral thought, namely that of the British empiricists, is a natural forerunner to the evolutionary approach.[41] Historically, you would expect this since the great British evolutionists of the nineteenth century were themselves well-steeped in empiricist thought. And in fact, you can see conceptually that suspicions based on history do have a strong claim to being correct. Most particularly, if you look at the work of David Hume, you see that he is the complete forerunner of the evolutionary ethical position sketched in this paper. Hume argued that morality is not some objective phenomenon but a question of feeling or sentiment that works between people in order to facilitate social mechanisms.[42]

This is entirely the position of the evolutionist. Moreover, one can trace Hume's ideas back at least to the position of Thomas Hobbes, who started with the supposition that humans are naturally opposed to each other and that morality must in some way come out as a compromise or result of individual self-interests. This, obviously, is the starting point of the Darwinian evolutionist.

Hence, I argue that evolutionary ethics is not some completely new phenomenon. It is the natural continuation of an approach to moral philosophy started by Hobbes, which found its pre-evolutionary flowering in the work of David Hume. Now, at last, we are in a position to carry forward the work of the empiricists. We can make clear and complete that which they could not because we (unlike them) are no longer ignorant of the fact and process of evolution.

CONCLUSION

This discussion has been partially empirical and partially philosophical. I argue that we are now at last in a position to grasp the essential outlines of the biological evolution of human morality. When one does this, one sees that morality has no objective existence of its own. It is purely an adaptive mechanism for facilitating cooperation between humans. As such, it is a collective illusion. But to argue this is neither to pitch oneself into a crypto-fascist view of human nature nor to commit appalling conceptual fallacies. It is, rather, to grasp the essential humanness of our nature. Moral philosophy can grow out of its Creationist Christian antecedents. At last, it can grapple realistically with the fact that we humans, like the rest of organic nature, are the end products of a long, slow process of evolution through natural selection. For myself, I find this a liberating and exhilarating beginning, not a morbid conclusion to all that I have hitherto held dear. To paraphrase St. Paul, the time has come to stop looking through a glass darkly and to grow up.

NOTES

1. Michael Ruse, *Can a Darwinian Be a Christian?* (Cambridge: Cambridge University Press, 2000).
2. Charles Darwin, *Descent of Man* (London: Murray, 1871); Michael Ruse, *Darwinism Defended: A Guide to the Evolution Controversies* (Reading, Mass.: Maddison-Wesley, 1982). See also D. Pilbeam, "The Descent of Hominoids and Hominids," Scientific *American* 250, no. 3 (March 1964): 87–97.
3. D. Johanson and M. Edey, *Lucy: The Beginnings of Humankind* (New York: Simon and Schuster 1981).
4. L-K. Konigsson, *Current Argument on Early Man* (Oxford: Pergamon, 1980).
5. F. J. Ayala and R. W. Valentine, *Evolving: The Theory and Processes of Organic Evolution* (San Francisco: Benjamin Cummings, 1979).
6. H. M. Morris, *Scientific Creationism* (San Diego: Creation-Life, 1974).
7. H. Putnam, *Reason, Truth and History* (Cambridge: Cambridge University Press, 1981).
8. A. G. N. Flew, *Evolution and Ethics* (London: Macmillan, 1967).
9. Ruse, *Darwinism Defended*; C. Russett, *Darwin in America: The Intellectual Response 1865–1912* (San Francisco: Freeman, 1976).
10. A. Quinton, "Ethics and the Theory of Evolution," in *Biology and Personality*, edited by I. T. Ramsey (Oxford: Blackwell, 1966).
11. D. Hume, *Treatise of Human Nature*, edited by P. Nidditch (Oxford: Oxford University Press, 1978).
12. G. E. Moore, *Principia Ethica* (Cambridge: Cambridge University Press, 1903).
13. M. Ruse, *Sociobiology: Sense or Nonsense!* (Dordrecht, Netherlands: Reidel, 1979).
14. M. Ruse, *The Philosophy of Biology* (London: Hutchinson, 1973).

15. T. Dobzhanslcy, F. Ayala, G. L. Stebbins and J. Valentine, *Evolution* (San Francisco: Freeman, 1971).
16. R. C. Lewontin, "Adaptation," *Scientific American* 239, no. 3 (September 1978): 212–230.
17. R. D. Alexander, *Darwinism and Human Affairs* (Seattle: University of Washington Press, 1971).
18. O. J. Flanagan, "Is Morality Epiphenomenal?" *Philosophical Forum* 2132 (1981): 207–225
19. C. J. Lumsden and E. O. Wilson, *Genes, Mind and Culture* (Cambridge, Mass.: Harvard University Press, 1980).
20. See, for example, Bert Olivier's account of the birth of subjectivity through language in the previous section (Eds.).
21. It is also important to note in this respect the role of language and history in orientating cognition, as explored by Martin Heidegger and Hans-Georg Gadamer (Eds.).
22. P. van der Bergh, "Human Inbreeding Avoidance: Culture in Nature," *Behavioural and Brain Sciences* 6, no. 1 (March 1983): 91–102.
23. M. S. Adams and J. V. Neel, "Children of Incest," *Pediatrics* 40 (1967): 55–62.
24. See in this respect K. R. Popper, *The Logic of Scientific Discovery* (London: Hutchinson, 1959).
25. S. Hampshire, "The Illusion of Sociobiology," *New York Review of Books* 25 (October 12, 1978): 64–69.
26. J. L. Mackie, *Ethics: Intending Right and Wrong* (Harmondsworth, U.K.: Penguin, 1977).
27. Ruse, *Sociobiology*.
28. A. O. Lovejoy, *The Great Chain of Being* (Cambridge, Mass.: Harvard University Press, 1936).
29. M. Ruse, "Is Rape Wrong on Andromeda? Philosophical Reflections on Extra-Terrestrial Life," in *The Search for Extra-Terrestrials*, edited by E. Regis (Cambridge: Cambridge University Press, 1984).
30. M. Midgley, *Beast and Man: The Roots of Human Nature* (Ithaca, N.Y.: CornellUniversity Press, 1978).
31. I. Kant, *Critique of Practical Reason*, translated by L. W. Beck (Chicago: University of Chicago Press, 1949).
32. J. Rawls, *A Theory of Justice* (Cambridge, Mass.: Belknap, 1971).
33. J. S. Mill, "Utilitarianism" (1863), reprinted in *Mill's Utilitarianism*, edited by J. M. Smith and E. Sosa (Belmont, Calif.: Wadsworth, 1963).
34. E. O. Wilson, *Sociobiology: The New Synthesis* (Cambridge, Mass.: Harvard University-Press, 1975).
35. Rawls, *A Theory of Justice*.
36. Wilson, *Sociobiology*.
37. P. W. Taylor, *Problems of Moral Philosophy* (Belmont, Calif.: Wadsworth, 1978).
38. Lewontin, "Adaptation."
39. P. Singer, *The Expanding Circle: Ethics and Sociobiology* (New York: Farrar, Straus, and Giroux, 1976).
40. J. Murphy, *Evolution, Morality, and the Meaning of Life* (Totowa, N.J.: Rowman& Littlefield, 1982).
41. Mackie, *Ethics*.
42. Hume, *Treatise of Human Nature*.

REFERENCES

Adams, M. S., and J. V. Neel. "Children of Incest." *Pediatrics* 40 (1967): 55–62.
Alexander, R. D. *Darwinism and Human Affairs*. Seattle: University of Washington Press, 1971.

Ayala, F. J., and R. W. Valentine. *Evolving: The Theory and Processes of Organic Evolution.* San Francisco: Benjamin Cummings, 1979.
Barash, D. *Sociobiology and Behavior*, 2nd edition. New York: Elsevier, 1982.
Darwin, C. *The Descent of Man.* London: Murray, 1971.
———. *On the Origin of Species.* London: Murray, 1859.
Dawkins, R. *The Selfish Gene.* Oxford: Oxford University Press, 1976.
Dobzhanslcy, T., F. Ayala, G. L. Stebbins, and J. Valentine. *Evolution.* San Francisco: Freeman, 1971.
Flanagan, O. J. "Is Morality Epiphenomenal?" *Philosophical Forum* 2132 (1981): 207–225.
Flew, A. G. N. *Evolution and Ethics.* London: Macmillan, 1967.
Gibbard, A. "Human Evolution and the Sense of Justice." In *Midwestern Studies in Philosophy* 7, edited by P. French et al., 31–46. Minneapolis: University of Minnesota Press, 1982.
Hamilton, W. D. "The Genetical Evolution of Social Behaviour." *Journal of the Theory of Biology* 7 (1964): 1–16.
Hampshire, S. "The Illusion of Sociobiology." *New York Review of Books* 25 (October 12, 1978): 64–69.
Himmelfarb, G. "Varieties of Social Darwinism." In *Victorian Minds.* London: Weidenfeld and Nicolson, 1968.
Hudson, W. D. *Modern Moral Philosophy.* London: Macmillan, 1970.
Hume, D. *Treatise of Human Nature.* Edited by P. Nidditch. Oxford: Oxford University Press, 1978.
Isaac, G. "Aspects of Human Evolution." In *From Molecules to Men*, edited by D. S. Bendall, 509–543. Cambridge: Cambridge University Press, 1983.
Johanson, D., and M. Edey. *Lucy: The Beginnings of Humankind.* New York: Simon and Schuster, 1981.
Kant, I. *Critique of Practical Reason.* Translated by L. W. Beck. Chicago: University of Chicago Press, 1949.
———. *Foundations of the Metaphysics of Morals.* Translated by L. W. Beck. Indianapolis: Bobbs-Merrill, 1959.
Konigsson, L-K. *Current Argument on Early Man.* Oxford: Pergamon, 1980.
Lewontin, R. C. "Adaptation." *Scientific American* 239, no. 3 (September 1978): 212–230.
Lovejoy, A. O. *The Great Chain of Being.* Cambridge, Mass.: Harvard University Press, 1936.
Lumsden, C. J., and E. O. Wilson. *Genes, Mind and Culture.* Cambridge, Mass.: Harvard University Press, 1980.
———. *Promethean Fire.* Cambridge, Mass.: Harvard University Press, 1983.
Mackie, J. L. *Ethics: Intending Right and Wrong.* Harmondsworth, U.K.: Penguin, 1977.
———. *Hume's Moral Theory.* London: Routledge and Kegan Paul, 1979.
Maynard Smith, J. "The Evolution of Behavior." *Scientific American* 239, no. 3 (1977): 176–193.
Mayr, E. *The Growth of Biological Thought.* Cambridge, Mass.; Harvard University Press, 1983.
Midgley, M. *Beast and Man: The Roots of Human Nature.* Ithaca, N.Y.: Cornell University Press, 1978.
Mill, J. S. *Utilitarianism* (1863). Reprinted in *Mill's Utilitarianism*, edited by J. M. Smith and E. Sosa. Belmont, Calif.: Wadsworth, 1963.
Moore, G. E. *Principia Ethica.* Cambridge: Cambridge University Press, 1903.
Morris, H. M. *Scientific Creationism.* San Diego: Creation-Life, 1974.
Murphy, J. *Evolution, Morality, and the Meaning of Life.* Totowa, N.J.: Rowman & Littlefield, 1982.
Pilbeam, D. "The Descent of Hominoids and Hominids." *Scientific American* 250, no. 3 (March 1964): 87–97.
Popper, K. R. *The Logic of Scientific Discovery.* London: Hutchinson, 1959.
Putnam, H. *Reason, Truth and History.* Cambridge: Cambridge University Press, 1981.

Quinton, A. "Ethics and the Theory of Evolution." In *Biology and Personality*, edited by I. T. Ramsey. Oxford: Blackwell, 1966.
Rawls, J. *A Theory of Justice*. Cambridge, Mass.: Belknap, 1971.
Ruse, M. *Can a Darwinian Be a Christian?* Cambridge: Cambridge University Press, 2000.
———. *The Darwinian Revolution: Science Red in Tooth And Claw*. Chicago: University of Chicago Press, 1979.
———. *Darwinism Defended: A Guide to the Evolution Controversies*. Reading, Mass.: Maddison-Wesley, 1982.
———. "Is Rape Wrong on Andromeda? Philosophical Reflections on Extra-Terrestrial Life." In *The Search for Extra-Terrestrials*, edited by E. Regis. Cambridge: Cambridge University Press, 1984.
———. *The Philosophy of Biology*. London: Hutchinson, 1973.
———. "Social Darwinism: The Two Sources." *Revista Di Filosofia* (1982): 22–23.
———. *Sociobiology: Sense or Nonsense!* Dordrecht, Netherlands: Reidel, 1979.
Russett C. *Darwin in America: The Intellectual Response 1865–1912*. San Francisco: Freeman, 1976.
Singer, P. *The Expanding Circle: Ethics and Sociobiology*. New York: Farrar, Straus, and Giroux, 1976.
Taylor, P. W. *Problems of Moral Philosophy*. Belmont, Calif.: Wadsworth, 1978.
Trigg, R. *The Shaping of Man*. Oxford: Blackwell, 1982.
Trivera, R. L. "The Evolution of Reciprocal Altruism." *The Quarterly Review of Biology* 46, no. 1 (March 1971): 35–57.
van de Bergh, P. *Human Family Systems: An Evolutionary View*. New York: Elsevier, 1978.
———. "Human Inbreeding Avoidance: Culture in Nature." *Behavioural and Brain Sciences* 6, no. 1 (March 1983): 91–102.
Wilson, E. O. *On Human Nature*. Cambridge, Mass.: Harvard University Press, 1978.
———. *Sociobiology: The New Synthesis*. Cambridge, Mass.: Harvard University Press, 1975.

Chapter Four

Return to the Enlightenment

Susan Neiman

Morality as a problem is a surprisingly recent phenomenon in human history. True, the ancient philosophers had run the gamut of ethical positions, ranging from a form of relativism (Heraclitus) to a form of absolutism (Plato, if you are in the Karl Popper camp). However, these tended to be intellectual exercises: until modernity, societies had generally been embedded in an accepted set of customs sanctioned by some or other form of divine power. In fact, Derek Parfit accounted for the lacunae in secular moral theory by pointing out that it was a relatively young field of inquiry.

The notion that morality can be liberated from its religious roots and placed on what is seen as a more reliable, or more authentic, foundation is a classic Enlightenment ideal. Enlightenment-era religious commentary was more or less a response to the conflict of the preceding century. During this period, scholars often sought to curtail the political power of organized religion and thereby prevent another age of seemingly endless conflict. Spinoza was determined to remove politics from contemporary and historical theology (and, by so doing, to disregard Judaic law). Mendelssohn advised affording no political weight to any organized religion and instead recommended that each person followed what they found most convincing. They believed a good religion was based in instinctive morals and a belief in God should theoretically not need force to maintain order in its believers. Both Mendelssohn and Spinoza judged religion on its moral fruits, not the logic of its theology.

There is much to be said for this approach, but the fact that there is room at all for a book such as this one indicates that this answer did not prove to be sufficient either. Kant, too, noticed the theoretical shortfall and attempted to formulate a watertight foundation for morality for rational beings, the famous categorical imperative and its reformulations. These formulations are not as watertight as Kant intended, but among his most important contributions to philosophy was his challenge to Westerners to achieve maturity: to think for themselves. Although Kant did not necessarily mean atheism, he did challenge his contemporaries to consider philosophical questions without reference to traditional authority.

Susan Neiman places herself in the tradition of Spinoza, Mendelssohn, and Kant. Drawing on the famous story of Abraham, she considers appeals to divine authority dangerous and argues that for all its shortcomings—as pointed out by, among others figures, Adorno, Foucault, and Derrida—we should reconsider the merits of the Enlightenment message and ground morality in pure reason alone.

—The Editors

Consider what you mean when you tell someone to be realistic. A good translation would be to decrease your expectations. The world is going to disappoint you, so you might as well forget about trying to realize your ideals. There usually follow a few clichés about human nature and other things that cannot be changed. Realistic is equivalent to resigned, which is equivalent to mature. Calling someone an idealist, on the other hand, has become equivalent to calling her a fool, and quite a lot of political and other arguments are won by calling one's opponent idealistic, without stopping to ask what it means. These are the kinds of metaphysical questions that determine our lives. Of course, the question "What is reality?" has led to a lot of pedantry, but your answer to that question may have very real consequences. If you believe that reality only consists of experience, you have no means with which to go beyond experience. If you believe that ideas too have reality and power, you can use them to change experience.

Let us look for a moment at Plato because both the concept of idealism and the scorn for idealists began in his masterpiece *The Republic*—the first great book with which Western philosophy begins. This book opens with a group of men trying to find a definition of justice. One example: justice is helping your friends and hurting your enemies. OK, answers Socrates, are we supposed to help our apparent friends or only our real ones, and how do we know the difference? Should we help our real friends if they do something wrong? And why should we be intent on hurting our enemies, when we know that even a dog becomes worse when you hurt it?

There follows a rather hapless discussion until Thrasymachus enters the scene—that postmodern young man who is almost 2,500 years old. He makes fun of his elders for what he calls their naïveté: why go to the bother of trying to define justice? Do not they know that justice is simply the justice of the winners of history, who preach a set of rules that are designed to keep them in power? Moral concepts are merely instruments of power that serve the self-interest of the stronger in exploiting the weaker. Anyone naïve enough to take them seriously is no better than the sheep who believes that the shepherd does his work for the welfare of the sheep—and goes on believing it all the way to the slaughterhouse.

This should sound familiar even if you haven't read a word of Plato—because every generation seems to find it necessary to invent its own Thrasymachus, who suddenly discovers that moral concepts are often abused and therefore decides to give up on them entirely. Every Thrasymachus believes he is being both brave and honest. Every new incarnation of him is convinced that he is the first one to recognize the lies that we poor misguided sheep fail to see. This insistence on demystification can occur in every political direction, but what worries me most is the popularity of Thrasymachus in the contemporary left.

The arguments he brings are always more historical than philosophical. In Western Europe, moral language was abused by the fascists as well as the church that did so little to oppose fascism. In Eastern Europe, the communist appeal to self-sacrifice on behalf of the common good served, after 1989, to make any such appeal seem faintly nauseating. Nor should we forget the way that the end of colonialism made clear how often simple greed and racism stood behind universalist rhetoric.

I have called Kant a grown-up idealist. There are many reasons to view Kant's work as a major source for progressive politics. He developed ideas of international law, a United Nations, and prefigured social democracy. But none of these ideas is as important as the idea of the idea itself—for without this basic metaphysics no other idea has a chance. Every proposal for change can be met with a shake of conservative heads. You have certainly heard claims like "Freedom and equality are nice in theory, but the hard facts of experience have shown that it is utopian to expect them in practice." Perhaps you have even made them yourself. It is interesting to learn that claims like these were already clichéd in 1793, when Kant wrote the essay "On the Old Saw: That May Be Right in Theory But It Will Not Work in Practice." In that essay as elsewhere, he turns the claims of the so-called realists upside down. Naturally, the ideas of reason conflict the facts of experience. That is what ideas are supposed to do. For it is reason's job to ensure that experience does not have the last word—and it is reason that drives us to widen the horizons of our experience by providing ideas that experience should obey. If enough of us do so, it will.

I call this idealism grown-up because it demands a great deal. Grown-up idealism demands that we recognize how much we are torn: the gap between the way the world is and the way the world should be is too great to ever disappear. I grant you: this is a standpoint that guarantees a lifetime of dissatisfaction. It is much easier to give up on ideals altogether. If you believe that universal justice is a childish fantasy, you have no obligation to work for it. In this sense, realism is a form of resignation. So the standpoint of Thrasymachus will probably always be with us: the rhetoric sounds brave and tough, but the practice is actually quite comfortable, demanding nothing but occasional criticism.

Don't ideals need foundations? Religion is often seen as the foundation of all moral concepts—and it is seen that way by both believers and atheists. The Bible, however, sees it differently. Let us turn to the story of Sodom and Gomorrah, often abused as a classic fundamentalist text. But the crimes that were committed there were not sexual license or even homosexuality. The Sodomites had the habit of gang-raping passing strangers to death. Most of us would agree with G-d that this should be punished, and G-d tells his favorite son, Abraham, that he plans to do just that. When he hears the plan to destroy both cities, Abraham—who otherwise accepts every word of the Lord without comment or complaint—speaks up. We can paraphrase his response like this: Is the judge of the world really going to destroy the innocent along with the guilty? That is hardly what justice looks like! The judge of the world agrees; if there are fifty just people in Sodom, he will leave the city alone. But the Lord is surely not a pedant! Would He destroy the cities for a mere lack of five? Indeed the Lord is not a pedant. If there are forty-five righteous men in Sodom and Gomorrah, the cities will be saved. A long discussion occurs in which Abraham bargains G-d down to ten, Scholars have argued about the reason for just this number; I think ten is small enough for those included to gather their things and run, which is just what happens in the end.

Three aspects of Abraham's behavior warm hearts like mine. The first is his universalism. His concern for innocent life here is not concern for his friends or his neighbors: he risks his life to argue for those who remain abstract and nameless. The second aspect is his courage. In arguing for the life of the innocents of Sodom, he is willing to risk his own. His world is not, after all, a democracy, yet he dares to tell the King of Kings that He's about to violate moral law. Third and perhaps most important: everything depends on detail. Numbers matter. Small differences matter. Abraham may sound like a merchant but he thinks like a moralist. If he can bring G-d to think about details, none of us is exempt. Moral judgments are complex, detailed, and seldom absolute. But through this exchange some moral principles become clear: rape is a crime—and so is collateral damage.

We have moral needs, needs so strong they can override our instincts for self-protection, as the story of Abraham shows. It also shows those needs are not based in religion or any form of divine command. They include the need to express reverence and the need to express outrage, the need to reject euphemism and cant and call things by their proper names. They include the need to see our own lives as stories with meaning—meanings we impose on the world, a crucial source of human dignity—without which we hold our lives to be worthless. Most basically and surprisingly, we need to see the world in moral terms. These needs are grounded in a structure of reason. While they may be furthered by religion or emotion, that is not what keeps them alive. They are based in the principle of sufficient reason that we use as a compass. Moral inquiry and political activism start where reason is missing. When righteous people suffer and wicked people flourish, we begin to ask why.

Abraham is the father of monotheism. According to all three Western religions, nobody ever had a more direct connection to G-d. Despite that connection, G-d is not the source of his moral consciousness; on the contrary, Abraham is prepared to give the Lord a lesson in ethics. Those who believe that religion is the motor of morality tend to forget this story in favor of one that is much better known: Abraham's willingness to sacrifice his own son. The binding of Isaac feeds fundamentalists of all kinds, who preach the conclusion: if Abraham was prepared to sacrifice his son without even a question, the rest of us should be willing to accept every lesser demand of religious authority.

Both stories stand at the beginning of the Bible, and all three Western religions have signposts pointing both ways. Fundamentalists view faith as obedience: to be a believer is to follow laws that you need not understand. Rationalists, by contrast—and they have been around in all three religions since the middle ages—view reason as one of G-d's gifts. (There are Jewish texts that show G-d laughing with pleasure because His children have defeated Him with a particularly good argument.) According to this tradition, our capacity to think about life and the meaning of it is another proof of the goodness of G-d. For no law interprets itself, and holy books have to be interpreted like any others. The great Jewish, Christian, and Muslim legal traditions were developed for this reason, with great influence on legal thinking to the present.

Remembering these facts should stop us from dividing the world along religious and secular lines. Many rationalist religious thinkers have more in common with secular Social Democrats than with fellow believers; many a fideist is closer to postmodern nihilism than he or she knows. Far less important than your belief that God exists, or that He does not, is what you think your belief entails. Does it direct your behavior by rules and commandments that are set out before you, or does it require you to think them through yourself? Does it require you to try to make sense of the world, or does it give up on sense itself?

The difference between the two moral paradigms is far more important than whether you call yourself religious or secular. Those paradigms could be described in drier terms, without mentioning Abraham or God at all. But the greatness of the Bible—even if you are not sure what it means to call it divine—is that it sets out the choices so starkly that nothing has come close to being as clear since. So let us call the first paradigm that of Abraham at

Sodom, who refuses to rest in the humility of resignation and demands that his world make sense. Those who subscribe to this paradigm hold fast to the principle that there must be reasons for everything that happens, and that those reasons are up to us to find. This is the fundamental law to which everyone, including God, must answer, and it leads us to seek not only justice but transparent justice. The second paradigm is that of Abraham at Mt. Moriah, who does not ask anything at all. This man of faith is certain: the demand to find reason after reason is at odds with a grateful acceptance of Creation and arrogant to boot.

The two Abraham stories are pages apart in the Bible and worlds apart in their message. One urges us to submit to God's orders; however outrageous they appear to be they will lead us right in the end. The other urges us to question, for even a message that comes in God's voice may need to be reconsidered. Both stories are deeply part of our repertoire, anchored firmly in the very first book of the Bible on which so many others depend. Even those who believe in biblical authority will not find it decisive here. They have to decide how the book should be read.

Any serious reading of it will raise the question: are things good because God loves them, or does God love them because they are good? As readers of Plato will remember, this question is not confined to monotheism. Socrates was executed for alleged impiety. His crime was not atheism—he really did worship the local gods—but insisting that reason be put before them. Goodness is not arbitrary. Things must be good in themselves, which is what makes the gods love them; the gods' choice cannot make something good that is evil just because they are gods.

Traditional religion paints a nightmare of anarchy and violence that erupts whenever divine authority is missing, and there are people who claim that they would up and kill their neighbors without religious prohibitions on murder. Yet we know they do not. Virtuous atheists have been around and been noticed for centuries, but most of them now suspect the language of virtue. Though they do not accept the idea that moral values are empty without religious ones, they accept no alternative framework. Worse than that: they have seen too many frameworks abused. Rules conceived as universal values have too often been used as sugarcoated ways of forcing one people's will on another. As a result, the rebuke "Don't be judgmental!" is now firmly embedded in American slang. Though it began in good conscience—to express the discovery that many of our judgments were based on assumptions the whole world does not share—it has ended by stifling conscience altogether. The resolve not to impose your moral worldview by force often ends with the resolve to make no judgments at all. For those who live without divine sanctions, judgments of good—and especially evil—are off-limits.

Both Abraham and Socrates offer another perspective. Whether the tradition is monotheist or pagan, it has central sources for denying that we need religious authority to maintain morality. The Abraham of Sodom and Gomorrah certainly did not; it was he who risked his life to give God lessons in ethics—and this story comes at the start of monotheistic tradition. Any ethics that needs religion is bad ethics; any religion that tries to play on this is bad religion. Of course there are plenty of both around, a practical question that must be dealt with practically. But first we must see that neither genuine religious nor genuine moral impulses are ever expressed in standpoints that tie the two essentially together.

Those who view religion as necessary for morality reduce us to the moral level of four-year-olds. If you follow these commandments, you will go to heaven, and if you do not, you will burn in hell is just a spectacular version of the carrots and sticks with which we raise our children: if you clean up your room, you will get the cookie, and if you do not, you will stay inside. Those of us who have raised them know that even if we rely on bribes and threats in the short term, the moral behavior we seek to instill requires us to get beyond them. We want to prepare our kids to be responsible and generous and straightforward even when rewards are not forthcoming, as they often are not in the parts of the world we do not control. Serious believers, on the other hand, despise the sort of faith that springs up in foxholes. The religious feeling they cherish is not about a Being who can be bribed: I will do whatever you say if only you will save me. They hold this attitude to be no better than that of a pagan who thinks the gods will protect him if only he serves up a particularly tasty bit of entrails. True faith, they think, is not a matter of bargaining but of gratitude—certainly for Creation and possibly for salvation as well.

If you acknowledge that serious religion and serious ethics are thus separate matters, you must believe things are good or evil independent of divine authority. At this point in the argument, many people turn to self-interest. Moderation, argued the former Greek slave Epicurus, is a virtue because gluttony and drunkenness are bad for your health. Enlightened self-interest, therefore, is all you need to be temperate. Keeping promises, said the Prussian philosopher Kant, is an expression of honesty, but it also builds strong communities. Or would you choose to live in a world where you could not take people at their word? Today evolutionary biologists argue that altruism has adaptive advantage; generous behavior will be selected because it increases the species' chances to survive. Richard Dawkins argues that you need not focus on the survival of the fittest species; altruistic behavior is already rewarded at the level of the gene pool. But he readily concedes that biological self-interest cannot account for the kinds of sacrifice we hold central to moral experience. At such points, many secular thinkers retreat to the view that the basis of morality is political, a system of law constructed—more or less nefariously—to maintain civil order.

All such arguments depend on the view that if religion does not tell us to be moral, something else has to do so; self-interest and order look like the sort of hard-nosed bases to which unsentimental souls can appeal. And it is certainly true that much—perhaps most—moral behavior is to our own and our communities' advantage. Honesty is often the best policy; kindness is often reciprocated. Even observing traffic rules creates a measure of order and safety that benefits us all. Hence a great many rules that are both ethical and useful have been shared and internalized throughout different times and cultures, so that we are socialized—perhaps hardwired—to do the right thing with astonishing frequency.

Yet sometimes morality and self-interest part company, and when they do, such arguments leave us helpless. For though they seemed sober and scientific, they implicitly rely on a notion of preestablished harmony that is both ancient and suspect. What a marvelous system that keeps our needs and the world so finely calibrated that self-interest and morality run on parallel tracks! Bishop Butler, the eighteenth-century founder of natural theology in England, did not know about gene pools, but he considered it self-evident that it is in our constitution to condemn falsehood, violence, and injustice. In his day, it was called Providence: the assumption that virtue and happiness are perfectly balanced by an invisible guiding hand. Even Job knew enough to question that.

If morality is settled neither by the claims of religion nor the claims of self-interest, must we believe there is an otherworldly standard of goodness, fixed and eternal in a transcendent world? Plato seemed to think so, and his metaphysics provided centuries of fuel for postmodernist fires. (Not all postmodernist claims are recent.) What was attacked was more fairy tale than Plato's own views; it is unlikely that he pictured ideas as ghostly objects in the heavens beaming down at the shadows below. Still he did believe that things are good or true or beautiful because they participate in ideas far above and beyond them. What all these views have in common is the thought that morality must be commanded—if not by God, then by nature; if not by nature, then by a supernatural metaphysics with the features of both. This will pose problems for anyone who rejects a particular source of commandment. Perhaps even more important: what about those who believe that being moral is not a matter of following orders, whether natural or supernatural, but about the dignity of freely choosing to do right?

With consequences too unhappy to be ironic, most voices willing to speak in (allegedly) universal moral terms at all now come from the right. And this is what's true in the claim that the left has trouble with values, a claim that can, understandably, make its targets' blood boil. Right-wing talk of moral clarity and honor and heroism is sometimes empty, but that is not the same as being meaningless. Empty concepts remain concepts, in search of an application. The left, by contrast, has deflated the concepts themselves and put nothing but irony in their place. What the left lacks is not values but a standpoint from which all those values make sense.

Two thousand years of religious war—whether fought by soldiers or scholars—should have convinced us by now that religion cannot be the basis of morality. Even the Bible often denies that, as the story of Abraham shows. For many people, religion remains a way to live out moral ideals, but it cannot ground them. This realization has often led philosophers to seek another metaphysical basis for morality—a long and often dull story that I do not want to examine here. What's interesting is our longing for commandments that determine morality—if not through religion, then perhaps through nature, as the attempts of many recent evolutionary psychologists show. These attempts reveal the wish to avoid the uncertainties that are present in moral reflection—even if your name happens to be Abraham or G-d.

Rather than looking for foundations, I prefer to speak of orientation. We can find orientation for moral concepts in the thought of the much-maligned Enlightenment—if we are prepared to look beyond its caricatures. Few things are trendier than Enlightenment bashing today, but none of the postmodern critics of the Enlightenment offer anything in its stead. A defense of the Enlightenment is a defense of the modern world—with all its possibilities for self-criticism and transformation. Much of the modern world deserves serious critique. But the possibilities for self-correction and change are missing in the other two alternatives: premodern nostalgia (everything used to be better; today we are decadent) or postmodern skepticism (decadence too is a category, like every other, that has been deconstructed). You can mourn the loss of the premodern world; you can yawningly accept the postmodern one—or you can defend and continue the modern.

What are the most common criticisms that have been made of it?

1. The Enlightenment believed that human beings are by nature good and endlessly getting better.
2. The Enlightenment believed that reason is unlimited and can solve every problem and paid no attention to the role of emotion.
3. The Enlightenment believed nothing was sacred and profaned everything.
4. The Enlightenment believed that progress was inevitable—and ended in Auschwitz and Hiroshima.

These claims are supported by no more than a few scraps of historical testimony, always torn out of context. This is not a matter of nuance: the Enlightenment is not only subtler than the caricatures of its critics; it was diametrically opposed to them. You need not be a scholar to figure this out. Forget about the archives and buy a paperback edition of *Candide*, the most-read book of the Enlightenment, and you will see that the most important attacks on the so-called Enlightenment came from the heart of the Enlightenment itself. *Candide* makes it clear that the Enlightenment opposed all the clichés that are attributed to it: it believed neither that human nature was benevolent nor that progress was inevitable, neither that human reason was unlimited nor science the answer to everything. If the Enlightenment did not rest on such weak and silly principles, what did it believe?

Tolerance and fairness are always mentioned as Enlightenment values, but it is important to focus on values that are more robust than these. Tolerance, in particular, is a negative value: it may prevent some of our worst excesses, but it will not move anyone to action. Even worse, we tolerate that which we do not like and cannot change: the headache that aspirin will not cure, the loud noise coming from a neighbor's apartment, the stink in the corner of the subway. Telling a racist to be more tolerant is only reminding her of her powerlessness. I want to concentrate, rather, on four modern values that are particularly important: happiness, reason, reverence, and hope.

The Enlightenment demanded a right to happiness, which may seem banal until you think about how happiness was viewed in the premodern world. Before the Enlightenment, happiness was put in the past—in a mythical paradise that our ancestors lost through one sin or another—or in the future—in a heavenly paradise that we might, with grace, reach after our death. For the present, the order of the day was suffering. Sickness and poverty were the consequences of sin or fate and therefore part of a cosmic order we had no right to judge.

The Enlightenment was hardly unaware that the world is full of suffering. No era devoted more reflection to the problem of evil. But to be committed to Enlightenment means to reject the view that suffering and injustice are punishments. Rather they are evils that can and should be addressed by human beings. Anyone who attempts to combat the injustices in the human world or the inadequacies in the natural world is acting on the assumption that all of us—however and wherever we were born—have the same right to happiness on earth. If you believe, by contrast, that life consists of suffering, you will be unlikely to do anything but sigh.

Happiness is a matter of right and not simply of luck. Our longing for happiness is neither a childish wish nor a weakness. Reason demands a balance between what you do in the world and what the world does to you. Of course you can say sentences like these: anyone who rapes and murders children should be rewarded with fame and fortune; anyone who protects children should be slowly tortured to death. You can say those sentences, but can you possibly mean them? Aren't they like Descartes's claim that, in principle, two and two could be five if G-d chose to make them so? A world in which righteous people always suffer and wicked people always triumph is a world that makes no sense. To be sure, there are days when the world looks just like that. That is why the claim that we have a right to happiness makes demands on the present. If happiness is a human right in a world in which so many people suffer, it is the task of human beings to work toward it.

If reason tells us that we have a right to happiness, only experience can tell us what will actually make us happy, and the Enlightenment's visions of happiness are as different as the thinkers of the Enlightenment themselves. But as different as those visions of happiness could be, they all had one thing in common: happiness is neither hedonism nor a blissful end state. If paradise were a place where all our wishes were satisfied, it would bore us to death. The good life can take many forms, but none of them is passive.

The Enlightenment conception of reason is just as active as its conception of happiness. The Enlightenment attacked the mechanical-instrumental conception of reason conceived by classical rationalism—not only because that conception is not in a position to explain the world but because it is neither free nor can it serve as an instrument of freedom. For that is its task: contrary to the Romantics, reason is not opposed to nature but to authority. Traditional authorities retain power by restricting the right to think to a small group of elites. In the eighteenth century, the authorities were the church-backed aristocracy; today they are more likely to be neoliberal economists or technocrats. Enlightenment thinkers were well aware that reason has limits; they just weren't prepared to let the authorities be the ones to set them. Everyone can think for themselves, and everyone can fail. To be grown-up means to take your own life in your hands. Precisely because it is able to go beyond experience, reason is able to ask the question: this could have been different, so why is it like this? Reason's guiding principle is the principle of sufficient reason—not as a statement that everything in the world has a reason but rather as a demand: find out what the reason is for the way things now are. Many things can count as reasons, but some things do not: that is just the way it is; it was always that way; they told me so. Our ability to find reasons for what is given is the basis both of scientific inquiry and of social justice. The personification of reason is not the rule-obsessed technocrat but rather Mozart's Figaro, who uses his reason against the aristocracy, not against his own passions but precisely in order to fulfill them.

I have sketched somewhat different pictures of Enlightenment conceptions of happiness and reason than those that are normally painted, but no one will be surprised to hear them listed as Enlightenment values. But reverence and Enlightenment do not seem to fit together. Both critics and defenders of Enlightenment come easily to the conclusion that the attack on religion and anything in its neighborhood is the central goal of Enlightenment.

It is true that every thinker of the Enlightenment fought against fanaticism and superstition, particularly since they were the most important means of mystification that allowed traditional governments to retain authority. But many Enlightenment thinkers attacked traditional religion on religious grounds: according to them, orthodox religion was not only immoral but blasphemous. A religion of justice should not lead to bloodshed; a religion of truth should not depend on superstition; a religion of reverence should not appeal to our basest instincts. Hume described the biblical G-d as being driven by the lowest of human passions: an endless appetite for applause.

Hume was one of the few genuine agnostics among Enlightenment thinkers, but the majority supported the kind of religion they sometimes called natural, sometimes reasonable. This religion would be based on ideas that do not require revelation but can be known to everyone through the use of reason—and consequently be a means to unite people rather than divide them. The achievements of science were viewed as a proof of G-d's greatness: Creation had been shown to be a miracle—as was indeed our ability to understand it.

Why should a modern view hang onto any sort of religion at all, even one that has been purified of fanaticism and superstition? The Enlightenment vision of happiness involved the bold sort of striving that goes beyond what we have been given; its vision of reason is one that refuses to accept the given as given. Reverence, by contrast, is the moment in which we are simply grateful for it. However you understand the Creation of the world, one thing is certain: you did not do it. However you understand the notion of G-d, one idea is contained in it: human beings have limits. Reverence has more than one opposite: contempt, scorn, indifference, and above all envy, one of the deadliest sins. Reverence contains awe and above all gratitude: for being itself and for the fact that we have been granted the chance to experience it. You may have reverence for G-d or for nature but also for ideals of goodness, truth, and beauty—everything that is, finally, beyond our own reach. Reverence is the value that gives us balance. Kant put this the best: "Two things fill the mind with awe and wonder the more often and more steadily we reflect on them—the starry heavens above me and the moral law within me." One shows me my limits; the other shows me my freedom and power. Being grown-up is a matter of staying aware of both.

The fourth Enlightenment value is hope—not to be confused with the optimism that was so clearly rejected in *Candide*. Optimism is a denial of facts; hope is the attempt to change them. In order to determine if you are making progress, you have to know where you began. Modern philosophers tried to do this by speculating about the original state of nature. It is common to ascribe two different possibilities to two different philosophers: Hobbes stands for the belief that the state of nature is a state of permanent war, which can only become civilized through submission to absolute authority; Rousseau stands for the belief that the state of nature was originally benevolent, and civilization is responsible for our misery. Neither of these philosophers ever held such a simple view, but this seems to make little difference: they are standardly described this way in both classrooms and editorials, usually with the comment that Hobbes's worldview is the realistic one and Rousseau's the utopian. What's important is the fact that neither of these alternatives, nor anything more sensible in between, can ever be proven—despite the best efforts of many scientists. We will never have access to the state of nature—not only because we can no longer find peoples without civilization but because every image we try to form is colored by our wishes and our fears. Long before Claude Levi-Strauss tried to confirm Rousseau's view of the state of nature by traveling to the Amazon, Rousseau had recognized that our speculations about the state of nature are both projections and propaganda. If you want to establish an authoritarian government, you will try to convince people that it is natural for people to slaughter each other without the intervention of a strong leader. If you want to found a social democracy, you will magnify every example of natural cooperation. Instead of futile attempts to find out the truth about the state of nature, Rousseau proposed radical honesty: our pictures of humankind's distant past are tools that we use to create our future. Which future do we want to work on?

Neither Rousseau nor any other serious modern thinker ever claimed that human beings are essentially good—only that they are not born in original sin, either in the biblical or the Hobbesian version. Rousseau's observation that even animals feel compassion has been confirmed by modern scientific research. Not only apes and elephants demonstrate compassion and kindness; rats stop eating when they discover that their taking of food sends an electric shock to other rats. Proofs that our capacities for compassion are fundamental and inborn have been recently offered by every field from child psychology to neurobiology—which has recently discovered what are called mirror neurons that react to the pain of others the way we react to our own. We have the tools to behave well. That we can behave badly hardly needs to be repeated.

And that is the question that is more interesting than all the questions we cannot answer: if our capacity for goodness is as evident as our capacity for evil, why are we so insistent on the latter? Pessimism is fashionable. Formerly it was the conservatives who insisted on pointing out just how bad the human race is—which was at least consistent with their own stated purposes, which involved rejecting any attempt to make things better since the best one could hope for was to prevent their getting worse. Today it is people who belong to what is sometimes called the progressive tradition who refuse to use the word "progress"—at least not without quotation marks, the ultimate postmodern gesture. That things we once thought would be progress turned out not to be progress is not open to doubt, but it is hardly an argument for the idea that progress is impossible. There is no such argument. If you ask for one, you are likely to get the suggestion that the only alternative to believing that progress is impossible is believing it is inevitable. There are a few texts of Hegel and Marx that suggest such a view, but no Enlightenment thinker ever believed that progress is necessary—only that it is possible. Why are we tempted to deny that?

Hobbes's view of human nature is part of a long and dismal tradition that seems to make us feel at home. Amazingly, many committed atheists hold fast to one of the more disturbing elements of Christianity, the doctrine of original sin. Christianity has made that doctrine familiar, but I do not believe Christianity is essential here. Original sin, in its many variations, doesn't feel comfortable because Christianity cultivated it; Christianity cultivated it because it is a useful explanation for the problem of evil. Religion, in the first instance, is an attempt to cope with that problem. Why is there such a gap between the way the world is and the way the world should be? The doctrine of original sin may give us responsibility, but it also gives us consolation, for it offers a reason for all the evils we experience: humankind is corrupt, and it has been that way from the start. Any explanation is better than no explanation at all, for that seems to imply that the universe is senseless—and we seem to be able to bear anything, including our own alleged guilt, better than sheer meaninglessness. Our inclination to believe the very worst about human nature has its roots not in fact but in faith.

If we can find out the facts about neither the essence of human nature nor the future of humanity, we should choose the conception of human nature that offers the most hope for its future. Original sin offers no prospects but grace or despair. If we are to act morally, we must believe that our actions can contribute to the progress of humankind. This is not wishful thinking but a condition on the possibility of any moral action. Kant called it rational faith. But even Kant knew that the abstract conviction that progress is possible is not always enough to sustain our actions when times are tough. At some point, one needs a sign that shows that progress is not only possible but occasionally also actual. His sign was so minimalist that it gives the lie to every caricature of Enlightenment optimism. Not the French Revolution itself, he wrote, but the fact that people all over the world looked to the French Revolution with disinterested hope was a sign that human beings are capable of making moral progress. That is not very much, but then Kant described himself as a melancholy sort of person.

I do not have much use for original sin, but I do keep noticing two pervasive character traits that seem fairly universal and fairly destructive: we have very short memories, and we're inclined to be ungrateful. Think back half a century: the war of all against all that Hobbes thought was natural took place in what's now called the European Union. Seen with a little historical perspective, the European Union is a miracle, but few Europeans believe it today. To point to the fact that Europe is a miracle is not to refrain from criticizing the gray and often self-serving, even self-destructive bureaucracy it has engendered. But without recognizing the achievement that Europe represents, we will never be able to make critique constructive nor realize its possibilities. Similarly, the idea that America would elect an African American president was barely imaginable before it happened. To be sure, Obama's election created a backlash that unleashed Donald Trump on the world. But the fact that Obama could be twice elected—and gain the respect and admiration of most of the world—is still a sign of progress for all that.

I like pointing to good news—not because I do not know the bad news but because it is too common and easy to point it out. More importantly, I believe that if we cannot celebrate our successes we will never go on to make more. I could reel off a list of major instances of human progress in my lifetime alone; few of them are unfamiliar, but all of them are things we're inclined to take for granted. But hope is a virtue, which means that it is not a given—it is something one often has to work hard to retain.

The point of pointing to signs of progress is not to let us rest on our laurels but to give us the courage to do more. It is easy to count off the signs of decline. Why do we enjoy doing so? Among other things, it is a form of self-protection: idealists will spend their whole lives struggling with disappointment, while pessimists can only be pleasantly surprised. Though so-called realists may claim to be tough, their position is far more comfortable: the rest of us are walking a tightrope all the time.

Idealism is a matter of dignity. We want to determine the world, not simply be determined by it. We want to stand above the things we sometimes want to consume. We are born and we die as part of nature, but we feel most alive when we go beyond it. To be human is to refuse to accept the given as given.

REFERENCES

Aristotle. *The Nicomachean Ethics*. Edited and translated by Robert C. Bartlett and Susan D. Collins. Chicago: University of Chicago Press, 2012.
The Holy Bible, New King James Version. Nashville: Thomas Nelson Publishers, 1982.
Kant, I. *Practical Philosophy*. In *The Cambridge Edition of the Works of Immanuel Kant in English*. Translated by Mary Gregor. Cambridge: Cambridge University Press, 1996.
———. *Religion and Rational Theology*. Translated by Allen Wood and George di Giovanni. Cambridge: Cambridge University Press, 1996.
Neiman, S. *Evil in Modern Thought*. Princeton, N.J.: Princeton University Press, 2015.
Plato, *The Republic*. Edited, translated, and with an interpretative essay by Alan Bloom. New York: Basic Books, 2016.

Part II

The Ambivalents

Chapter Five

No Science of Morality

Steven Weinberg

In an age in which the argument that science can decide matters like the nature of the good life is frequently made, it is important to listen to what scientists themselves have to say on the subject. Without the voices of those who practice the natural sciences, the debate about whether science or religion should be the final arbiters of morality can become empty and overly theoretical. It is interesting to note that some of the fiercest conflicts between science and religion occur in philosophy: most theologians stick to the grand narrative contained in the ancient texts. The majority of natural scientists, too, are well aware of the limits of a purely empirical approach.

Steven Weinberg is one such scientist. A Nobel laureate, member of the Royal Society, and recipient of the Benjamin Franklin Medal, he is considered by many to be the preeminent theoretical physicist alive today. He is known, among other things, for his contributions with Abdus Salam and Sheldon Glashow to the theory of the unified weak and electromagnetic interaction between elementary particles. One may have expected Weinberg to uphold a position similar to that of Sam Harris and defend the natural sciences as being able to serve as a complete foundation for human morality.

Contrary to expectations, Weinberg adheres to Stephen Jay Gould's classic formulation for what he considered to be the authentic relationship between science and religion, namely Non-Overlapping Magisteria, or NOMA, according to which science and religion are two distinct domains, each with their own tools for determining veracity and value. But Weinberg does not simply repeat Gould. In contrast to Harris, he accepts Hume's classic fact/value distinction and holds that while science can provide interesting observations with respect to morality, it is best to accept the moral consensus which that developed over the centuries in a painful but productive fashion.

—*The Editors*

Science cannot give us any help in discovering the principles on which we ought to base our actions. It seems to me, as it did to David Hume, that there is an unbridgeable gulf between the "is" and the "ought." Science does have a morality of its own—a commitment to honesty, an aversion to wishful thinking—but it cannot without circularity justify itself.

I would go further: moral principles can never be established by any systematic mode of thought. I wish I could prove this—it would save a good deal of argument—but I can at least throw the burden of proof on those who think that there is some line of reasoning on which one can base moral principles. No one has ever succeeded in finding such a justification.

Not that they haven't tried. Most often, those who have made these attempts have started with an ungrounded assumption about a goal that people ought to pursue and then worked out rationally how to achieve that goal. Thus Aristotle, in *The Nicomachean Ethics*, took it for granted without argument that the goal is human happiness (*eudaimonia*). Although differently formulated, it was also the assumed goal of the utilitarianism of Bentham and Mill. No justification was offered, nor could one be offered, for though reason can perhaps tell us what will make people happy, it cannot tell us that this ought to be our goal.

E. O. Wilson and other biologists have sought to explain altruism as a result of natural selection. It's an interesting possibility, and I wouldn't be surprised if they were right, but it has nothing to do with whether we ought to be altruistic. Thus I disagree with Michael Shermer, who in *The Science of Good and Evil*, seeks a basis for moral judgments in evolution. Science may indeed help us to understand how our moral principles evolved through natural selection, but how does the origin of behavior in evolution give it any moral authority? Polygamy may have its roots in human evolution (as it did in the evolution of lions), but does this mean we ought to be polygamous?

None of this matters. At least now, in the West, there is a broad measure of agreement, not in some set of underlying moral postulates, but at least in a general sense of what is right. There is a general sense that knowledge is better than ignorance, that truth is better than lies, and that, other things being equal, the more happiness the better. Of course, other things are not always equal, and we have no moral calculus that tells us how to choose among these good things, but that should not stop us from joining together to pursue the goals we share, while we squabble over the details.

I see no logical necessity for us to base moral judgments on the maximization of any one quantity, whether happiness or well-being or anything else. Most people manage to balance a number of values—happiness, honesty, loyalty, justice, and so on.

For brevity, in what follows, I will refer to this widespread though imprecise general agreement about moral values as the "enlightenment consensus."

It is shared even by some who continue to seek underlying moral principles on which to base our actions. For instance, in *The Moral Landscape*, Sam Harris has replaced the "happiness" of Aristotle and the utilitarians with "human well-being" as the thing to be maximized. But the notion of "human well-being" is sufficiently flexible that it can avoid any conflict with the enlightenment consensus, without giving us much help in resolving its ambiguities.[1]

In opposition to the enlightenment consensus are various schemes based on clear moral principles, some of which lead to very different judgments about how to behave. One of them is utilitarianism. The novel *Brave New World* by Aldous Huxley presents a powerful example of how the unqualified pursuit of happiness can lead to what, from the viewpoint of the enlightenment consensus, seems a nightmare. In Huxley's future world, everyone except a few misfits is happy. The alphas, who run things, are kept happy with sports, drugs, and sex. The betas and lesser breeds who have to do menial work have their intelligence chemically reduced before birth and are conditioned from childhood on to be happy with their status. It is a world that repels us, a world of sex without passion, of entertainment without culture, and of contentment without justice.

More relevant to the world today are the many people who continue to base their moral principles on obedience to the supposed will of God, as revealed in sacred writings. We can leave aside the question of whether to believe in God or in the authenticity of these writings. Even for those who believe in an all-powerful, all-knowing God who created the universe and has made His will known to humans, there is a logical gap here: why should we adopt God's moral judgments as our own? Indeed, from the point of view of the enlightenment consensus, any god who sends honest skeptics to hell does not merit our respect and obedience. From our moral standpoint, even those who think Sharia is God's will should know that it is wrong to kill infidels and apostates.

In this respect, the pagan Greeks were closer to the enlightenment consensus. The Olympian Gods had the power to punish Prometheus for giving fire to humanity by chaining him to a rock in the Caucasus where vultures would tear at his liver, but Aeschylus did not think that this was right. I cannot find any logical argument against accepting God's will as the basis of our moral code, but this acceptance is a free moral judgment, not forced on anyone by any chain of argument.

Those like myself who are skeptical about moral philosophy are not thereby required to reject morality itself. Just as there is no logical argument for any moral principle, there is also no logical argument that tells us that we should not be guided by own moral judgments, even where these judgments cannot be grounded in general principles. There certainly is no logical argument that requires us to consent to the moral judgments of other cultures when we feel they are wrong, to consent for instance to slavery or the oppression of women.

Without a coherent moral philosophy, we soldier on, trying to do whatever at the moment seems right to us. We may try to convince others to share our moral judgments, using whatever arguments come to hand, but we cannot fool ourselves that these arguments have any scientific or logical basis. Instead, we accept the lack of ultimate justification for what seem to us our noblest actions, as one of the irreducible perplexities of human life.

NOTE

1. To be sure, Aristotle's *eudemonia* would translate better as "well-being," and "happiness" is closer to Sam Harris's brand of utilitarianism (Eds.).

REFERENCES

Aristotle. *The Nicomachean Ethics*. Edited and translated by Robert C. Bartlett and Susan D. Collins. Chicago: University of Chicago Press, 2012.
Hume, D. *Treatise of Human Nature*. Edited by P. Nidditch. Oxford: Oxford University Press, 1978.
Shermer, M. *The Science of Good and Evil*. New York: Henry Holt and Company, 2004.
Wilson, E. O. *On Human Nature*. Cambridge, Mass.: Harvard University Press, 1978.
———. *Sociobiology: The New Synthesis*. Cambridge, Mass.: Harvard University Press, 1975.

Chapter Six

Misunderstanding Moral Psychology

Jonathan Haidt

Just as surprising as is the case with Steven Weinberg, Jonathan Haidt is also reluctant to give an easy answer as to the origins of morality. In his own words: "I study morality from every angle I can find." He was named one of the "top global thinkers" by Foreign Policy *magazine and proclaimed to be one of the "top world thinkers" by* Prospect *magazine. He is one of the participants in the new field of "positive" psychology, which emerged during the 1990s, and it led to Haidt producing leading research in the field, culminating in two bestsellers,* Flourishing *in 2003 and* Happiness *in 2006.*

Haidt is a moral intuitionist and understands the origins of and variation in human moral reasoning on the basis of innate, modular foundations. Unlike his more explicitly atheistic colleagues, Haidt takes more of a holistic approach. Like Sara Algoe, Haidt argues that exposure to stories about moral beauty (the opposite of moral disgust) can cause a common set of responses, including warm, loving feelings; calmness; and a desire to become a better person. He calls the emotion "moral elevation," as a tribute to Thomas Jefferson, who had described the emotion in detail in a letter discussing the benefit of reading great literature.

In his original research, conducted with Jesse Graham, Haidt identified five pairs of "foundations" that (taking into account cultural differences) Haidt considers to be "innate." The original theory proposed five foundations: Care/Harm, Fairness/Cheating, Loyalty/Betrayal, Authority/Subversion, and Sanctity/Degradation; however, its authors envisioned the possibility of including more.

These qualities may be regarded as a fragmented or refracted "conscience," and it should be clear that no single classical moral theory, be it deontological or utilitarianism or even virtue ethics, is sufficient to explain the wide variety of phenomena that make up the human instinct. Haidt is unwilling to engage in any kind of reductionism and is willing to acknowledge the role of religion in the formation of the psyche.

—The Editors

I study morality from every angle I can find. Morality is one of those basic aspects of humanity, like sexuality and eating, that cannot fit into one or two academic fields. I think morality is unique, however, in having a kind of spell that disguises it. We all care about morality so passionately that it is hard to look straight at it. We all look at the world through some kind of moral lens, and because most of the academic community uses the same lens, we validate each other's visions and distortions. I think this problem is particularly acute in some of the new scientific writing about religion.

When I started graduate school at Penn in 1987, it seemed that developmental psychology owned the rights to morality within psychology. Everyone was either using or critiquing Lawrence Kohlberg's ideas, as well as his general method of interviewing kids about dilemmas (such as: should Heinz steal a drug to save his wife's life?). Everyone was studying how children's understanding of moral concepts changed with experience. But in the 1990s, two books were published that I believe triggered an explosion of cross-disciplinary scientific interest in morality, out of which has come a new synthesis—very much along the lines that E. O. Wilson predicted in 1975.

The first was Antonio Damasio's *Descartes' Error* in 1994, which showed a very broad audience that morality could be studied using the then-new technology of fMRI and also that morality, and rationality itself, were crucially dependent on the proper functioning of emotional circuits in the prefrontal cortex. The second was Frans de Waal's *Good Natured*, published just two years later, which showed an equally broad audience that the building blocks of human morality are found in other apes and are products of natural selection in the highly social primate lineage. These two books came out just as John Bargh was showing social psychologists that automatic and unconscious processes can and probably do cause the majority of our behaviors, even morally loaded actions (like rudeness or altruism) that we thought we were controlling consciously.

Furthermore, Damasio and Bargh both found, as Michael Gazzaniga had years before, that people couldn't stop themselves from making up post-hoc explanations for whatever it was they had just done for unconscious reasons. Combine these developments and suddenly Kohlbergian moral psychology seemed to be studying the wagging tail rather than the dog. If the building blocks of morality were shaped by natural selection long before language arose, and if those evolved structures work largely by giving us feelings that shape our behavior automatically, then why should we be focusing on the verbal reasons that people give to explain their judgments in hypothetical moral dilemmas?

In my dissertation and my other early studies, I told people short stories in which a person does something disgusting or disrespectful that was perfectly harmless (for example, a family cooks and eats its dog, after the dog was killed by a car). I was trying to pit the emotion of disgust against reasoning about harm and individual rights.

I found that disgust won in nearly all groups I studied (in Brazil, India, and the United States), except for groups of politically liberal college students, particularly Americans, who overrode their disgust and said that people have a right to do whatever they want, as long as they don't hurt anyone else.

These findings suggested that emotion played a bigger role than the cognitive developmentalists had given it. These findings also suggested that there were important cultural differences and that academic researchers may have inappropriately focused on reasoning about harm and rights because we primarily study people like ourselves—college students and also children in private schools near our universities, whose morality is not representative of the United States, let alone the world.

So, in the 1990s, I was thinking about the role of emotion in moral judgment; I was reading Damasio, De Waal, and Bargh; and I was getting very excited by the synergy and consilience across disciplines. I wrote a review article called "The Emotional Dog and Its Rational Tail," which was published in 2001, a month after Josh Greene's enormously influential *Science* article. Greene used fMRI to show that emotional responses in the brain, not abstract principles of philosophy, explain why people think various forms of the "trolley problem" (in which you have to choose between killing one person or letting five die) are morally different.

Obviously I'm biased in terms of what I notice, but it seems to me that the zeitgeist in moral psychology has changed since 2001. Most people who study morality now read and write about emotions, the brain, chimpanzees, and evolution, as well as reasoning. This is exactly what E. O. Wilson predicted in *Sociobiology*: that the old approaches to morality, including Kohlberg's, would be swept away or merged into a new approach that focused on the emotive centers of the brain as biological adaptations. Wilson even said that these emotive centers give us moral intuitions, which the moral philosophers then justify while pretending that they are intuiting truths that are independent of the contingencies of our evolved minds.

And now, forty-five years later, Josh Greene has a paper in press where he uses neuroscientific evidence to reinterpret Kantian deontological philosophy as a sophisticated post-hoc justification of our gut feelings about rights and respect for other individuals. I think E. O. Wilson deserves more credit than he gets for seeing into the real nature of morality and for predicting the future of moral psychology so uncannily. He's in my pantheon, along with

David Hume and Charles Darwin. All three were visionaries who urged us to focus on the moral emotions and their social utility.

I recently summarized this new synthesis in moral psychology with four principles.

1. Intuitive primacy but not dictatorship. This is the idea, going back to Wilhelm Wundt and channeled through Robert Zajonc and John Bargh, that the mind is driven by constant flashes of affect in response to everything we see and hear.

Our brains, like other animal brains, are constantly trying to fine-tune and speed up the central decision of all action: approach or avoid. You can't understand the river of fMRI studies on neuroeconomics and decision-making without embracing this principle. We have affectively valenced intuitive reactions to almost everything, particularly to morally relevant stimuli such as gossip or the evening news. Reasoning by its very nature is slow, playing out in seconds.

Studies of everyday reasoning show that we usually use reason to search for evidence to support our initial judgment, which was made in milliseconds. But I do agree with Josh Greene that sometimes we can use controlled processes such as reasoning to override our initial intuitions. I just think this happens rarely, maybe in 1 or 2 percent of the hundreds of judgments we make each week. And I do agree with Marc Hauser that these moral intuitions require a lot of computation, which he is unpacking.

Hauser and I mostly disagree on a definitional question: whether this means that "cognition" precedes "emotion." I try never to contrast those terms because it is all cognition. I think the crucial contrast is between two kinds of cognition: intuitions (which are fast and usually affectively laden) and reasoning (which is slow, cool, and less motivating).

2. Moral thinking is for social doing. This is a play on William James's pragmatist dictum that thinking is for doing, updated by newer work on Machiavellian intelligence. The basic idea is that we did not evolve language and reasoning because they helped us to find truth; we evolved these skills because they were useful to their bearers, and among their greatest benefits were reputation management and manipulation.

Just look at your stream of consciousness when you are thinking about a politician you dislike or when you have just had a minor disagreement with your spouse. It is like preparing for a court appearance. Your reasoning abilities are pressed into service generating arguments to defend your side and attack the other. We are certainly able to reason dispassionately when we have no gut feeling about a case and no stake in its outcome, but with moral disagreements that's rarely the case. As David Hume said long ago, reason is the servant of the passions.

3. Morality binds and builds. This is the idea stated most forcefully by Emile Durkheim that morality is a set of constraints that binds people together into an emergent collective entity.

Durkheim focused on the benefits that accrue to individuals from being tied in and restrained by a moral order. In his book *Suicide*, he alerted us to the ways that freedom and wealth almost inevitably foster anomie, the dangerous state where norms are unclear and people feel that they can do whatever they want.

Durkheim didn't talk much about conflict between groups, but Darwin thought that such conflicts may have spurred the evolution of human morality. Virtues that bind people to other members of the tribe and encourage self-sacrifice would lead virtuous tribes to vanquish more selfish ones, which would make these traits more prevalent.

Of course, this simple analysis falls prey to the free-rider problem that George Williams and Richard Dawkins wrote so persuasively about. But I think the terms of this debate over group selection have changed radically in the past ten years, as culture and religion have become central to discussions of the evolution of morality.

I'll say more about group selection in a moment. For now, I just want to make the point that humans do form tight, cooperative groups that pursue collective ends and punish cheaters and slackers, and they do this most strongly when in conflict with other groups. Morality is what makes all of that possible.

4. Morality is about more than harm and fairness. In moral psychology and moral philosophy, morality is almost always about how people treat each other. Here's an influential definition from the Berkeley psychologist Elliot Turiel: morality refers to "prescriptive judgments of justice, rights, and welfare pertaining to how people ought to relate to each other."

Kohlberg thought that all of morality, including concerns about the welfare of others, could be derived from the psychology of justice. Carol Gilligan convinced the field that an ethic of "care" had a separate developmental trajectory and was not derived from concerns about justice.

Okay, so there are two psychological systems: one about fairness/justice and one about care and protection of the vulnerable. And if you look at the many books on the evolution of morality, most of them focus exclusively on those two systems, with long discussions of Robert Trivers's reciprocal altruism (to explain fairness) and of kin altruism and/or attachment theory to explain why we don't like to see suffering and often care for people who are not our children.

But if you try to apply this two-foundation morality to the rest of the world, you either fail or you become Procrustes. Most traditional societies care about a lot more than harm/care and fairness/justice. Why do so many societies care deeply and morally about menstruation, food taboos, sexuality, and respect for elders and the gods? You can't just dismiss this stuff as social convention. If you want to describe human morality, rather than the morality of educated Western academics, you've got to include the Durkheimian view that morality is in large part about binding people together.

From a review of the anthropological and evolutionary literatures, Craig Joseph (at Northwestern University) and I concluded that there were three best candidates for being additional psychological foundations of morality, beyond harm/care and fairness/justice. These three we label as ingroup/loyalty, which may have evolved from the long history of cross-group or subgroup competition, related to what Joe Henrich calls "coalitional psychology"; authority/respect, which may have evolved from the long history of primate hierarchy, modified by cultural limitations on power and bullying, as documented by Christopher Boehm; and purity/sanctity, which may be a much more recent system, growing out of the uniquely human emotion of disgust, which seems to give people feelings that some ways of living and acting are higher, more noble, and less carnal than others.

Joseph and I think of these foundational systems as expressions of what Dan Sperber calls "learning modules"—they are evolved modular systems that generate, during enculturation, large numbers of more specific modules that help children recognize, quickly and automatically, examples of culturally emphasized virtues and vices. For example, we academics have extremely fine-tuned receptors for sexism (related to fairness) but not sacrilege (related to purity).

Virtues are socially constructed and socially learned, but these processes are highly prepared and constrained by the evolved mind. We call these three additional foundations the binding foundations because the virtues, practices, and institutions they generate function to bind people together into hierarchically organized interdependent social groups that try to regulate the daily lives and personal habits of their members. We contrast these to the two individualizing foundations (harm/care and fairness/reciprocity), which generate virtues and practices that protect individuals from each other and allow them to live in harmony as autonomous agents who can focus on their own goals.

My UVA colleagues Jesse Graham and Brian Nosek and I have collected data from about seven thousand people so far on a survey designed to measure people's endorsement of these five foundations. In every sample we've looked at, in the United States and in other Western countries, we find that people who self-identify as liberals endorse moral values and statements related to the two individualizing foundations primarily, whereas self-described conservatives endorse values and statements to all five foundations. It seems that the moral domain encompasses more for conservatives—it is not just about Gilligan's care and Kohlberg's justice. It is also about Durkheim's issues of loyalty to the group, respect for authority, and sacredness.

I hope you'll accept that as a purely descriptive statement. You can still reject the three binding foundations normatively—that is, you can still insist that in-group, authority, and purity refer to ancient and dangerous psychological systems that underlie fascism, racism, and homophobia, and you can still claim that liberals are right to reject those foundations and build their moral systems using primarily the harm/care and fairness/reciprocity foundations.

But just go with me for a moment that there is this difference, descriptively, between the moral worlds of secular liberals on the one hand and religious conservatives on the other. There are, of course, many other groups, such as the religious left and the libertarian right, but I think it is fair to say that the major players in the new religion wars are secular liberals criticizing religious conservatives. Because the conflict is a moral conflict, we should be able to apply the four principles of the new synthesis in moral psychology.

In what follows, I will take it for granted that religion is a part of the natural world that is appropriately studied by the methods of science. Whether or not God exists (and as an atheist, I personally doubt it), religiosity is an enormously important fact about our species. There must be some combination of evolutionary, developmental, neuropsychological, and anthropological theories that can explain why human religious practices take the various forms that they do, many of which are so similar across cultures and eras. I will also take it for granted that religious fundamentalists, and most of those who argue for the existence of God, illustrate the first three principles of moral psychology (intuitive primacy, post-hoc reasoning guided by utility, and a strong sense of belonging to a group bound together by shared moral commitments).

But because the New Atheists talk so much about the virtues of science and our shared commitment to reason and evidence, I think it is appropriate to hold them to a higher standard than their opponents. Do these New Atheists' books model the scientific mind at its best? Or do they reveal normal human beings acting on the basis of their normal moral psychology?

1. Intuitive primacy but not dictatorship. It is clear that Richard Dawkins (in *The God Delusion*) and Sam Harris (in *Letter to a Christian Nation*) have strong feelings about religion in general and religious fundamentalists in particular. Given the hate mail they receive, I do not blame them. The passions of Dawkins and Harris do not mean that they are wrong or that they can't be trusted. One can certainly do good scholarship on slavery while hating slavery.

But the presence of passions should alert us that the authors, being human, are likely to have great difficulty searching for and then fairly evaluating evidence that opposes their intuitive feelings about religion. We can turn to Dawkins and Harris to make the case for the prosecution, which they do brilliantly, but if we readers are to judge religion, we will have to find a defense attorney. Or at least we will have to let the accused speak.

2. Moral thinking is for social doing. This is where the scientific mind is supposed to depart from the lay mind. The normal person (once animated by emotion) engages in moral reasoning to find ammunition, not truth; the normal person attacks the motives and character of her opponents when it will be advantageous to do so. The scientist, in contrast, respects empirical evidence as the ultimate authority and avoids ad hominem arguments. The metaphor for science is a voyage of discovery, not a war. Yet when I read the New Atheist books, I see few new shores. Instead I see battlefields strewn with the corpses of straw men. To name three:

1. The New Atheists treat religions as sets of beliefs about the world, many of which are demonstrably false. Yet anthropologists and sociologists who study religion stress the role of ritual and community much more than of factual beliefs about the creation of the world or life after death.
2. The New Atheists assume that believers, particularly fundamentalists, take their sacred texts literally. Yet ethnographies of fundamentalist communities (such as James Ault's *Spirit and Flesh*) show that even when people claim to be biblical literalists, they are in fact quite flexible, drawing on the Bible selectively—or ignoring it—to justify humane and often quite modern responses to complex social situations.
3. The New Atheists all review recent research on religion and conclude that it is an evolutionary by-product, not an adaptation. They compare religious sentiments to moths flying into candle flames, ants whose brains have been hijacked for a parasite's benefit, and cold viruses that are universal in human societies. This denial of adaptation is helpful for their argument that religion is bad for people, even when people think otherwise.

I quite agree with these authors' praise of the work of Pascal Boyer and Scott Atran, who have shown how belief in supernatural entities may indeed be an accidental output of cognitive systems that otherwise do a good job of identifying objects and agents. Yet even if belief in gods was initially a byproduct, as long as such beliefs had consequences for behavior, then it seems likely that natural selection operated upon phenotypic variation and favored the success of individuals and groups that found ways (genetic or cultural or both) to use these gods to their advantage, for example as commitment devices that enhanced cooperation, trust, and mutual aid.

3. Morality binds and builds. Dawkins is explicit that his goal is to start a movement, to raise consciousness, and to arm atheists with the arguments they'll need to do battle with believers. The view that "we are virtuous and our opponents are evil" is a crucial step in uniting people behind a cause, and there is plenty of that in the New Atheist books. A second crucial step is to identify traitors in our midst and punish or humiliate them. There is some of that too in these books—atheists who defend the utility of religion or who argue for disengagement or détente between science and religion are compared to Chamberlain and his appeasement of Hitler.

To my mind, an irony of Dawkins's position is that he reveals a kind of religious orthodoxy in his absolute rejection of group selection. David Sloan Wilson has supplemented Durkheim's view of religion (as being primarily about group cohesion) with evolutionary analyses to propose that religion was the conduit that pulled humans through a "major transition" in evolutionary history.

Dawkins, along with George Williams and most critics of group selection, acknowledge that natural selection works on groups as well as on individuals and that group selection is possible in principle. But Dawkins relies on Williams's argument that selection pressures at the individual level are, in practice, always stronger than those at the group level: free riders will always undercut Darwin's suggestion that morality evolved because virtuous groups outcompeted selfish groups.

Wilson, however, in *Darwin's Cathedral*, makes the case that culture in general and religion in particular change the variables in Williams's analysis. Religions and their associated practices greatly increase the costs of defection (through punishment and ostracism), increase the contributions of individuals to group efforts (through cultural and emotional mechanisms that increase trust), and sharpen the boundaries—biological and cultural—between groups. Throw in recent discoveries that genetic evolution can work much faster than previously supposed and the widely respected work of Pete Richerson and Rob Boyd on cultural group selection, and suddenly the old consensus against group selection is outdated.

It is time to examine the question anew. Yet Dawkins has referred to group selection in interviews as a "heresy," and in *The God Delusion*, he dismisses it without giving a reason. In chapter 5, he states the standard Williams free-rider objection, notes the argument that religion is a way around the Williams objection, concedes that Darwin believed in group selection, and then moves on. Dismissing a credible position without reasons and calling it a heresy (even if tongue in cheek) are hallmarks of standard moral thinking, not scientific thinking.

Morality is about more than harm and fairness. In *Letter to a Christian Nation*, Sam Harris gives us a standard liberal definition of morality: "Questions of morality are questions about happiness and suffering. . . . To the degree that our actions can affect the experience of other creatures positively or negatively, questions of morality apply." He then goes on to show that the Bible and the Koran, taken literally, are immoral books because they're not primarily about happiness and suffering and, in many places, they advocate harming people.

Reading Harris is like watching professional wrestling or the Harlem Globetrotters. It is great fun, with lots of acrobatics, but it must not be mistaken for an actual contest. If we want to stage a fair fight between religious and secular moralities, we can't eliminate one by definition before the match begins. So here's my definition of morality, which gives each side a chance to make its case:

> Moral systems are interlocking sets of values, practices, institutions, and evolved psychological mechanisms that work together to suppress or regulate selfishness and make social life possible.

In my research, I have found that there are two common ways that cultures suppress and regulate selfishness, two visions of what society is and how it ought to work. I'll call them the contractual approach and the beehive approach.

The contractual approach takes the individual as the fundamental unit of value. The fundamental problem of social life is that individuals often hurt each other, and so we create implicit social contracts and explicit laws to foster a fair, free, and safe society in which individuals can pursue their interests and develop themselves and their relationships as they choose.

Morality is about happiness and suffering (as Harris says and as John Stuart Mill said before him), and so contractualists are endlessly trying to fine-tune laws, reinvent institutions, and extend new rights as circumstances change in order to maximize happiness and minimize suffering. To build a contractual morality, all you need are the two individualizing foundations: harm/care and fairness/reciprocity. The other three foundations, and any religion that builds on them, run afoul of the prime directive: let people make their own choices, as long as they harm nobody else.

The beehive approach, in contrast, takes the group and its territory as fundamental sources of value. Individual bees are born and die by the thousands, but the hive lives for a long time, and each individual has a role to play in fostering its success. The two fundamental problems of social life are attacks from outside and subversion from within. Either one can lead to the death of the hive, so all must pull together, do their duty, and be willing to make sacrifices for the group. Bees don't have to learn how to behave in this way, but human children do, and this is why cultural conservatives are so heavily focused on what happens in schools, families, and the media.

Conservatives generally have a more pessimistic view of human nature than do liberals. They are more likely to believe that if you stand back and give kids space to grow as they please, they'll grow into shallow, self-centered, undisciplined pleasure seekers. Cultural conservatives work hard to cultivate moral virtues based on the three binding foundations: in-group/loyalty, authority/respect, and purity/sanctity, as well as on the universally employed foundations of harm/care and fairness/reciprocity. The beehive ideal is not a world of maximum freedom; it is a world of order and tradition in which people are united by a shared moral code that is effectively enforced, which enables people to trust each other to play their interdependent roles. It is a world of very high social capital and low anomie.

It might seem obvious to you that contractual societies are good, modern, creative, and free, whereas beehive societies reek of feudalism, fascism, and patriarchy. And as a secular liberal, I agree that contractual societies such as those of Western Europe offer the best hope for living peacefully together in our increasingly diverse modern nations (although it remains to be seen if Europe can solve its current diversity problems).

I just want to make one point, however, that should give contractualists pause: surveys have long shown that religious believers in the United States are happier, healthier, longer-lived, and more generous to charity and to each other than are secular people. Most of these effects have been documented in Europe too. If you believe that morality is about happiness and suffering, then I think you are obligated to take a close look at the way religious people actually live and ask what they are doing right.

Don't dismiss religion on the basis of a superficial reading of the Bible and the newspaper. Might religious communities offer us insights into human flourishing? Can they teach us lessons that would improve well-being even in a primarily contractualist society?

You can't use the New Atheists as your guide to these lessons. The New Atheists conduct biased reviews of the literature and conclude that there is no good evidence on any benefits except the health benefits of religion. Here is Daniel Dennett in *Breaking the Spell* on whether religion brings out the best in people:

> Perhaps a survey would show that as a group atheists and agnostics are more respectful of the law, more sensitive to the needs of others, or more ethical than religious people. Certainly no reliable survey has yet been done that shows otherwise. It might be that the best that can be said for religion is that it helps some people achieve the level of citizenship and morality typically found in brights. If you find that conjecture offensive, you need to adjust your perspective.[1]

I wish to emphasize two themes that show ordinary moral thinking rather than scientific thinking. The first is Dennett's claim not just that there is no evidence but that there is *certainly* no evidence, when in fact surveys have shown for decades that religious practice is a strong predictor of charitable giving. Arthur Brooks recently analyzed these data (in *Who Really Cares*) and concluded that the enormous generosity of religious believers is not just recycled to religious charities. Religious believers give more money than secular folk to secular charities and to their neighbors. They give more of their time, too, and of their blood. Even if you excuse secular liberals from charity because they vote for government welfare programs, it is awfully hard to explain why secular liberals give so little blood. The bottom line, Brooks concludes, is that all forms of giving go together, and all are greatly increased by religious participation and slightly increased by conservative ideology (after controlling for religiosity). These data are complex and perhaps they can be spun the other way, but at the moment it appears that Dennett is wrong in his reading of the literature. Atheists may have many other virtues, but on one of the least controversial and most objective measures of moral behavior—giving time, money, and blood to help strangers in need—religious people appear to be morally superior to secular folk.

My conclusion is not that secular liberal societies should be made more religious and conservative in a utilitarian bid to increase happiness, charity, longevity, and social capital. Too many valuable rights would be at risk, too many people would be excluded, and societies are so complex that it is impossible to do such social engineering and get only what you bargained for. My point is just that every long-standing ideology and way of life contains some wisdom, some insights into ways of suppressing selfishness, enhancing cooperation, and ultimately enhancing human flourishing.

But because of the four principles of moral psychology, it is extremely difficult for people, even scientists, to find that wisdom once hostilities erupt. A militant form of atheism that claims the backing of science and encourages "brights" to take up arms may perhaps advance atheism. But it may also backfire, polluting the scientific study of religion with moralistic dogma and damaging the prestige of science in the process.

NOTES

Reprinted by kind permission from the Edge Foundation.
1. Daniel Dennett, *Breaking the Spell: Religion as a Natural Phenomenon* (London: Penguin, 2007), 55.

REFERENCES

Brooks, A. C. *Who Really Cares: The Surprising Truth about Compassionate Conservatism.* New York: Basic Books, 2007.
Damasio, A. *Descartes' Error: Emotion, Reason, and the Human Brain.* New York: Putnam Books, 1994.
Dawkins, R. *The God Delusion.* New York: Transworld, 2009.
De Waal, F. *Good Natured: The Origins of Right and Wrong in Humans and Other Animals.* Cambridge, Mass.: Harvard University Press, 1997.
Dennett, D. *Breaking the Spell: Religion as a Natural Phenomenon.* London: Penguin, 2007.
Harris, S. *Letter to a Christian Nation.* New York: Transworld, 2011.

———. *The Moral Landscape*. New York: Transworld, 2011.
Mill, J. S. *Utilitarianism* (1863). Reprinted in *Mill's Utilitarianism*, edited by J. M. Smith and E. Sosa. Belmont, Calif.: Wadsworth, 1963.

Chapter Seven

The Use and Abuse of Naturalism for Morality

Louise Mabille

Louise Mabille revisits the old Voltairean jibe that "if God did not exist, He would have to be invented" and finds an answer as to why this is the case in the most unlikely person imaginable: Friedrich Nietzsche. Contrary to popular perception, Nietzsche did not simply rejoice in what he described as the "death of God." This concept differs from the more philosophically conventional discussions of God, in that it concerns itself less with the existence of God and more with the meaning of God. According to Nietzsche, the Western "will to truth"—the preoccupation with truth—has led to an untenable state of perpetual skepticism, which he describes as "nihilism"—the "uncanny guest at the door" (of the West) that eventually leads to the ultimate devaluation or erasure of all values:

> In the horizon of the infinite. We have left the land and have embarked. We have burned our bridges behind us indeed, we have gone farther and destroyed the land behind us. Now. little ship, look out! Beside you is the ocean: to be sure, it does not always roar, and at times it lies spread out like silk and ·gold and reveries of graciousness. But hours will come when you will realize that it is infinite and that there is nothing more awesome than infinity. Oh, the poor bird that felt free and now strikes the walls of this cage! Woe, when you feel homesick for the land as if it had offered more freedom and there is no longer any "land." (The Gay Science, 124)[1]

Mabille demonstrates that the entire conversation or debate that we have hitherto enjoyed falls within the perimeters that have already been drawn by Christianity, and that much of what passes as a universal morality, such as Kantian deontology and British utilitarianism, are in fact products of a preexisting worldview, informed by Christian "prejudices" such as the Augustinian notion of equality before God. Drawing on Nietzsche, she shows that secularism or humanism provides neither a universal moral code nor an "escape" from Christianity; it is simply a secular variant of Christian ethics that refuses to acknowledge its original roots. This also goes for the "New Atheists" (now over a decade old), who are taken here as the latest representatives of a utilitarian tradition more than two centuries old, much as they express their ideas in Darwinian idiom.

To be sure, Nietzsche identifies a particularly difficult aspect of Christianity, namely that it upholds moral standards of such a high nature that it turns upon its own immoralities—a state of affairs that led to the emergence of secularism and its problematic legacy in the West. However, it is demonstrated that secular humanism itself falls prey to this phenomenon and—as Nietzsche acknowledges—leaves no grounding for morality at all. Following Nietzsche's genealogical example, Mabille argues that a purely naturalistic, in particular a utilitarian, ethic is bound to implode upon itself.

—The Editors

Only a God can save us now. —Martin Heidegger, *Der Spiegel*, 1957

One of the strangest aspects of the contemporary humanist movement is that its central ambition appears to be to turn the human being into an animal. Ever since Darwin, we have become accustomed to hearing that there is no comfortable divide between the natural world and ourselves, but that we exist on a single continuum with all living organisms. One's first impulse today is to regard the abolition between man and animal as a great step forward. For centuries, humanity treated both his fellow creatures and the world in which he lived as objects, pieces of property, and few would deny that there is room for improvement when it comes to the treatment of nonhuman life. However, given that according to the naturalist model, literally everything we know about humanity—its needs, desires, passions, and intellect—emanates from nature, the attempt to account for our moral impulses seems rather tautologous. As every evolutionist knows, both our negative and positive qualities are natural. Given the general amoral character of nature, the insistence upon finding a moral "sky-hook" in nature is ultimately self-defeating. Richard Dawkins writes:

> The total amount of suffering per year in the natural world is beyond all decent contemplation. During the minute that it takes me to compose this sentence, thousands of animals are being eaten alive, many others are running for their lives, whimpering with fear, others are slowly being devoured from within by rasping parasites, thousands of all kinds are dying of starvation, thirst, and disease. It must be so. If there ever is a time of plenty, this very fact will

automatically lead to an increase in the population until the natural state of starvation and misery is restored. In a universe of electrons and selfish genes, blind physical forces and genetic replication, some people are going to get hurt, other people are going to get lucky, and you won't find any rhyme or reason in it, nor any justice. The universe that we observe has precisely the properties we should expect if there is, at bottom, no design, no purpose, no evil, no good, nothing but pitiless indifference.[2]

Despite admitting to a practically amoral universe, Dawkins, like Peter Singer, Sam Harris, and others, insists upon an entirely natural explanation for what we have commonly come to regard as "morality." They usually account for morality in terms of a self-identical moral instinct that is more or less equated with altruism.

Atheists both old and new have always been fond of pointing to nonbelievers like the poet Shelley, who found a new religion in natural beauty, when accused of nihilism or rationalistic rigidity. For them, Nature is everything, as well as good and noble, and it is the unnatural elements of culture that have been responsible for all the hardship that man suffers. It is their very own version of the Fall, and it was made famous by Jean Jacques Rousseau and poets like Shelley and Byron. Since nature is all that we have, according to the atheist definition, much depends on the atheist showing that the natural world is not only good and inspiring but the source of all genuine goodness.

Richard Dawkins, for one, is at pains to show that there is a world of difference between the harsh world of selfish genes and the nobler world of human ideals. As valuable as her refusal to bow to scientific reductionism otherwise is, in her criticism of Dawkins, the otherwise astute philosopher of science Mary Midgely *has* misunderstood what Dawkins intended in *The Selfish Gene*. Dawkins distinguishes between the urge to survive on gene level and the unpleasant psychological trait that some human beings exhibit when they focus on their own self-interest to the detriment of their fellows. One can easily see where the misunderstanding has crept in: Midgely has simply confused the parts with whole. The "selfishness" in question refers only to the gene, that unit of genetic material that determines the inheritance of a particular characteristic. Genes are carried by chromosomes in the cell nucleus and are arranged in a line along each chromosome. Genes are therefore not isomorphically equivalent to the individual that they constitute, nor the group or species to which the individual belongs. They are players in the game of natural selection, and their ultimate aim is to survive for as many generations as possible. So selfishness on gene level is not a problem. The genes are excused.

Dawkins's attempt to account for moral goodness on a higher level is far less convincing. It is, as a matter of fact, utterly pointless. Beginning again at gene level, he admits that programming the individual organism to be selfish, and so ensure its own survival, is indeed a successful tactic of some genes to ensure their survival in the successful organism. Fortunately, it does not end there. Genes can also influence behavior toward the altruistic.

> There are circumstances—not particularly rare—in which genes ensure their own selfish survival by influencing organisms to behave altruistically. These circumstances are now fairly well understood and they fall into two main categories. A gene that programs individual organisms to favour their genetic kin is statistically likely to benefit copies of itself. Such a gene's frequency can increase in the gene pool to the point where kin altruism becomes the norm. Being good to one's children is the obvious example, but it is not the only one. Bees, wasps, ants, termites and, to a lesser extent, certain vertebrates such as the naked mole rats, meerkats, and acorn woodpeckers have evolved societies in which elder siblings care for younger siblings (with whom they are likely to share the genes for doing the caring).... Animals tend to care for, defend, share resources with, warn of danger, or otherwise show altruism towards close kin, because of the statistical likelihood that kin will share copies of the same genes.[3]

Then there is the obvious Darwinian example of reciprocal altruism that does not depend upon genes. First introduced by Robert Trivers, this is often expressed in the mathematical language of game theory or, in biology, simply symbiosis. This occurs when different species work together for mutual benefit. Sam Harris calls this the tit-for-tat mechanism, or strong reciprocity. Obvious examples are oxpeckers that eat the ticks of the great mammals, especially bovines. They get rid of parasites, and the oxpeckers are fed in the process. Bees pollinate flowers, and they gain nectar in the process. Any functioning ecosystem will have examples of this because, as Dawkins says, of asymmetries in needs and capacities to meet them. Reciprocal altruism is an obvious survival mechanism. If you do not have something that you desperately need, it only makes sense to try and obtain it from someone else. However, as you will see below, there is no such thing as a free lunch: no one is going to aid your chances of survival without wanting his pound of flesh in return. As Harris points out, this phenomenon is generally found throughout society, and it appears to be as universal as cultural phenomena can get, given the rich cultural diversity on our little blue planet: "You show me some kindness, and I am eager to return the favor; you do something rude or injurious, and the temptation to respond is difficult to resist."[4]

Dawkins adds an extension to the reciprocal altruism explanation. While in the animal kingdom and primitive societies, one may be generous with an eye to immediate reciprocation, in human societies with the sophisticated language and communication mechanisms, reputation is of cardinal importance. As societies grow, it is important not only to be generous but also to have a reputation for generosity. It is a smart survival strategy: those who are known for doling out rewards are more likely to be recipients of societal benefits. Even today our society pages are graced with celebrities famed for not only their talents or beauty but also their open purses.

What strikes one at once in the naturalistic accounts of morality hitherto encountered—not only by Richard Dawkins but in this volume also Sam Harris and even our more skeptical contributors like Michael Ruse and Steven Weinberg—is the tendency to equate morality with altruism, the disinterested concern for the well-being of others. Despite claims to a strong adherence to evolutionary logic, there is a strange reluctance to engage the developmental potential that the theory of evolution brings, and reciprocal altruism is treated like a solid-self-identical phenomenon *sub specie aeternitatis*—much like the old metaphysical chimera of the Will. It is yet another instance of what Nietzsche identifies as the inability to identify the origin and the result of the development of an idea. At the heart of our utilitarians' simplicity lies the inability to take the implications of Darwin's claims truly seriously: they confuse the end result of a long developmental struggle between organism and organism, organism and environment, as well as competing value systems, with the timeless essence of the participants in this struggle—a classic Platonic prejudice. As a result, they appear to be blissfully ignorant what their pseudo-Darwinian account of the origins of late-modern middle-class morals actually prove.

The most obvious question that presents itself when confronted with the notion of an "instinct" for the Good is this: if we are primarily other-directed, ethical beings whose goodness, based upon reciprocal altruism, has been bred into us, where does evil then come from? And indeed, where do those religious impulses that the New Atheists fight with tooth and claw originate? It appears that all the Dawkinites have succeeded in doing is to create a civil war within modern man, asking one impulse to obliterate the others.

Among the greatest problems that occur when scientists try to think is that they are committed to the principle of self-identity. That is to say, they think of phenomena in terms of single unified entities that fit preestablished categories without excess or remainder. Where identity is concerned, it is simply a question of locating that entity and observing it. They believe in treating the self like a patient for whose problems they just need to find the right cure. For them the self is ready-made and given: the only thing that remains is to diagnose the problems and curb the excesses that prevent the ready-made self from fitting into the perfect rational order. For the Dawkinites, it is just a question of liberating that natural instinct for the Good, hiding inside of all of us, and all will be well.

The problem, however, is that the Good is not alone in there. Dawkins himself states, as we have seen, that "natural selection, in ancestral times, when we lived in small and stable bands like baboons, programmed into our brains altruistic urges, xenophobic urges and so on."[5] It is a very significant statement, one whose possibilities clearly escape Dawkins. He admits that we are a plurality of urges or drives. Aside from the much vaunted instinct for the Good, there are plenty of other urges or drives: sexual, xenophobic, probably hunger, "and so on." How many instincts or urges are there, exactly?

It is for this reason that Nietzsche rejects any simple metaphysical construct such as the Good or the Will. Like Darwin, Nietzsche discards the notion of a pure, atemporal, autonomous self, and both endorse a developmental view of human and its morality. They both locate the apparently pure and noble sentiments of contemporary morality in less than noble origins. Unlike Darwin, however, Nietzsche did not fall into a naïve Romanticism based upon utilitarian motifs.

Even Schopenhauer, a far more sophisticated thinker than the simple utilitarians, had it wrong. There is no such thing as the Will, any more than there is an instinct of the Good. There is no presiding ego that dictates when a drive or instinct can proceed and seek its ends and when it must step back and allow time and resources for the discharge of another. Nietzsche instead imagines a constant struggle between drives or urges and that a drive expresses itself only at the cost of all the others. Each drive or instinct therefore does not only seek to discharge itself but also to dominate the others so that it can reach its goals more often. In this process, drives synthesize themselves into individuals and communities, so that it appears that there is such a thing as a unified ego or instinct.

Earlier, Sam Harris has given an overview of the development of altruism as an evolutionary mechanism along lines very similar to Dawkins and other evolutionists like Daniel Dennett and Steven Pinker. We have seen in Bert Olivier's essay that the process of becoming human can be rather painful and that, even if altruism plays a decisive role in the development of the moral consciousness, it is far from as clear cut and ahistorical as our utilitarian friends presuppose. Nor does it provide a purer motive for the moral life than the ones presupposed by Christian morality.

To begin, all three "hermeneuticians of suspicion," Nietzsche, Marx, and Freud, and their biological wingman, Charles Darwin, all agree on this: no moral system can be maintained without the existence of memory. This much should be obvious: reciprocal altruism depends upon the remembering of good turns. One can hardly repay a favor if one has forgotten it completely. The same goes for bad turns. But as the evolutionist well knows, one is not simply endowed with memory—it developed over time. In one of the most infamous essays ever written on the origins of morality, Nietzsche gives us an account of the painful origin of memory. According to the second essay of *On the Genealogy of Morals*, at one stage, a certain animal developed greater intellectual capacities and made the leap into humanity. It was far from a simple affair though: no system of reciprocal obligations can exist without the operation of painful mnemotechnics. To be a remembering animal stands as a kind of paradox in nature, what Aristotle would have called a *para physin*, something unnatural. Whereas all other animal life is known for their ability to forget easily, man alone has developed the opposing capacity for remembering. Goldfish, for example, are noted for their short memories (although it is in really closer to five months than three seconds), and even elephants, which are proverbially the animal famed for its grudge-bearing ability, can hardly compete with the human ability to store experience, events, and ideas. Forgetting is not simply erasure or repression but the condition for the bodily drives or instincts to discharge themselves directly, without delay, in response to excitations received from other drives or instincts, from other bodies (e.g., the sexual impulse), or from natural forces in the environment (e.g., the so-called fight-or-flee impulse). Although animals of course remember on the most instinctual level basic things like associations with the obtaining of food (think of the famous Pavlov experiments), it is only in the human being that the automatic capacity for forgetting has been deliberately curtailed. For Nietzsche, not unlike Freud (as we have seen in Olivier's Lacanian account), human reality begins with a denial of sensuous animality and the imposition of checks, detours, and delays upon the expenditure of bodily drives. In other words, you become human as soon as you learn to think, however briefly, before you act. Before this is possible, one has to remember enough so that one can measure new experiences against an already existing framework. This implies the active desire not to rid oneself of a former impression, a desire for the continuance of something desired once developed as human society progressed. Man is the only living being who has had to make himself into a calculable (*berechenbar*), regular being who is able to keep his word. Nietzsche calls this the transformation into the animal who is able to keep promises.

Rendering himself calculable, however, has not been the quaint picture of reciprocal assistance that Dawkins and Singer insist upon painting. Quite the contrary: "There was nothing more fearful and uncanny in the whole prehistory of man than his mnemotechnics: If something is to stay in the memory it must be burned in: only that which never ceases to hurt stays in the memory—this is the main clause of the oldest . . . psychology on earth."[6] Pain is the most powerful aid to mnemotechnics. You never forget the terror of having pain inflicted upon yourself, even if the memory of the pain itself eventually disappears. It can even be communicated over generations, as the legacy of slavery proves.

What has been blissfully ignored in every account of reciprocal altruism hitherto discussed is the uncomfortable fact that the moment one begins to trade in favors, one is trading. As soon as reciprocal altruism sprang into action in *Homo sapiens*, other values besides the desire to benefit immediately were born. No one said that if you bring food to a fellow primitive human on a particular day, he has to repay the favor immediately. Every evolutionist ought to know that ideas do not develop one at a time or in isolation. We are social beings and, as such, develop our ideas in a social setting. This means that more than one idea develops at a given time. With the idea of trading in favors and the stretching of our concept of time came the idea of debt. As soon as the original favor was repaid with the promise to reciprocate in the future, debt was born and with it the need to remember. It is in the creditor-debtor relationship that the first promise was made and that *Homo sapiens* eventually began to understand himself across time as a future-orientated being, Debt is a complex problem: one has to ensure, for one, that the debtor understands and remembers what is owed. To inspire trust in his promise to repay, as proof that he understood the meaning of the pact, the first debtor promised his creditor that should he fail to repay, he would substitute something else that he "owned" or something he had control over: his body, his wife, his freedom, or even his life. Nietzsche writes:

> Consider the old German punishments: for example, stoning . . . breaking on the wheel . . . piercing by stakes . . . tearing apart or trampling by horses . . . boiling of the criminal in wine or oil . . . the popular flaying alive . . . cutting flesh from the chest, and also the practice of smearing the wrongdoer with honey and leaving him in the blazing sun for the flies. (*Genealogy of Morals*, II.3)[7]

What angered them to go to this kind of extreme is precisely this: failure to repay, the ultimate breach of promise. Whoever breaks his word will be broken. As *Homo sapiens* became stronger and more self-aware, so did his truth-telling standards. The apparently simple tit-for-tat transaction was nothing like the kind, mutually beneficial gift giving that latter-day utilitarians like to portray. Instead of the romantic picture of mutually beneficial cooperation, we find that a much more banal structure informs our most fundamental relationship: trade. With the advent of debt came hierarchical relationships, feelings of guilt, and the phenomenon of punishment. Rather than simply blame the ills of the modern world on their favorite target, religion, one can argue that the harsh God of the Abrahamic religions developed precisely among those people with the most severe ethic of trade. In that case, trade precedes religion, and since it has a natural origin, it makes no sense to hold them accountable for their so-called stupidity. It should also be noted that it is in trade that differentiation occurs: the strong begin to overtake the weak, and since they are free to call the shots, a harsh ethic of honesty and strength develops. It is as much of a morality as any other, and as Nietzsche shows, this ethic dominated the ancient pagan world before the advent of Christianity. While this ethic shares a great deal with the moralities that followed it (it too objected to the usual suspects like murder, theft, and lying), there is a great deal that separated this ethic from the quaint post-

Christian secular liberal humanism that Richard Dawkins, Daniel Dennett, and especially Harris appear to take *as* morality. As you will see in the final section of this essay, there are indeed quite a few obvious taboos that are, for all practical purposes, pretty much universal. This, however, does not mean that the reasons for their prohibition do not differ radically and that the worldviews that engendered them can be equally legitimate. Consider for now how early man gave his own particular twist to that ethic of reciprocal altruism:

> The free man, the owner of an enduring unbreakable will, also acquires his own standard of value: he looks out from himself at others and confers respect or contempt. And just as it will be necessary for him to honour those like him, the strong and dependable (who are entitled to make promises)—in other words, everyone who makes promises like a sovereign, seriously, rarely, and slowly, who is sparing with his trust, who honours another when he does trust, who gives his word as something reliable, because he knows he is strong enough to remain upright even when opposed by misfortune, even when "opposed by fate"—in just the same way it will be necessary for him to keep his foot ready to kick the scrawny unreliable men, who make promises without being entitled to, and to hold his cane ready for the liar, who breaks his word in the very moment it comes out of his mouth. (*Genealogy of Morals*, II:2)[8]

Marx was wrong: there is an inescapable primitive capitalist logic that long precedes the more sophisticated exchange systems criticized by the German materialist. And the pain necessary for the development of this system is equally inescapable: you never forget the terror of having pain inflicted upon yourself, even if the memory of the pain itself eventually disappears. Pain can be remembered across generations—again, as the horrible example of slavery testifies—and it is to be found at the bottom of every foundation myth.

Ever the biologist, Dawkins offers a fourth explanation for human altruism, the so-called potlatch effect, after Pacific chieftains who vied with each other to present the richest and most ruinous feasts. According to Dawkins, this is a variation of the well-known desire to demonstrate superiority or dominance and therefore suitability for mating—standard Darwinian fare. Strong individuals demonstrate their wealth or strength by acting generously, saying in effect, "Look how strong and confident I am. I can afford to be generous." Dawkins uses the findings of the Israeli zoologist Amotz Zahavi as example. He found that Arabian babblers demonstrate their superiority by feeding their subordinates. Such birds would in effect say: "Look how superior I am. I can afford to offer you food." Or: "See! I am not afraid. I can afford to make myself vulnerable to predators by acting as a look-out for the rest of you." Everybody loves a hero!

It appears that he is under the impression that Zahavi's explanation of generosity as a sign of strength or self-confidence is something new, "radically unexpected." For a reader whose frame of reference stretches beyond the biological, there is nothing new about this, nor does this very human phenomenon need to be justified by turning toward the biological. Such an ethic of generosity lies at the heart of any virtue-based system of ethics from Aristotle (which would by implication include the great Scholastics) and forms the core of Nietzsche's ethics. While most people associate Nietzsche with a brute admiration of power, what he actually advocates is a celebration of personal strength and—running the risk of crudely reducing Nietzsche to a simple dictum—the cultivation of individuals strong enough to bear the burdens of others, the Supermen. This is in fact his ethical ideal. Unlike most ethical ideals hitherto, the ideal espoused by Nietzsche does not try to get rid of weak, unsavory, or even "dangerous" elements. It can be said that the ability to bear parasites is for Nietzsche a sign of health and strength: "The parasite is the lowest species; he, however, who is of the highest species feedeth most parasites." We will return to virtue ethics and its essential link to freedom in the final chapter. Now, however, we have to make a rather startling statement. Nothing that Dawkins has hitherto said about altruism is of the slightest ethical significance. As a matter of fact, it is not even clear whether he has been talking about altruism at all. After all, altruism is usually defined as an attitude or way of behaving marked by unselfish concern for the welfare of others. Not a single one of the acts that Dawkins describes qualifies, the "care" that is given is not genuine selfless care but mere biological pragmatism. Obviously, as we have noted, we can discount either "selfishness" or "selflessness" on the gene level since what we are seeing there are biological mechanisms vying for survival and cannot be described in terms of psychological traits or ethical positions. But neither is there anything ethical about the notion of reciprocal altruism, be it in the animal world or the more elevated level of human relationships toward which Dawkins is ultimately aiming the argument. In the first instance, it is simply the mirror image of the calculating believer, which would definitely not qualify as truly moral:

> Do you really mean to tell me that the only reason you try to be good is to gain God's approval and reward, or to avoid his disapproval and punishment? That is not morality, that is just sucking up, apple-polishing, looking over your shoulder at the great surveillance-camera in the sky, or the still small wiretap in your head, monitoring your every move, even your every base thought. As Einstein said: "If people are good only when they feel punishment, then we are a sorry lot indeed."[9]

If one acts altruistically only because one expects to get something in return, it is not altruism. In fact, it has nothing whatsoever to do with being moral and cannot therefore be seen as the "ancestor" of what we today call morality. As long as it merely serves the agent in enhancing his chances to survive, it is purely self-serving. In the purely pragmatic Darwinian domain, it has nothing whatsoever to do with morality, but as soon as one tries to put a moral spin upon it, we are talking about a form of dishonest greed. If cooperation for mutual benefit forms the cornerstone for our morality, we are a sly lot indeed.

In the most formal philosophical sense, one can only truly begin to speak of morality when the language of benefit, whether immediate or long-term, is transcended. Unlike the utilitarians, the German idealists made it a point of honor to define the human being, whether in his epistemological or moral capacity, in terms that put him at a considerable distance from his animal nature. The ethic of reciprocal benefit espoused by our utilitarians violates the tenets of what is arguably the most sophisticated secular ethical formulation ever devised. It is, of course, the Categorical Imperative. When this stern formulation of the requirements for a truly moral act is cited, the first formulation that comes to mind is of course the Golden Rule: "Act only according to that maxim whereby you can at the same time will that it should become a universal law."[10] It seems like a formal restating of what the Dawkinites take as pretty much common sense, and they usually take it that Kant's ethics simply concur with their own. This is, however, only one formulation of the Categorical Imperative and is known as the Formula of the Universal Law. Kant is far too civilized merely to lay down a formulation to distribute happiness evenly. The Categorical Imperative needs to be grounded but certainly in something more than mere utility. Kant seeks something that is absolutely and necessarily valuable, regardless of whether it is recognized by all human beings as such. If there is such an end, then any action needed for the attainment of that end would be required of all beings, regardless of whether the action contributes to their happiness.

For Kant, there is something that is absolutely and unconditionally valuable. "Now I say that man, and in general every rational being, exists as an end in himself, not merely as a means for arbitrary use by this or that will: he must in all his actions, whether they are directed to himself or to other rational beings, always be viewed at the same time as an end." That the rational nature sees itself as an end in itself serves as a grounding for all moral thinking. Each individual is a person, not a means to another's well-being or even survival. Kant believes that we draw upon this principle every time we distinguish between a thing and a person. The value of our personhood consists in our being rational agents of worth. All rational agents have unconditional value in themselves as ends. Thus spoke reason itself.

Kant is seen—with good reason—as one of the most difficult thinkers on ethics and morality of all time. Unlike the poetic Greeks or more literary authors like Nietzsche, his prose is dry and often obscure. But it is clear that

Kant intends that we treat all rational beings as ends-in-themselves without making arbitrary distinctions between them that would reduce some to the status of mere things. The link with the first formulation of the Categorical Imperative is clear: the principle of universalizability demands that whatever we consider as moral behavior in one rational agent must be conceived as such in all of them. Importantly, however, it must be emphasized that the raison d'être of the Categorical Imperative does not lie in its demand for universalizability but in the value of the agent uttering the command. The second formulation of the Categorical Imperative is a principle that most philosophers today agree is the most fundamental principle of morality. It is known as the Formula of Humanity and runs as follows: "Act in such a way that you always treat humanity, whether in your own person, or in the person of any other, never simply as a means, but always at the same time as an end."[11] Note that this injunction does not require us to refrain from treating others as a means in all possible circumstances. Ordinary human interaction sometimes demands this. This principle only prohibits us from using others merely as a means to some or other end, such as when we use others as the means for our survival without recognizing that they, too, are rational agents. It is the moral law that inheres in them that renders them absolutely valuable for their own sake. Only when we do this can we begin to speak of morality because morality is a matter between rational agents. Instinct is not morality. If it were, we need not have wasted your time with an argument on the nature of morality. We would all have agreed what it is.

Contrary to the cliché, Nietzsche thinks that it is the English-speaking world that includes the great sensualists, at least where philosophy is concerned. The Englishman is, after all, according to Nietzsche, "gloomier, more sensual, and stronger of will than the German."[12] The famous Empiricists, such as John Locke, George Berkeley, and David Hume, all hold that knowledge is ultimately based upon human experience, in other words, our "sensations" or "impressions" or observations of the external world. In more technical terms, knowledge is a posteriori, or something only achieved after the relevant experience. Although no sophisticated empiricist today, like Daniel Dennett, believes that the mind is a blank slate or a tabula rasa, it is easy to trace the lines from the Dawkinites to their more illustrious forebears.

Characteristic of the empiricist approach is a tendency to describe morality in terms of bodily effects. Hume famously rejected, along with other metaphysical concepts, the idea of an innate moral "sense." For him, all judgments, be they moral or aesthetic, are based neither on reason nor understanding, but simply on feelings of pain and pleasure: "Pleasure and pain, therefore, are not only the necessary attendants of beauty and deformity, but constitute their very essence. . . . An action, or sentiment, or character, is virtuous or viscous; why? Because its view causes a pleasure or uneasiness of particular kind."[13]

This raises an interesting problem with respect to the very real autonomous faculty, which, as you have seen above, Dawkins identified as a product of evolution. Either we have an innate moral faculty, or we do not. If the various atheists differ so much among themselves upon this cardinal issue, how can anybody be faulted for appealing to divine authority in the face of this massive self-contradiction?

The empiricist approach stimulated the development of utilitarianism, which became the backbone philosophy of the British Empire during the Victorian age. Jeremy Bentham developed Hume's picture of moral judgement in terms of the human capacity for pain and pleasure. In his exposition of his utilitarianism, he sought to devise a scale of pleasures and pains, rating them in terms of their intensity, propinquity or remoteness, certainty, purity, duration, fruitfulness, and the extent to which pleasure and pain are shared among fewer or more people.

No matter how it is formulated, for the utilitarian, everything is determined by pleasure and pain. As we have seen in Harris's introduction, Bentham wrote,

> Nature has placed mankind under governance of two sovereign masters, pain and pleasure. It is for them alone to point out what we ought to do, as well as to determine what we shall do. On the one hand, the standard of right and wrong, the chain of causes and effects are fastened to their throne. They govern us all in what we do, what we say, in all we think: every effort we can make to throw off our subjection, will serve but to demonstrate and to confirm it. In other words, a man may pretend to abjure their empire: but in reality, he will remain subject to it all the while.
>
> Pleasure and freedom from pain are the only things desirable as ends; and that all desirable things are desirable either for the pleasure inherent in themselves or as means to the promotion of pleasure and the prevention of pain.[14]

Utilitarianism, in step with the Darwinistic moralism that characterized the late Victorian era, relegated man to the animal domain by referring to the immediate sensations of pain and pleasure as the ultimate standards of good and evil. It is the scientist's morality, born from observing the interaction between the human being and his physical environment. Sam Harris has simply taken this to the next logical level and speaks of the "scientific account of human values—i.e. one that places them squarely within the web of influences that link states of the world and states of the human brain."[15]

According to Harris himself, he defends a very simple thesis: "that human well-being entirely depends upon events in the world and on states of the human brain. Consequently, there must be scientific truths to be known about it." It only makes sense, therefore, that "science can in principle help us to understand what we should do and what we should want—and therefore what other people should do and want in order to live the best lives possible."[16]

Sam Harris's position on morality is nothing else than standard utilitarianism couched in the language of brain states. It is not even a true update but simply a restatement of the tired utilitarian ethics in terms that his Victorian predecessors lacked. Whereas John Stuart Mill used terms like "happiness," Harris chose "well-being" as the be-all-and-end-all of moral righteousness. Like his Victorian predecessors, he also thinks that it is quite easy to find the rules to distinguish right from wrong. Using two extreme examples, he seeks to prove that "The Bad Life" is easily distinguishable from "The Good Life":

> The Bad Life
> You are a young widow who has lived her entire life in the midst of civil war. Today, your seven-year-old daughter was raped and dismembered before your eyes. Worse still, the perpetrator was your fourteen-year-old son, who was goaded to this evil at the point of a machete by a press-gang of drug-addled soldiers. You are now running barefoot through the jungle with killers in pursuit. While this is the worst day of your life, it is not entirely out of character with the other days of your life: since the moment you were born, your world has become a theatre of cruelty and violence. You have never learnt to read, taken a hot shower, or traveled beyond the green hell of the jungle. Even the luckiest people you know have known little more than an occasional respite from chronic hunger, fear, apathy, and confusion. Unfortunately, you have been very unlucky, even by these bleak standards. Your life has been one long emergency, and now it is nearly over.

After this bleak picture, he gives us another view, bleak in its own particular kind of way:

> The Good Life
> You are married to the most loving, intelligent and charismatic person you have ever met. Both of you have careers that are intellectually stimulating and financially rewarding. For decades, your wealth and social connections have allowed you to devote yourself to activities that bring you immense personal satisfaction. One of your greatest sources of happiness has been to find creative ways to help people who have not had your good fortune in life. In fact, you have just won a billion-dollar grant to benefit children in the developing world. If asked, you would say that you could not imagine how your time on earth could be better spent. Due to a combination of good genes and optimal circumstances, you and your closest friends and family will live very long healthy lives, untouched by crime, sudden bereavements and other misfortunes.[17]

One is at a loss to see why this would be relevant as an introduction to a book on moral issues. What he has given us is a picture of the unfortunate and fortunate lives. He has committed a gigantic category mistake: goodness and good fortune are two entirely different things; likewise evil and bad fortune. The comfortable life is not necessarily moral, and the terrible life is not necessarily evil. Just because there is a correlation between a certain brain state and a certain event on the outside does not mean that the occurrence of that event was indeed something of which one can give unconditional moral approval.

With insistence that morality is simply a question of the "well-being of conscious creatures," all that he has in effect done is to emphasize the most basic facet of the human condition: that we are sensual beings who respond to external stimuli. Some are pleasurable; others are painful; some cause indifference; others mild irritation; others a warm, fuzzy feeling of contentment; and so on. At best, he has given us an overview of what it means to exist as a bodily being in our kind of world. One could say that all of human culture begins at this level. As Nietzsche said, "Initially, we organic beings have no interest in a thing, other than in its relationship to us with regard to pleasure and pain." Fortunately, it does not end there. Humanity only truly begins when the bounds of pain and pleasure are exceeded. It is downright horrifying to think what Aristotle would have made of utilitarianism. As is well known, Aristotle understood ethics in terms of virtue. That is, the good life is one that has been shaped in such a way that it reaches its fullest potential. If we measure Harris's crude pain/pleasure ethic against the Greek ideal of achievement and take it to its ultimate conclusion, we arrive at an even cruder result: it would appear that the noblest act for the New Atheist would be masturbation, since it harms no one, there are no risks or possibilities involved, and the pleasure involved is undeniable. In other words, it is the perfect New Atheist virtue—safe, nice, and private. It is hard to imagine why anyone would want to do anything else.

Harris's position on pain and pleasure can be compared to that of the clergyman who, when asked about his opinion on sin, just replied that he was "against it." This is no moral position but merely a pragmatic one, one of practical import and of no genuine interest to ethics. Nowhere does Harris state what pain is or why it should be avoided. He merely takes it as an obvious point of departure, that we should all avoid pain and aim for "well-being" as much as possible. The question that now presents itself is this. If this is such an obvious and universal premise for all rational creatures (that is, all of humanity, let no one accuse the New Atheists of elitism), then why do not all of humanity automatically gravitate toward this facile utilitarianism? Why do the New Atheists feel the need to constantly tell the world that the principles of morality are obvious and universal, if they are so obvious and universal? Why is it that there is no automatic universal consensus as to what is right and how we should live?

The simplicity of Harris's argument cannot but fail to astonish, especially when read in the light of the Romantic lineage that precedes modern atheism. Harris appears to think that pain and pleasure represent exact opposites and that they are easily distinguishable. One wonders how he would account for the phenomenon named after that one atheist the New Atheists are so loathe to include in their intellectual ancestry: de Sade. Ever since de Sade, every thinker that took questions of identity, pain and pleasure seriously. This charming atheist held that it is always by way of pain that one arrives at pleasure. From the Marquis's slap and tickle to Goethe's *Sorrows of Young Werther*, from the Victorian melancholic to the tiresome hypochondriac that enjoys the attention his illnesses bestow upon him, pleasure and pain have always been deeply intertwined. In fact, suffering and pleasure go together like a horse and carriage. This phenomenon is not limited to either heartache or leather clubs: in the contemporary political world, no one gets as much attention as the sufferer. There is no better way to instant credibility.

The following passage by Nietzsche, however, says it all:

> What? The ultimate goal of science is to create for man the greatest possible amount of pleasure and the least possible amount of pain? But suppose pleasure and pain were so linked together that he who wants to have the greatest amount possible of the one must have the greatest amount of the other also? And perhaps that is how things are! The Stoics, at any rate, thought so, and were consistent when they desired to have the least possible amount of pleasure in order to have the least possible amount of pain from life. Today, too, you have the choice: either as little pain as possible, in short painlessness, or as much pain as possible, as the price of an abundance of subtle joys and pleasures hitherto rarely tasted.[18]

One of the main reasons why utilitarianism arrived so late in history, and remains a distinctly English phenomenon, is because there is no universal consensus about the role of pain. Throughout history, people have endured, and have been willing to endure, a great deal of pain, whether for their principles or beliefs, for others, or even for progress: the voyages of discovery, for example, were anything but a cakewalk. It is possible to doubt that the modern middle class would be able to endure what Columbus, Magellan, da Gama, and Scott did. Pain had never been a problem for humanity until the nineteenth century. Up to that era, it was commonly accepted that pain and pleasure were deeply intertwined and that many great achievements demand great sacrifice and often a great deal of pain and suffering. Freud argues that civilization itself demands a great deal of suffering: the suppression of instinct can be one of the worst forms of torture imaginable. As history's long list of martyrs proved, with a clear goal in mind, man could reconcile himself to suffering surprisingly well, provided that it had a clear purpose. Nietzsche writes:

> The suffering itself was not his problem, but rather the fact that he lacked an answer to the question he screamed out, "Why this suffering?" Man, the bravest animal, the one most accustomed to suffering, does not deny suffering in

itself. He desires it, he seeks it out in person, provided that people show him a meaning for it, the purpose of suffering. (*Genealogy of Morals*, III, 28)[19]

Whatever one wants to say about pain, its avoidance can by no means serve as the basis for morality. Sam Harris's description of morality as that which brings about the "good" life as opposed to the "bad" life by no means engages the matter of morality but merely indicates the perimeters of the human comfort zone. Consider the following examples. It is Saturday night and you are without a date. Luckily for you, so is your dog. You decide to have sex with her right there in the living room. No one happens to be hurt in the process. Or imagine the following scenario: you are employed at a slaughterhouse, and your job is to slaughter pigs. You figure the poor sentient creatures may just as well have a good time before they are dispatched to become the best part of ham sandwiches. In fact, from Sam Harris's point of view, it is much more moral to copulate with pigs than to eat them. It may even be argued that you are a healthy nonconformist. So you give them a good seeing-to. From Harris's perspective, you would be contributing to the well-being of sentient beings. Everything is, after all, only a matter of brain states.

But what would the situation be if only one party to the act is sentient? Imagine this scenario. You are employed at a mortuary, and one of the dead bodies looks, well, really hot. There is no one around, and you end up copulating with a corpse. A dead body is not sentient and cannot therefore experience pain or humiliation. The act certainly contributes to the well-being of the only sentient creature in the room: you, because you achieved sexual release (a great contributor to well-being) without harming another sentient being. The obvious response will be that violating a corpse hurts the feelings of his or her next of kin. But why is this the case? Would this mean that it would be perfectly acceptable to have sex with the dead body of a homeless man with no family? Or that it would be acceptable as long as family are not aware of such corpse violation? Finally, let us bring the two scenarios together. According to Sam Harris's credo that morality is what promotes the well-being of sentient creatures, it would be perfectly acceptable to achieve sexual release with the dead bodies of animals.

One can hopefully presume that most readers will be pretty disgusted by now. Yet this is to what a purely utilitarian ethic amounts. This is why one of the earliest objections to utilitarianism was that it was a doctrine unworthy of humanity. Even John Stuart Mill himself was aware of this. He was not willing to accede to a world of pure pleasure. Importantly, however, he had to justify his unease in terms other than pure utilitarianism: "To suppose that life . . . has no higher end than pleasure—no better and nobler object of desire and pursuit—they designate as utterly mean and grovelling; as a doctrine worthy of swine."[20] Given our slaughterhouse example above, he may well have had a point.

Mill of course objected that human beings had faculties that far exceeded those of animals and were subject to higher pleasures of the intellect and imagination, which were considerably more than "mere sensation." This distinction between the "higher" and "lower" pleasures depends upon an aesthetic distinction, however, not a moral one. As soon as we bring questions of virtue, quality, and nobility into the discussion, we are no longer in the domain of utilitarianism.

One of the biggest problems with respect to both the Victorian utilitarians and their New Atheist inheritors is their conception of the human being. Unlike Mill, the New Atheists are far from keen to draw a distinction between animal and human life. Richard Dawkins even prides himself upon being an "African ape."[21]

One of the most important consequences of Darwin was the erasure of the definite distinction between human and animal life. What we have now, instead, is a biological continuum, one ontological category with various degrees of rationality. This, too, is currently under attack. Researchers assail us with new findings every day that show that there is but a miniscule difference between our DNA and that of the great apes and no true grounds for viewing us in terms of two separate domains. This means that we, just like the animals who are our kin, are then not truly subject to the demands of ethics. We do not blame a cat for catching a mouse, even if she cruelly plays with it first. The natural world is after all only subject to the laws of physics and instinct. But if we are part of that world, how can anyone then expect us to be moral? Morality is by no means purely natural but only develops when man exceeds nature.

NOTES

1. F. Nietzsche, *The Gay Science*, translated by Walter Kaufman (New York: Vintage, 1957), 124.
2. Richard Dawkins, "God's Utility Function," *Scientific American* (November 1995): 85.
3. Richard Dawkins, *The God Delusion* (London: Transworld, 2009), 247.
4. Sam Harris, *The Moral Landscape* (London: Bantam, 2011), 99.
5. Dawkins, *The God Delusion*, 253.
6. Friedrich Nietzsche, *The Genealogy of Morals and Other Writings*, edited by Keith Ansell-Pearson and Carol Diethe (Cambridge: Cambridge University Press, 2000), 61.
7. Nietzsche, *The Genealogy of Morals*, 41.
8. Nietzsche, *The Genealogy of Morals*, 37.
9. Dawkins, *The God Delusion*, 259.
10. Immanuel Kant, *Ethical Philosophy: Grounding for the Metaphysics of Morals* (1785), translated by J. W. Ellington (Indianapolis,: New Hackett, 1995), 30.
11. Kant, *Ethical Philosophy*, p. 36.
12. Friedrich Nietzsche, *Beyond Good and Evil: Prelude to a Philosophy of the Future*, edited by Rolf-Peter Horstman and translated by Judith Norman (Cambridge: Cambridge University Press, 2002).
13. David Hume, *Enquiry Concerning Human Understanding*, edited by Selby-Bigge (Oxford: Clarendon Press, 1902), section 10.

14. Jeremy Bentham, "An Introduction to the Principles of Morals and Legislation," in *The Works of Jeremy Bentham*, Vol I. (New York: Russell & Russell, 1962), 11.
15. Harris, *The Moral Landscape*, 13.
16. Harris, *The Moral Landscape*, 28.
17. Harris, *The Moral Landscape*, 15, 16.
18. Nietzsche, *The Gay Science*, 85.
19. Friedrich Nietzsche, *On the Genealogy of Morality*, translated by C. Diethe (Cambridge: Cambridge University Press, 1990), 120.
20. John S. Mill, *The Collected Works of John Stuart Mill*, edited by J. M. Robson (London: Routledge and Kegan Paul, 1963), X:210.
21. As Dawkins declared on Twitter on May 13, 2015, "We are African apes and are descended (as are chimpanzees) from extinct apes" (https://twitter.com/richarddawkins/status/598523097843671040).

REFERENCES

Bentham, J. "An Introduction to the Principles of Morals and Legislation." In *The Works of Jeremy Bentham*, Vol I. New York: Russell & Russell, 1962.
Dawkins, R. *The God Delusion*. New York: Transworld, 2009.
———. "God's Utility Function." *Scientific American* (November 1995).
Harris, S. *Letter to a Christian Nation*. New York: Transworld, 2011.
———. *The Moral Landscape*. London: Bantam, 2011.
Hume, D. *Enquiry Concerning Human Understanding*. Edited by Selby-Bigge. Oxford: Clarendon Press, 1902.
Kant, I. *Critique of Practical Reason*. Translated by W. S. Pluhar. Indianapolis: Hackett, 2002.
———. *Ethical Philosophy: Grounding for the Metaphysics of Morals*. Translated by J. W. Ellington. Indianapolis: New Hackett, 1995.
Mill, J. S. = *The Collected Works of John Stuart Mill*. Edited by J. M. Robson. London: Routledge and Kegan Paul, 1963.
———. "Utilitarianism" (1863). Reprinted in *Mill's Utilitarianism*, edited by J. M. Smith and E. Sosa. Belmont, Calif.: Wadsworth, 1963.
Nietzsche, F. *Beyond Good and Evil: Prelude to a Philosophy of the Future*. Edited by Rolf-Peter Horstman and translated by Judith Norman. Cambridge: Cambridge University Press, 2002.
———. *The Gay Science*. Translated by Walter Kaufman. New York: Vintage, 1957.
———. *The Genealogy of Morals and Other Writings*. Edited by Keith Ansell-Pearson and Carol Diethe. Cambridge: Cambridge University Press, 2000.
———. *On the Genealogy of Morality*. Translated by C. Diethe. Cambridge: Cambridge University Press, 1990.

Part III

The Theists

Chapter Eight

My God-Given Conscience

Henk Stoker

In a rather bold Kantian move, Henk Stoker argues that the phenomenon of the human conscience—that uncanny "dialogue between me and myself," as Hannah Arendt once described our capacity to decide between what is right and wrong—runs counter to our immediate instinctual responses. But unlike Kant, Stoker chooses to describe this phenomenon in terms of the Christian faith. He also refrains from appealing to other purely humanist constructs such as the Romantic notion (made famous by Rousseau and popularized by poets like Shelley and Wordsworth) that the sometimes demanding voice at the back of our heads is just an "innate" faculty. On the contrary, he holds that there is something decidedly different about this inner voice: it is so unquestioningly good, that when it is silenced, the consequences are terrible. Such an unambiguous good can only be identified with God. Through a phenomenological description of the human conscience, Stoker traces the origins of morality to the divine.

In contrast to Susan Neiman, who also finds the origins of morality in categorical obligations, Stoker holds that the force of the human conscience is just too compelling to be of purely human origin. It is as difficult to define it as to avoid it—it is, as Stoker argues, the ultimate first-person experience: communicating the experience of the guilty conscience almost defies human effort. This is because the conscience is one of the most precious aspects of human existence, the small sliver at the back of the human mind that links the human subject with a power beyond him- or herself.

There may be those who will argue that the conscience may just as well be described in purely naturalist terms and that natural selection is sufficient to account for the emergence of the conscience as a strategy of social cohesion, or that such a move on Stoker's part indicates a lack of historical awareness, perhaps the complementary side to Harris's innate pain/pleasure principle. However, such criticism would be premature: Stoker describes the experience of guilt in its most fundamental sense and strives to unlock the essence (what Aristotle or, more recently, Husserl or Brentano may have said), the hyle *of the experience of the guilty conscience. Why are we so in thrall to this mysterious inner voice? Even if it is accepted that the conscience is subject to development over time, it does not preclude the possibility of its divine origin. Even more important, such a move would signify animal nature breaking through the ceiling leading to humanity.*

Such criticism would also miss the central thrust of Stoker's argument: that the operation of the conscience exceeds all utilitarian logic, that it is arguably the most solitary of all experience possible; the narrator of the tale that opens Stoker's essay stands completely alone in his act of making a moral choice. That we are capable of doing this at al, is in itself a miracle, one that we far too often take for granted.

To be sure, it is in this very solitary act that the narrating self also encounters the ultimate Other: not the object of his help in the form of the victim but the very Originator of the human condition as such: the God that created humanity with the capacity to experience a scintilla of His own goodness.

—The Editors

> My conscience hath a thousand several tongues,
> And every tongue brings in a several tale,
> And every tale condemns me for a villain.
> —William Shakespeare, *Richard III*, V.iii

Late afternoon.
I am on my way home through the nearly empty streets of our South African university town. It is only myself and one other person who has just passed me on a bicycle. The students' exams are over and they have returned home. Most of the other residents have left for the Christmas vacation. My own vacation has just started, and I cannot wait to get home and relax with my family around a barbecue. It was a crazy year. . . .
Suddenly a car comes around the corner at a high speed, hits the bicycle, and drives off. The cyclist flies through the air and lands besides the road, bloodied and broken. I had a tough year, I am tired, and I am quite well-dressed—I don't want to get blood on my clothes. I know my family has been waiting for the entire year for this day, and besides, I don't want to end up having to testify in a court of law about what happened. So I decide to just walk past the victim. Perhaps I can call an ambulance after all. . . . But only when I have turned off caller ID.
No—something kicks in—my conscience. It forces me to act in a way antithetical to what I really want. I quickly approach the scene and call the ambulance. Upon closer inspection, I notice that the injured bears more than a passing resemblance to a police description of a person suspected of stealing bicycles

> *in our neighbourhood. I wonder fleetingly whether the man does not have AIDS; I do not have any gloves. Nevertheless, I bend down, support his neck with my one hand, while I open his collar to aid the difficult breathing. Then I begin to remove blood and clothes to see whether I can find the origin of the bleeding.*

I am sure you know why the narrator in the story had done what he had done—even if he did not want to do it. We call the source of his unselfish acts his conscience. Everyone has it: a fundamental sense of right and wrong that forces us in the opposite direction and is really in opposition to the New Atheistic view of morals as driven by a "selfish gene" or by "survival of the fittest." We know, for example, that self-sacrifice is regarded as more moral than selfishness, that courage is better than cowardice, even that love is superior to hate.

It does not stop at mere knowledge. People act according to their conscience. As illustrated in the narration above, one's conscience is so much more than consciousness of what human beings ought and ought not to do. While assuming a certain basic moral knowledge, humanity's conscience has the compelling nature to force—even against an individual's will—a person to what seems to be good and right and proper. It brings a sense of how one ought to act, but it is also more than just a feeling. It is an inner reaction of the individual against the evil or selfishness in him- or herself.[1]

CONSCIENCE AND THE EXPERIENCE OF GUILT GO HAND IN HAND

If, in the example above, the narrator would walk past the injured person as he actually wanted to do, it is likely that he would feel a deep sense of guilt, a guilt which in all likelihood would not be short-lived but one that would have a big impact on him and would likely influence his experiences of that evening as well as his vacation negatively. Through his conscientious reaction to the injured, the narrator saved himself from the dreadful feelings of a guilty conscience afterward.

But how did it happen? Not because he consciously wanted to avoid the experience of a guilty conscience. The moment when he had to make that moral choice, his conscience kicked in spontaneously, and he experienced guilt upon the desire not to help. In everyday life experience, our conscience does not kick in merely when an expert explains *theoretically* what one should and should not do. It is only in the moment when one knows one is acting or wants to act contrary to what one ought that one experiences conscientious reproaches or conscientious coercion—a heartfelt experience of and feeling of guilt.

That experience of guilt when not helping a person in need is not a feeling of guilt toward oneself. Quite the opposite because it holds potential negative consequences for the narrator that he really would prefer to escape—including AIDS, court cases, a busy evening, spoiled clothing. It is clear that these feelings of guilt for not helping are not toward oneself because through helping one actually harms oneself. These feelings are also not directed toward the injured because he has no direct claim upon one's time and, moreover, may well be the person who is victimizing the neighbourhood. The experience of the guilty conscience that forced the narrator to do good against his will and advantage implies a power beyond mere humanity.

Going against someone's will tells us that the human conscience is not just a subjective opinion but the very basis for being a moral being. Most people would, for instance, agree that it was the right thing to do when the narrator, as the only other person around, tried to help the injured person. People know that they should help a person in dire need if they are in the position to do so. Some people might deny their responsibility and try to ignore the accident and the injured man, but when they are confronted with their lack of positive action, they are likely to recognize their failure *as* moral failure and are likely to immediately try to give a reason for not helping. Deep in their hearts, they *know* that a refusal to help in one way or another is wrong—even if they claim not to feel remorse. The refusal to help those in dire need if I can and am the only one around is immoral for everyone, everywhere, now and forever, like all other basic moral obligations. Such moral obligations form the basis of our shared human conscience and imply obligations that were made part of human lives (even against our will) by the Giver of life.

EXPERIENCE OF THE GUILTY OR CLEAR CONSCIENCE

One's conscience can be activated before or after an action. If it is before or during an action, his or her conscience serves to warn the individual against and/or motivate such an individual for acting in a particular way. In the case mentioned above, the narrator's conscience warned him against ignoring the injured and moved him to become physically involved. The same would be true when your conscience reacts after the fact to your handling of a particular event and could manifest itself in the form of either a guilty or clear conscience, leading to an unpleasant or a pleasant experience.

The existence of the guilty conscience is usually seen as good. If the narrator of the story refused to help the injured and experienced no feelings of guilt afterward, it would be considered abnormal and inappropriate. The word "conscience" is usually framed in a negative fashion, for example, in a question: "Doesn't the person have a conscience?" or in remarks like "His conscience haunts him" and "I hope his conscience will kick in."

A guilty conscience can be described as the unpleasant feeling of dissatisfaction, restlessness, and inner disapproval that a person experiences about his actions or lack of action. The possibility of having a guilty conscience makes it possible that what is morally good finally triumphs over what is morally evil. A good example of this occurs when the biblical Nathan, in 2 Samuel 12, portrayed to David through a fictional story the evil he did to Uriah and Bathsheba. The workings of David's conscience and very real feelings of guilt can be clearly seen when Psalm 51 is read.

The experience of guilt through one's conscience may be said to be based on a personal sense of *evil*. Although it can be assumed that most people who were in the same position of the author of the story told in the beginning in some way would have helped the injured person, even if it was not what they planned for that late afternoon or really wanted to do, it must also be assumed that not all people would have helped. The person in the car, for example, who caused the accident and could be expected even legally to help, did not help but sped away. The fact that there are differences in guilty feelings and what ought to be done, however, does not erase that people do have what may be called an intersubjective sense of immorality, evil, and guilt, what we commonly know as the conscience.

The opposite of a guilty conscience is a clear conscience. Both are a reaction to a desire to act contrary to what I actually know ought to happen. The more I come under the impression of my own actions as wrong or even evil, the more authentic the experience of my guilty conscience and the stronger the desire to correct it. However, where a person did not submit to the desire to act against what he felt he should do (as in the example above where the injured person was assisted), the person experienced a clear conscience.

A clear conscience is not something that occurs when a person is experiencing a good day at work, even if it makes him or her feel good or satisfied. A clear conscience comes into play only where there is an internal conflict in a person to do things that should not be or not to do what should be done. Only when there is a desire to do evil, or to transgress norms, does conscience comes to the fore. This underlines the fact that there is a standard of ought and ought not, of right and wrong, that comes from outside humankind and became part of us through the inner workings of our conscience. Even where people's actions go to the contrary, their reactions to accusations show that they know about it. In the words of C. S. Lewis: "Human beings, all over the earth, have this curious idea that they ought to behave in a certain way, and cannot really get rid of it."[2]

A clear conscience brings a calmness and even a sense of inner peace when doing what should be done, precisely when you (as in the example above) do not feel at all like doing it and would prefer to have a good enough reason for not doing it. However, a clear conscience by no means necessarily assures that my actions or the result thereof are by definition good. The narrator of the above story could, for instance, in the process of supporting the neck of the injured, have caused the person to become paralyzed—one of the unfortunate limitations of a purely utilitarian ethic! A clear conscience makes someone feel not only no guilt about his or her actions but even pleased and happy to have made the sacrifice. Note, however, that a clear conscience is not a feeling of one's own goodness, while a guilty conscience, on the other hand, includes the experience of our own moral depravity.

The question that now arises is how it is possible that man, who is, according to Christian doctrine, in his deepest being sinful and self-centered or, according to evolutionists and New Atheists, deeply driven by selfish genes and survival instincts, is at all able to experience (through the conscience) such a real and profound sense of own debt and guilt? Why is it that the deeper our experience of evil, the more we *value* this conscience? Why do my conscientiously good acts that go against my own immediate interests not generate the same intense experience of well-being, as the feelings of guilt that could drive people into despair when they wronged someone? One would surely think that the psychological experience of personal goodness should have the same value or even higher value as an experience of moral lack. Does it not point to a lack of moral equilibrium that one's conscience will condemn one continuously but will not praise one in a similar fashion? Is it even possible to imagine a happiness with the same intensity of the guilt displayed by a Meursault or a Jean Valjean?

This unequal experience may be said to have an ontic[3] foundation because it lies in the fundamentally unequal relationship with God. If what I am and what I have is not the doing of God, my conscience would not have been so one-sided—or it would be one-sided to the selfish side . . . and even proud of it from a survival-of-the-fittest position. Our pursuit of doing good—even to our own disadvantage—cannot come from our own selfish or self-focused desires that are part of us from very small. It makes more sense to see it as something our Creator has made an intrinsic part of us, for us to function in a moral and responsible fashion as human beings. To go around and praise oneself for helping an injured man would bring a bad taste in the narrator's and other people's mouths. Why? Because he just did what he should do. When you honestly think about it you realize that the good actions were not due to yourself (because self-focused man would like to put his interests first) but to a conscience that was created in us and works against our selfish nature. However, if the narrator gave in to self-benefit and just walked pass the injured, he could only blame himself and not God. By God's grace, we are not at the mercy of selfishness, even though it plays such a big role in people's lives that evolutionists reduce behavior to survival of the fittest and selfish genes.

A WARNING CONSCIENCE

A warning conscience is not simply an instrument to warn me to avoid wrong and to do what should be done in order not to feel guilty. It is something that makes a person hesitate before acting contrary to what ought. The warning conscience does not conduct a moral inquiry into the desirability of an action, but suppose we already know that the planned action is wrong (cf. Socrates's *daemon*). To use the example with which we started again: the warning conscience tells the narrator that it would be wrong to give in to the desire to ignore the accident and go home. It does not argue for pros and cons and whether it is really immoral but speaks to the desire and intent to do wrong. It specifically targets the will or desire to do evil, an intent to commit real immoral actions, even though the person might misunderstand the evil.

A warning conscience usually warns against doing something wrong (e.g., stealing, lying, or murder), but it can also warn against failing to do something that *should* be done, for example, the unwillingness to help someone in need as in the example at the beginning. In the latter case, the conscience may almost be described as an inner injunction order, compelling the individual to act in a particular way, whether the individual desires to do so or not.

The personal experience of evil is an essential element of a warning conscience. This experience of the immorality of a planned action provides the basis for the response by the conscience experienced by the individual. Personal experience adds the further advantage in that it leads people to experience a deepening and intensification in their moral life, and growth in this cardinal part of their real (and ontic-intended) humanity. It goes against the more basic human impulse for self-interest and is independent of the individual's will because it was *created* to go against an individual's desire. It just starts working without the individual asking for it. "Conscience is an emotional power, which observes and betrays the secrets and confidences that lie in the innermost depths of our heart, so that nothing evil can remain shrouded in darkness."[4]

A true conscience is a real, inner, personal revelation. It is true in the sense that it is not thought out or merely a subjective feeling. It is internal because it originates spontaneously from the inner depths of the human soul and is emotional in nature. It is personal because only our *own* evil causes the conscience to respond. True, the conscience rebukes the individual but does so only when there is a real relationship to *personal* evil. If man emerged by chance and is driven by his desire for survival, for his own benefit, for happiness and pleasure, or selfish genes drive him as contemporary atheists argue, the existence of the conscience does not make sense. It only makes sense when it is recognized and acknowledged that there are phenomena such as good and as evil—a distinction and measure that exists independently of and outside human beings, which does not come from us but often goes against what we want—and exerts a powerful influence on our lives. He who created it in us is wholly good and the source of this check on an otherwise sinful nature. He gave us an understanding of the nature of goodness, thus making man a moral being, able to distinguish between good and evil. In other words, He provided us with the ability to distinguish conceptually between virtue and vice, making us distinct from the rest of the animal kingdom and truly *human*.

OUGHT DEMANDS

That the question of what man ought to do (*to deon* in Greek, whence the term "deontics") exists at all is an important aspect of understanding the essence of humanity and our thinking about morality. What man "ought" to do supposes something or someone requiring or demanding it. According to Christian understanding, deontics finds its origin in the ontic relationship between man (or the subject) on the one hand and God and cosmos (matter, plants, animals, and man) on the other hand. The very field of deontics is a divine gift to man, without which the human being as such cannot be human. Man's insight into what should be is distracted or derived from the ontological aspects of what ought. This positivation of deontics formulated by man (when for instance, promulgating laws of state, as formulated by Kant) presupposes the ontic nature of deontics and ought to correspond to them. In other words, the reality of the moral law precedes any formulation of it— goodness has a pre-phenomenal character.

WHAT ONE *MAY*

While animals can do things according to their nature and kind, it would not make sense to dictate to animals what they may or should do. The uniqueness of humans lies in the fact that we may not necessarily do everything that we are able to do or that we should not necessarily do everything that we are able to do. "May" refers to the lawful: that which is permissible for us, that which we have a right to, the privileges we were given as humans. It therefore focuses on the legal foundation of human actions, while should or ought go further and emphasize what is moral or proper.

Man has a choice between what he may do and may not do. When looking at the world from a phenomenological point of view, it is clear that the distinction between what is allowed and what is not allowed comprises an intrinsic part of human life. Without this distinction, people would not be able to live together; humans would not even be able to ensure their own safety or general well-being. What is allowed must thus be enforceable and be based on an authority system.

What man is allowed or not has theistic origins and derives from God's purpose with man. According to the theistic approach, people are expected to acknowledge their justified claims (as well as those of others) on what they either individually or jointly may do and undertake not to undermine these rights.

WHAT ONE *OUGHT*

What *ought* (German: *sollen*) to be done, or categorical obligations, are mostly tasks or duties that man encounters that demand from him reflection and reaction. These are matters that speak or should speak to man, demanding from him or her responsible action. People may legitimately appeal to that support that people should give to one another and may ask for help (even extraordinary help) from each other in situations of distress. The mere situation in which a person finds himself (as in the example at the beginning) can as such be a call for help and put a sense of duty to someone's conscience.

The question is: what brings about this normative claim to human conscience and why do people feel compelled to pay attention to it and deal with them? What authority lies behind this experience of duty and what does it tell us about human beings that they will comply with this at the expense of themselves? A purely evolutionary or naturalistic justification of self-interest and even group interest as the deepest motivation offers no realistic explanation because such altruistic behavior typically contradicts the selfishness of the "survival of the fittest" approach.

For Christians, the experience of what one ought to do originates in the ontic sense in God. It also offers an explanation for the fact that when this obligation is not met, or when a person succumbs to improper behavior, that person experiences guilt. This experience of missing one's purpose can be captured in the term *sin*. This involves both doing what ought not to be done and the failure to meet one's obligations.

OUGHT FREES

Morality, that what man ought to do, is based on two important assumptions. Firstly, it presupposes that man has a deontic choice vis-à-vis whether he will submit himself to the norms concerned or disobey them. On account of this latter possibility, man is not only accountable for his actions but also responsible, and he may be called on to answer for his actions. The possibility of choice is a first condition of human freedom (but not freedom itself), and this obedience to what ought to be is the second. Human freedom may be realized only on account of man's choice between his possibilities (or tasks) and his submission (obedience) to the determinants concerned.

CHOICE AND LIMITATION

An atheistic approach that reduces humans to physical-chemical reaction at the molecular level logically brings about the destruction of the once free and accountable human beings, who are now reduced to their biological urges—hence Dawkins's view of man who is manipulated and managed by his selfish genes. Atheism thus cannot free man but enslave him. Even the well-functioning conscience is distorted and twisted by a naturalistic worldview to become a deterministic self-centered genetic reaction. The paradox and antinomy of what we actually experience is clear. So is the logical destruction of moral obligations that accompanies this worldview. Man's ability to choose within the boundaries of what ought to be and is morally proper is a basic condition for human freedom. Where either choice or restraint is overemphasized or ignored, human freedom itself is in jeopardy.[5]

DETERMINISM, INDETERMINISM, AND SELF-DETERMINISM

In deterministic approaches, reality is reduced either to cause and effect or to determinism by natural law. Where the former proposes that everything is causally determined, the latter states that fixed laws govern everything so that there is neither the possibility of acting differently nor even any exceptions. When man is seen as deterministic, the freedom of man is sacrificed on a conceptual level. If man is not free and does not have the possibility of choice, questions about what he should do or what is morally proper become superfluous and the human conscience can hardly be said to play a role. "What ought" and the concomitant obligation that the conscience puts on a person (as in the narrative at the beginning) cannot be derived from any mere set of facts (see also Weinberg and Lennox on this matter).

Contrary to rigid determinism, indeterminism emphasizes the freedom of the individual to make arbitrary choices according to his own will. Indeterminism provides the opportunity for reflection and discussion on obligation, but taken to its radical extreme, indeterminism ends in relativism. There can be no objective right and wrong but only preference. But as we have seen, mere preference is insufficient for explaining the actions of the narrator at the beginning.

Because determinism and indeterminism either eliminate freedom or redirect freedom to coincidence and arbitrariness, self-determinism arose (especially with absolute idealists like Bradley, Bosanquet, and Green[6]) as a third category that wants to position itself between determinism and indeterminism. In self-determinism, the subject must fulfill his nature according to humanist principles in his or her social context. Self-realization is thus a realization of the subject within his or her social context. The problem is, however, that self-determinism also reduces what ought to be done to the subject alone—even if it is in a wider society—and derives it only from popular consensus. It still fails to explain either the force of the demands themselves or why humans feel compelled to comply (even at their own expense).

Categorical obligations—what ought to be done—cannot be based upon man alone but find their origin in the One who made man in this particular way, to have a conscience and to make responsible choices, namely God. Human freedom is possible only if man, on the basis of his conscience and possibility of choice, does what he as human being ontically ought to do and in applying these norms to him as a specific human being and to what his specific situation asks from him (as also seen in the story at the beginning). What man can, should, and ought to do is not based on an accidental development in man himself but the guidance of God, which determines the nature of man and his place and role in the cosmos and toward each other. Moral obligations and what ought are thus situated in the origin of man and in his deepest reason for existence.

FREE OR SLAVE

Freedom is not opposed to bondage—quite the contrary—but to slavery. If man refuses to accept God or the boundaries He set to humanity, he will only set his own boundaries through a combination of his own prejudices, judgments of others that are perceived as significant, the influence of the community, his own situation, or whatever he may need to determine what falls within the boundaries of arbitrary, and could in principle take any direction.

Humanity can only be free, according to the Christian worldview, when they adhere to the ontic, that is, the *real* intentions of God. Through the appearance of sin and evil in the world, human desire clashes with God's intentions, and as a result, freedom is often defined as freedom from any restraints, norms, and authority. When man seeks freedom within himself, he enslaves himself (ironically enough) to those desires, tries to counter the force of his conscience, and in the process ends up losing that very freedom he so coveted. By deciding to legislate his own moral norms, he develops a slave mentality. Then he is able to pass by the injured in the road at the beginning of this essay as if he is free from all obligations. By doing so, he absolves himself of moral agency and the duty to live morally, in order to satisfy his own selfish desire for immediate comfort. This is by no means freedom but enslavement to fickle cravings. As long as the human being is faithful to his ontic determination as a moral being and does what he ought to do, such an individual reaches his aim or *telos* as a mature rational being. If alcohol, for example, is used correctly, it serves the purposes of the user. However, when used incorrectly, the user eventually becomes its slave. The capacity to choose between good and evil therefore does not constitute freedom in itself but is only a precondition *for* freedom.

Through the Fall in Genesis—and the concomitant sin and evil that followed—disorder appeared in the universe, which in turn broke and distorted the relationship between humans. Humanity has been endowed with the faculties of conscience and freedom to choose precisely to counter this powerful force that can so easily get humanity within its grip. It is through the possession of this inner moral power that the human being is capable of using freedom in order to make good choices, resulting in a clean conscience and an unblemished existence. The warning conscience kicks in even when and where it would be easiest to ignore it—where no one sees it. It is precisely when it is the most difficult to be good that the conscience is at its most active.

A logical question that follows now is: what exactly motivates one to act in a particular way? The operation of the conscience is hardly a simple phenomenon. With respect to the example above, one has to ask what exactly would motivate me to help and what exactly would lead me to simply pass by and go home. Motive can be divided into two parts, namely *rationale* and *incentive*. Rationale refers to the external factor or phenomenon to which I react. With respect to the example above, one might say that if the man who hit the bicycle afterward lost control over his vehicle, stopped against a tree, jumped out, and tried to run away, the immoral nature of his conduct might have motivated me to attack him verbally and even to stop him physically if he is close enough. However, if that which motivates me to act at that stage is an uncontrolled reaction, it can consume my life to such an extent that I fail to help the injured. Then I am overpowered and enslaved by my incentive to combat the immoral behavior of the other. Even an incentive to do good (injustice must be countered) can become so powerful that it takes over one's entire behavior and thus becomes wrong and enslaving (think again of *Les Misérables*, this time of Javert).

It is also possible to put it in more psychological terms: drives or incentives emanate from the human being him- or herself. In contrast to even the most romanticized version of the "selfish gene" (as found among the "New Atheists"), drives are often enslaving powers that are bad or unbalanced to such an extent that they can consume the self entirely. These includes drives like the lust for power, the sex drive, the survival instinct, and drives toward honor, glory, and possessions. To the extent that such drives push one toward the illegitimate, such drives can lead to enslavement. If one were to succumb purely to the drives or instincts (or, in more Freudian terms, the id), that person is no longer in control of himself: instead of doing what ought to be done, the drive itself becomes autonomous, forces the person into that which rationally ought to be avoided, and thus enslaves the individual. Evil and sin enslave people to such an extent that they become blind to the claims of morality or, in the words of Jesus Christ, "see but don't see" (Matthew 13:13).

In the first two chapters of the Christian Bible's description of man as created in the image of God, one encounters four types of action that are implied by that status, namely *govern*, *create*, *care*, and engage in *relationship* with God and fellow human beings. When the ontic potential of these actions is correctly realized, the human being also realizes the full potential of his or her existence. When it is realized in a wrong and sinful way, one encounters falsification and enslavement. The duty to *govern* becomes either tyranny or the half-hearted following of moral rules, which permits the operation of evil. When enslavement is involved in the *creation* of culture, one finds a false or pseudo-culture. Enslavement with respect to *care* manifests itself in neglect or even deliberate destruction. Enslavement in the context of *relationship* shows itself as disobedience or even a betrayal of God or the abuse of or by people.

The need for restoration becomes all the more urgent as evil continues to create chaos. As the sinful human being is still a moral being and is still in possession of a conscience that pressures him or her to do good, we find among people the sense to combat evil and restore the good. While this striving toward self-improvement has been an aspect of human existence for a long time, human beings remain inclined toward self-advancement and one-sidedness and will often differ in their views and insights on what is right and what ought to happen. Any process of restoration will therefore remain imperfect and will always retain something of the original evil.

Everywhere in the world we find a struggle that aims to repair the ontological breach that occurred with the Fall, however different the motivations may be in every case. For instance, people from different backgrounds and presuppositions are in a variety of ways equally concerned about the damage being done to the environment—air, water, and earth. There are widespread attempts to save animals and plants on the brink of extinction and to assist the thousands of refugees struggling to find new homes. On the other hand, most of these problems are created by humans. As can be seen throughout the world, there is a perpetual struggle between good and evil in and around man, a struggle that affects humanity to such an extent that even Paul in Romans 7:19 had to acknowledge that the best of human intentions are often led awry: "For I do not do the good I want, but the evil I do not want is what I keep on doing." A familiar struggle!

Against the utopian view of the victory of good over evil on earth, the Bible makes it clear that humanity alone will never be able to rid the world of evil. There will be an ongoing struggle for the good against evil around and within us. Each point of restoration is always preliminary in the sense that it can never be final. This does not change the fact that God has made human beings to be in perpetual struggle against the evil found within and around us, even if we all know that all humans (albeit to different degrees) are still inclined toward self-interest. What is more, every attempt toward restoration and reparation can only occur within the particular as a wrong can never be repaired in its entirety (e.g., air pollution or shoplifting). The moral human's convictions thus motivate him or her to continue the struggle against evil as much as possible, while we know that only the final redemption and restoration that will occur one day will be perfect in nature.

God reveals in his Word that in Christ man is saved from sin and evil. At his second coming, Creation in its entirety will be made new, free from evil and sin. But the Bible calls for a struggle for the promotion of the good against evil and injustice already within the current state of affairs. Intuitively, the human being *knows* that the *good* is his duty and task, and he has been endowed with the faculty of conscience in order to keep this in mind.

OUGHT TASKS

What man "ought" to do is equivalent to his duty: a genuine (real and true) performance of duty presupposes love; for wherever love prevails, no demanded efforts are too great; whereas wherever love is wanting, the claims of duty are experienced as artificial, coerced from without. In the story that was told in the beginning, the narrator's love for the good prompted him to help the injured, even though he did not know him and even though the person could have been a thief.

QUESTION OR ANSWER?

While a rational science-based perspective would describe humanity as essentially a questioner—as someone who confronts the cosmos with his questions—it would be even more accurate to describe the human being as fundamentally an *answerer*. It is precisely because the cosmos confronts him, makes an appeal to him, that he feels obliged to respond, to come to conclusions, do science, and provide answers. The situation at the beginning makes certain demands upon the narrator and puts a question to him that demands an answer. The question as to why the author acted in the way that he did—

seeking the good of the injured person even at the risk of his own comfort, happiness, and safety—follows upon the answer that was given by him to the situation.

Reality is created in such a fashion and humanity shares in it in such a way that it is never merely passive but asks certain questions, gives certain choices, and then demands responsibility from the subject. As a moral being, the human is the original responder to everything that is asked and demanded from him. In every type of freedom (ruling, creating, caring), the human being is the original responder. This state belongs to the original character of human freedom and accounts for the desire of man *as* moral being to struggle to do what is good.

This answers at once the question as to "why are we good" or, better still, "why do we want to be good": the human being is ontically speaking the one who finds the question unavoidable. It is the human of whom it is expected to live in the world: to handle things, create what is necessary, and react to situations and care in a proper way. With the questions that face him, the human being is perpetually challenged to *act* and do it right and proper. Fortunately, the ultimate responsibility for humanity lies with the One that originally created everything—created it well and harmonious and with a distinct purpose—and placed potential in this world for human beings to find and unlock.

Through his responses, the human being arrives at his ultimate purpose and nature. All the possibilities of and for the human being, together with all the moral claims, appeals, and demands—that is everything that appears to the human being as question or appeal—reflect authority beyond humanity and even beyond creation and may therefore be seen in the most complete sense as that which God demands from the individual and humanity. The Christian regards the voice of the conscience as the voice of God. Its call is intensely personal and so is responding to it: a personal answer to God within His all-encompassing service. It is applicable everywhere and valid for all time. Serving God in fulfilling his or her calling gives temporary as well as eternal meaning to human life and may therefore be described as providing the ultimate sense of human existence and action.

Through the fulfillment of his calling, the human being becomes part of a God-determined project encompassing all things, among others the struggle for good against evil. However, like most things, the fulfillment of this calling may be achieved in a right or wrong way, in a good or bad way, properly or improperly. This brings us to the aspect of good and evil.

GOOD OR EVIL

Evil may be seen as a factor affecting the given order of reality, leading to chaos. In the cosmos, the tension between good and evil is such a reality that every religion and philosophical tradition had to consider the origin and consequences of evil and, along with that, the question of recovery, restoration, and overcoming of evil. According to the Christian understanding of reality, the dilapidated cosmos and fallen humanity are unable to totally overcome the evil inherent in the world, without the intervention by God through the redemption of man and the restoration of the cosmos in Christ.

The three foundational questions in the Christian history of the respective fields of inquiry into good and evil concern the nature and kinds of evil, the origin of evil, and the victory over evil. These questions take the good as for granted, viewing it as fundamental, ontologically privileged, that which *ought* to be, the self-evident, that which was originally intended. The question of "intended" immediately raises the question of an "intender." Evil is a new factor in addition to the given order, which upsets the designated order, leaving chaos within its wake. This brings us at once to the question and struggle about morality.

With respect to the cosmos we are living in, good and evil are easily distinguishable, but good is ontologically primary. Most people have a natural ability to distinguish between the two. Illness, for example, constitutes an evil that has to be countered in order to achieve good health, an undeniable good. The complexity of reality suggests that Buddhism is correct in that it (like Spinoza) holds that evil is merely an illusion and does not possesses genuine existence (i.e., no genuine ontological status).

Experience demonstrates that, not only are good and evil real, but also that good and evil are qualitative distinguishable and exclusionary. While Leibniz views good and evil only in quantitative and relative terms (saying that good is slightly less evil, and evil slightly less good), he still makes a clear phenomenological distinction between good and evil and upholds the qualitative distinction between good and evil. It is clear that good *ought* to exist but evil not. The motorist that just drove away after injuring the bike rider commits evil, while the person coming to the aid of the accident victim does good (even if he could argue that he is not directly involved in the event). Evil should not exist, and there rests an ontological duty upon the human being to fight it all the way.

The value *good* emerges when something complies with its ontological essence, when the purpose of something is reached, and when the laws governing a phenomenon are obeyed. Failure to answer these three allows for the manifestation of their counterpart—evil, improper, and unlawful. When a marriage, for example, meets all three criteria, it manifests the value of *good*. When a marriage fails to fulfill these demands, it acquires the quality of an unhappy marriage. Marriage is subject to a certain set of norms for marriage relationships. If a marriage fulfills these norms, it is good. If it fails to meet these norms, something ought to be done about it. Again, it leads to the conclusion that Someone has given everything its nature, purpose, and norms—which the Bible clearly identifies in its first chapter as God.

Good and evil are two contradictory and opposing powers. The human being does not only experience him- or herself as called toward the good but also to actively combat evil. Many such efforts toward restoration unfortunately generate a new evil: thus we see workers who fairly and justly receive an increased wage may eventually generate higher inflation, which in turn leads to new pressures on workers, resulting in new strikes. The Christian view is that it is the task of every individual to continue to fight evil even while realizing that evil will not be totally defeated. Only from the Origin of all (God) can evil be finally erased from the earth.

According to the optimistic view of humanity found within certain rationalistic traditions, the Enlightenment, and certain sociological circles, humans are born good and evil is the result of a lack of knowledge or the result of certain forms of civilization that were enforced upon people (as can be seen in the social justice debates that rage at most universities these days, South African ones in particular). Consequently, evil can be overcome through education, the operation of reason, or a return to nature and the natural. Society can be improved through good education or the removal of what is perceived to be "colonial education."

It is also possible to find a more pessimistic version, which holds that it is not possible to overcome evil and that all that humanity can really do is to learn to live with it as best as possible. Where humanity is unwilling to acknowledge the role of God and his relationship to all things (including human sin and evil), it is never possible to have anything more than reductionistic and cosmos-centric answers with respect to the problem of evil. The Christian view admits that humanity itself is sinful and lives in a broken cosmos. This understanding prevents a falling into either a pessimism where nothing can be done about it or a shallow optimism that education or a return to nature will provide a solution. Instead, it lives within the realism that evil is to be countered while expecting the return of Christ, when the cosmos will be re-created and humanity can live free from its selfishness and sin.

GUILT AND RESPONSIBILITY

Humanity initiates actions on the basis of choice. If the human being does not chose what he *ought* to choose with respect to his relationship with God, the world, and his fellow human beings, he does not only generate division, chaos, and disorder, but he also violates the deontic—that which *ought to be*.

With this, guilt makes its appearance and may lead to a guilty conscience, as discussed above. However, the human being may be guilty whether or not he or she is conscious of it or acknowledges it.

When the human being does not fulfill his purpose, discontentment and guilt make their appearance. As man may choose (whether he acts, what he does, how he does it, etc.) and is burdened with guilt if he chooses wrong (as the personal conscience often experiences guilt and discontentment on a personal level), a mere sense of guilt cannot be the ultimate reason for this awareness. As soon as the deontic is transgressed, *moral guilt* appears and should appear. What he ought to be defies the human being as moral being and requires obedience—he *ought* to obey. If the human being, with his possibility of choice transgresses, he is not only culpable but responsible for his misstep and has to answer to a higher power.

Why a higher power? The human being cannot hold himself accountable for misdeeds (otherwise it would divide him into a Kafkaesque guilty and an innocent part). The human being is also not simply guilty before the law as the law itself cannot hold anyone accountable—humanity is held to be guilty *in terms* of the law and before the law; it is the judge that acts according to the law that finds someone guilty or not. Thus the human being is not guilty before his compatriots, the church, or even humanity (the so-called sin against humanity). The Person to whom one is accountable must be above humanity, above deontological principles, and more than mere abstract norms. This brings Christians to the awareness that they are finally and fully accountable to their Creator, so that they stand in the most absolute sense responsible for their actions before God.

CONCLUSION

We have been endowed with a conscience in order to lead us to responsibility. In the example we started with, even if the narrator was not guilty of a crime before the law by virtue of his actions, if he had not helped the injured, he would still have been guilty before his own conscience. Other people with whom he shared the experience would be able to join in condemning his self-centered actions. The awareness of injustice, as well as the struggle of good against evil, is part and parcel of man as moral being to such an extent that even the transgressor understands (or is capable of understanding after explanation) that he has done something wrong. With the possibility of being held accountable, along with his capacity for choice and this conscience to alert him as to what he ought to do, human beings are created by God with the possibility and even the desire to act and be treated in accordance with the deontic—to do and to expect what is good and right and proper.

NOTES

1. "Genuine phenomena of conscience are such moral and religious phenomena as exhibit an experience of a real personal relationship to evil, or, more concisely—genuine conscience is the real inner revelation of personal evil." H. G. Stoker, *Conscience: Phenomena and Theories* (Notre Dame, Ind.: University of Notre Dame Press, 2018), 228.
2. C. S. Lewis, *Mere Christianity* (London: Harper One, 2001), 8.
3. "Ontic" refers to relating to the reality (or "realness") of beings or ideas and the facts about them, relating to real as opposed to phenomenal existence. "Ontological" refers to the study of reality.
4. Stoker, *Conscience*, 229.
5. The following can serve as examples of the overemphasis on the human choice at the expense of the deontic (what ought to be/"categorical obligation"):

- For Sartre, human freedom is equal to human choice. This is something he cannot escape; he cannot but choose. Unfortunately, he does not see what ought to happen as a condition of human freedom, with the result that his freedom becomes arbitrary.
- According to Kant, the human will is reasonable. The reason imposes on humans the necessary general laws according to which they should act. This redirected what "ought to" to fairly volutantive self-regulation and eliminates the duty aspect.
- The absolute idealists (neo-Hegelians) as Green and Bosanquet want to find what ought to be done to in self-realization in a social context. They ground it in man and overestimate the goodness of his choice.
- Utilitarians also depart from human choices and define what ought to as "the greatest happiness of the greatest number." What should is then not about what is right or proper but what makes the masses happy. Obligation then varies from century to century and from country to country.

On the other hand, human freedom is also distorted and even destroyed through the overemphasis of people's distance from what determines their choice. The following can be used as examples:

- Naturalists deliver human beings and their actions to physicochemical laws. This eliminates the basic aspect of human freedom, namely the possibility to plan, to decide on actions, and to take responsibility.
- Materialists assume the physical causal relationship in which every consequence (including human actions) is determined by a preceding cause and therefore by a physical law, which does not allow any exception. The consequence is that the moral and normative disappear. From animals and humans can the same "responsibility" be expected, amounting essentially to the dehumanization of man.

6. F. H. Bradley (1846–1924), Bernard Bosanquet (1848–1923), T. H. Green (1836–1882), British philosophers who rejected the mainstream utilitarianism and empiricism of traditional British philosophy.

REFERENCES

Lewis, C. S. *Mere Christianity*. London: Harper One, 2001.
Kant, I. *Practical Philosophy*. In *The Cambridge Edition of the Works of Immanuel Kant in English*, translated by Mary Gregor. Cambridge: Cambridge University Press, 1996.
———. *Religion and Rational Theology*. Translated by Allen Wood and George di Giovanni. Cambridge: Cambridge University Press, 1996.

Stoker, H. G. *Conscience: Phenomena and Theories.* Notre Dame, Ind.: University of Notre Dame Press, 2018.

Chapter Nine

Theism as Meta-Ethical Foundation for Morality

William Lane Craig

And Rakitin does dislike God. Ough! doesn't he dislike Him! That's the sore point with all of them. But they conceal it. They tell lies. They pretend. "Will you preach this in your reviews?" I asked him. "Oh, well, if I did it openly, they won't let it through," he said. He laughed. "But what will become of men then?" I asked him, "without God and immortal life? All things are lawful then, they can do what they like?" "Didn't you know" he said laughing, "a clever man can do what he likes," he said. "A clever man knows his way about, but you've put your foot in it, committing a murder, and now you are rotting in prison." He says that to my face! A regular pig! I used to kick such people out, but now I listen to them.[1]

William Lane Craig is no enemy to reason. During his very public career, he has made it clear upon numerous occasions not only that faith and reason are compatible but that reason may provide a path toward becoming a very intellectually satisfied believer. As noted in the introduction, he shares with the Enlightenment Project defender Susan Neiman a commitment to the notion of an objective reality that is independent from human interpretation, but to which humans nevertheless have access. In metaphysical terms, one could say that both thinkers aim at a position of "neutrality" or "objectivity," a position that does not sit easily with Marxists, postmodernists, or even some phenomenologists.

However, Craig is firmly in the analytical tradition and a thinker who views the values of the modern West—individual freedom, the universal recognition of the value of every human life, and even the pursuit of happiness—as compatible with biblical teachings. Unlike Neiman, Craig does not find the objectivity of these values to be absolute or binding in their own right. For Craig, the acts we normally regard as good are not only compatible with Christian teaching but ultimately impossible without it. Craig's position amounts to a version of divine command theory, or theological voluntarism. His version is of course not absolute. He regards the Euthyphro dilemma as false: God does not stand at a distance from the Good; there is no need to wonder whether God commands the Good because of its intrinsic nature or whether we attach the signifier "Good" to a value commanded by God. He is in good company: thinkers as diverse as Augustine, Duns Scotus, William of Ockham, and Søren Kierkegaard all embraced a version of this position. So does Paul Copan, but Craig's position amounts more to a kind of meta-ethical position, arguing that theism serves as a meta-ethical foundation for the good life. In other words, God acts as a kind of guarantor for the value of morality. Not only that, but for Craig the existence of objective moral values points to the reality of their Originator.

Although written in more analytical language, Craig's position with respect to morality is similar to that of Dostoyevsky: there is no neutral point that would justify morality in its own right. For morality to really count as morality, we need God to justify it. We may well engage in behavior with pleasant consequences, but it would be impossible to count it as moral. Craig does not refer to him anywhere in this particular text, but he is in fact acknowledging the same problem that Nietzsche did, that without God to serve as setting limits to the endless possibilities that confront us every day, we are bound to fall into nihilism.

—The Editors

Can we be good without God? At first the answer to this question may seem so obvious that even to pose it arouses indignation. For while those of us who are Christian theists undoubtedly find in God a source of moral strength and resolve that enables us to live lives that are better than those we should live without a deity, nevertheless it would seem arrogant and ignorant to claim that those who do not share a belief in God do not often live good, moral lives—indeed, embarrassingly, lives that sometimes put our own to shame.

But wait! It would, indeed, be arrogant and ignorant to claim that people cannot be good without *belief* in God. But that was not the question. The question was: can we be good without God? When we ask that question, we are posing in a provocative way the meta-ethical question of the objectivity of moral values. Are the values we hold dear and that guide our lives mere social conventions akin to driving on the left versus right side of the road or mere expressions of personal preference akin to having a taste for certain foods? Or are they valid independently of our apprehension of them, and if so, what is their foundation? Moreover, if morality is just a human convention, then why should we act morally, especially when it conflicts with self-interest? Or are we in some way held accountable for our moral decisions and actions?

I want to argue that if God exists, then the objectivity of moral values, moral duties, and moral accountability is secured, but that in the absence of God, that is, if God does not exist, then morality is just a human convention, that is to say, morality is wholly subjective and nonbinding. We might act in precisely the same ways that we do in fact act, but in the absence of God, such actions would no longer count as good (or evil) since if God does not exist, objective moral values do not exist. Thus, we cannot truly be good without God. On the other hand, if we do believe that moral values and duties are objective, that provides moral grounds for believing in God.

THEISM AS A META-ETHICAL FOUNDATION

Objective Moral Values

Consider, then, the hypothesis that God exists. First, if God exists, objective moral values exist. To say that there are objective moral values is to say that something is morally good or bad independently of whether anybody believes it to be so. It is to say, for example, that Nazi anti-Semitism was morally evil, even though the Nazis who carried out the Holocaust thought that it was good; and it would still be evil even if the Nazis had won World War II and succeeded in exterminating or brainwashing everybody who disagreed with them, so that everybody agreed that anti-Semitism is good.

On the theistic view, objective moral values are rooted in God. As St. Anselm saw, God is by definition the greatest conceivable being and therefore perfectly good. Indeed, He is not merely perfectly good; He is the paradigm of moral value. God's own holy and loving character supplies the absolute standard against which all things are measured. He is by nature loving, generous, faithful, kind, and so forth. Other things are good insofar as they resemble God. Thus, if God exists, moral values are objective, being wholly independent of human beings.

Objective Moral Duties

Moreover, God's moral nature is expressed in relation to us in the form of divine commands that constitute our moral duties or obligations. Far from being arbitrary, God's commands must be consistent with His holy and loving nature. Our duties, then, are constituted by God's commands, and these in turn reflect His essential character. In the Judeo-Christian tradition, the whole moral duty of man can be summed up in the two great commandments: first, you shall love the Lord your God with all your strength and with all your soul and with all your heart and with all your mind, and, second, you shall love your neighbor as yourself. On this foundation, we can affirm the objective rightness of love, generosity, and self-sacrifice and condemn as objectively wrong selfishness, hatred, abuse, and oppression.

Moral Accountability

Finally, on the theistic hypothesis, God holds all persons morally accountable for their actions. Wrongdoing will be punished; righteousness will be vindicated. Good ultimately triumphs over evil, and we shall finally see that we do live in a moral universe after all. Despite the inequities of this life, in the end the scales of God's justice will be balanced. Thus, the moral choices we make in this life are infused with an eternal significance. We can with consistency make moral choices that run contrary to our self-interest and even undertake acts of extreme self-sacrifice, knowing that such decisions are not empty and ultimately futile gestures. Rather our moral lives have a paramount significance. So I think it is evident that theism provides a sound foundation for morality.

ATHEISM AS A META-ETHICAL FOUNDATION

Objective Moral Values

Contrast theism with the atheistic hypothesis. First, if atheism is true, it is plausible that objective moral values do not exist.[2] For if God does not exist, then what is the foundation for objective moral values? More particularly, what is the basis for the objective value of human beings? If God does not exist, then it is difficult to see any reason to think that human beings are morally special or that their morality is objectively true. Philosopher of science Michael Ruse writes,

> The position of the modern evolutionist . . . is that humans have an awareness of morality . . . because such an awareness is of biological worth. Morality is a biological adaptation no less than are hands and feet and teeth. . . . Considered as a rationally justifiable set of claims about an objective something, ethics is illusory. I appreciate that when somebody says "Love they neighbor as thyself," they think they are referring above and beyond themselves. . . . Nevertheless, . . . such reference is truly without foundation. Morality is just an aid to survival and reproduction, . . . and any deeper meaning is illusory.[3]

As a result of socio-biological pressures, there has evolved among *Homo sapiens* a sort of "herd morality" that functions well in the perpetuation of our species in the struggle for survival. But there does not seem to be anything about *Homo sapiens* that makes this morality objectively true.

The objective worthlessness of human beings on a naturalistic worldview is underscored by two implications of that worldview: materialism and determinism. Naturalists are typically materialists or physicalists, who regard man as a purely animal organism. But if man has no immaterial aspect to his being (call it soul or mind or what have you), then he is not qualitatively different from other animal species but simply possessed of a relatively more complex nervous system. For him to regard human morality as objective is to fall into the trap of speciesism. Secondly, if there is no mind distinct from the brain, then everything we think and do is determined by the input of our five senses and our genetic makeup. There is no personal agent who freely decides to do something. But without libertarian freedom, none of our choices is morally significant. They are like the jerks of a puppet's limbs, controlled by the strings of sensory input and physical constitution. And what moral value does a puppet or its movements have?

Objective Moral Duties

Second, on the atheistic view, there is no divine lawgiver. But then what source is there for objective moral duty? Obligations and prohibitions plausibly arise as a result of imperatives issued by a qualified authority. On this basis, we can make sense of our societal and legal obligations. But whence the source of our moral obligations? Richard Taylor explains,

> A duty is something that is owed. . . . But something can be owed only *to* some person or persons. There can be no such thing as duty in isolation. . . .
> The idea of political or legal obligation is clear enough. . . . Similarly, the idea of an obligation higher than this, and referred to as *moral* obligation, is clear enough, provided reference to some lawmaker higher . . . . than those of the state is understood. In other words, our moral obligations can . . . be understood as those that are imposed by God. This does give a clear sense to the claim that our moral obligations are more binding upon us than our political obligations. . . . But what if this higher-than-human lawgiver is no longer taken into account? Does the concept of a moral obligation . . . still make sense? . . .
> The concept of moral obligation [is] unintelligible apart form the idea of God. The words remain, but their meaning is gone.[4]

He concludes,

> The modern age, more or less repudiating the idea of a divine lawgiver, has nevertheless tried to retain the ideas of moral right and wrong, not noticing that, in casting God aside, they have also abolished the conditions of meaningfulness for moral right and wrong as well. . . .
> Contemporary writers in ethics, who blithely discourse upon moral right and wrong and moral obligation without any reference to religion, are really just weaving intellectual webs from thin air; which amounts to saying that they discourse without meaning.[5]

Even more than the objectivity of moral values, the objectivity of moral duties seems difficult to explain given atheism.

KEEPING CLEAR

Now it is important that we remain clear in understanding the issue before us. The question is *not*: must we believe in God in order to live moral lives? There is no reason to think that atheists and theists alike may not live what we normally characterize as good and decent lives. Similarly, the question is *not*: can we formulate a system of ethics without reference to God? If the nontheist grants that human beings do have objective value, then there is no reason to think that he cannot work out a normative system of ethics with which the theist would also largely agree. Or again, the question is *not*: can we recognize the existence of objective moral values and duties without reference to God? The theist will typically maintain that a person need not believe in God in order to recognize, say, that we should love our children. Rather, as humanist philosopher Paul Kurtz puts it, "The central question about moral and ethical principles concerns this ontological foundation. If they are neither derived from God nor anchored in some transcendent ground, are they purely ephemeral?"[6]

If there is no God, then any ground for regarding the herd morality evolved by *Homo sapiens* as objectively true seems to have been removed. After all, what is so special about human beings? They are just accidental by-products of nature that have evolved relatively recently on an infinitesimal speck of dust lost somewhere in a hostile and mindless universe and that are doomed to perish individually and collectively in a relatively short time. Some action, say, incest, may not be biologically or socially advantageous and so in the course of human evolution has become taboo; but there is on the atheistic view nothing really *wrong* about committing incest. If, as Kurtz states, "The moral principles that govern our behavior are rooted in habit and custom, feeling and fashion,"[7] then the nonconformist who chooses to flout the herd morality is doing nothing more serious than acting unfashionably.

Thus, if naturalism is true, it becomes impossible to condemn war, oppression, or crime as evil. Nor can one praise brotherhood, equality, or love as good. It does not matter what values you choose—for there is no right and wrong; good and evil do not exist. That means that an atrocity like the Holocaust was really morally indifferent. You may think that it was wrong, but your opinion has no more validity than that of the Nazi war criminal who thought it was good. In his book *Morality after Auschwitz*, Peter Haas asks how an entire society could have willingly participated in a state-sponsored program of mass torture and genocide for more than a decade without any serious opposition. He argues that far from being contemptuous of ethics, the perpetrators acted in strict conformity with an ethic which held that, however difficult and unpleasant the task might have been, mass extermination of the Jews and Gypsies was entirely justified. . . . The Holocaust as a sustained effort was possible only because a new ethic was in place that did not define the arrest and deportation of Jews as wrong and in fact defined it as ethically tolerable and even good.[8]

Moreover, Haas points out, because of its coherence and internal consistency, the Nazi ethic could not be discredited from within. Only from a transcendent vantage point that stands above relativistic, socio-cultural mores could such a critique be launched. But in the absence of God, it is precisely such a vantage point that we lack. One rabbi who was imprisoned at Auschwitz said that it was as though all the Ten Commandments had been reversed: thou shalt kill, thou shalt lie, thou shalt steal. Mankind has never seen such a hell. And yet, in a real sense, if naturalism is true, our world *is* Auschwitz. There is no good and evil, no right and wrong. Objective moral values and duties do not exist.

Atheistic Moral Platonism

Some philosophers, unwilling to affirm that acts like rape or torturing a child are morally neutral actions, have tried to affirm the objective reality of moral values in the absence of God. Theirs is a sort of atheistic moral Platonism.[9] Atheistic moral Platonists affirm that objective moral values do exist and are not dependent upon evolution or human opinion, but they insist that they are not grounded in God. Indeed, moral values have no further foundation. They just exist.

It is difficult, however, even to comprehend this view. What does it mean to say, for example, that the moral value *Justice* just exists? It is hard to know what to make of this. It is clear what is meant when it is said that a person is just; but it is bewildering when it is said that in the absence of any persons, *Justice* itself exists. Moral values seem to exist as properties of persons, not as mere abstractions—or at any rate, it is hard to know what it is for a moral value to exist as a mere abstraction.[10] Atheistic moral Platonists seem to lack any adequate foundation in reality for moral values but just leave them floating in an unintelligible way.

Second, the nature of moral duty or obligation seems incompatible with atheistic moral Platonism. Let us suppose for the sake of argument that moral values do exist independently of God. Suppose that values like *Mercy, Justice, Love, Forbearance*, and the like just exist. How does that result in any moral obligations for me? Why would I have a moral duty, say, to be merciful? Who or what lays such an obligation on me? Moreover, on atheistic moral Platonism, moral vices such as *Greed, Hatred, Sloth*, and *Selfishness* also presumably exist as abstract objects. Why am I obligated to align my life with one set of these abstractly existing objects rather than any other? As Taylor clearly sees, in the absence of a divine lawgiver, there simply is no ground for duty, even if moral values somehow exist.[11]

Thirdly, it is fantastically improbable that just that sort of creatures would emerge from the blind evolutionary process who correspond to the abstractly existing realm of moral values. This seems to be an utterly incredible coincidence when one thinks about it. It is almost as though the moral realm *knew* that we were coming. It is far more plausible to regard both the natural realm and the moral realm as under the hegemony of a divine Creator and Lawgiver than to think that these two entirely independent orders of reality just happened to mesh.[12]

Thus it seems that atheistic moral Platonism is not as plausible a view as theism but serves as a convenient halfway house for philosophers who do not have the stomach for the moral nihilism that atheism seems to imply. Some philosophers, equally averse to abstractly existing moral values as to theism, try to salvage the existence of objective moral principles or properties in the context of a naturalistic worldview. But the advocates of such theories are typically at a loss to justify their starting point. If their approach to meta-ethical theory is to be serious metaphysics rather than just a shopping-list approach, whereby one simply helps oneself to the supervenient moral properties or principles needed to do the job, then some sort of explanation is required for why moral properties supervene on certain natural states or why such principles are true. It is insufficient for the naturalist to point out that we do, in fact, apprehend the goodness of some feature of human existence, for that only goes to establish the objectivity of moral values and duties, which the proponent of theistic ethics is eager to affirm.

Moral Accountability

Finally, if atheism is true, there is no moral accountability for one's actions. Even if there were objective moral values and duties under naturalism, they are irrelevant because there is no moral accountability. If life ends at the grave, it makes no difference whether one lives as a Stalin or as a saint. As the Russian writer Fyodor Dostoyevsky rightly said: "If there is no immortality, then all things are permitted."[13]

The state torturers in Soviet prisons understood this all too well. Richard Wurmbrand reports,

> The cruelty of atheism is hard to believe when man has no faith in the reward of good or the punishment of evil. There is no reason to be human. There is no restraint from the depths of evil which is in man. The Communist torturers often said, "There is no God, no hereafter, no punishment for evil. We can do what we wish." I have heard one torturer even say, "I thank God, in whom I don't believe, that I have lived to this hour when I can express all the evil in

my heart." He expressed it in unbelievable brutality and torture inflected on prisoners.[14]

Given the finality of death, it really does not matter how you live. So what do you say to someone who concludes that we may as well just live as we please, out of pure self-interest? This presents a pretty grim picture for an atheistic ethicist like Kai Nielsen of the University of Calgary. He writes,

> We have not been able to show that reason requires the moral point of view, or that all really rational persons should not be individual egoists or classical amoralists. Reason doesn't decide here. The picture I have painted for you is not a pleasant one. Reflection on it depresses me. . . . Pure practical reason, even with a good knowledge of the facts, will not take you to morality.[15]

Somebody might say that it is in our best self-interest to adopt a moral lifestyle. But clearly, that is not always true: we all know situations in which self-interest runs smack in the face of morality. Moreover, if one is sufficiently powerful, like a Ferdinand Marcos or a Papa Doc Duvalier or a Kim Jong-un, then one can pretty much ignore the dictates of conscience and safely live in self-indulgence. Historian Stewart C. Easton sums it up well when he writes, "There is no objective reason why man should be moral, unless morality 'pays off' in his social life or makes him 'feel good.' There is no objective reason why man should do anything save for the pleasure it affords him."[16]

Acts of self-sacrifice become particularly inept on a naturalistic worldview. Why should you sacrifice your self-interest and especially your life for the sake of someone else? There can be no good reason for adopting such a self-negating course of action on the naturalistic worldview. Considered from the socio-biological point of view, such altruistic behavior is merely the result of evolutionary conditioning that helps to perpetuate the species. A mother rushing into a burning house to rescue her children or a soldier throwing his body over a hand grenade to save his comrades does nothing more significant or praiseworthy, morally speaking, than a fighter ant that sacrifices itself for the sake of the ant hill. Common sense dictates that we should resist, if we can, the socio-biological pressures to such self-destructive activity and choose instead to act in our best self-interest. The philosopher of religion John Hick invites us to imagine an ant suddenly endowed with the insights of socio-biology and the freedom to make personal decisions. He writes:

> Suppose him to be called upon to immolate himself for the sake of the ant-hill. He feels the powerful pressure of instinct pushing him towards this self-destruction. But he asks himself why he should voluntarily . . . carry out the suicidal programme to which instinct prompts him? Why should he regard the

future existence of a million million other ants as more important to him than his own continued existence? . . . Since all that he is and has or ever can have is his own present existence, surely in so far as he is free from the domination of the blind force of instinct he will opt for life—his own life.[17]

Now why should we choose any differently? On atheism, prudential value and moral value are on a collision course. The atheist may choose to adopt a moral lifestyle if he likes, but it will be imprudent to do so. Thus the absence of moral accountability from the philosophy of naturalism makes an ethic of compassion and self-sacrifice a risky and imprudent choice. R. Z. Friedman rightly concludes, "Without religion the coherence of an ethic of compassion cannot be established. The principle of respect for persons and the principle of the survival of the fittest are mutually exclusive."[18]

SUMMARY

We thus come to radically different perspectives on morality depending upon whether or not God exists. If God exists, there is a sound foundation for morality. If God does not exist, then, as Nietzsche saw, we are ultimately landed in nihilism.

Moral Grounds for Theism

But the choice between the two need not be arbitrarily made. On the contrary, the very considerations we have been discussing can constitute moral justification for the existence of God.

Objective Moral Values

For example, if we do think that objective moral values exist, then we shall be led logically to the conclusion that God exists. And could anything be more obvious than that objective moral values *do* exist? The reasoning of Ruse is at worst a textbook example of the genetic fallacy and at best only proves that our subjective perception of objective moral values has evolved. But if moral values are gradually discovered, not invented, then such a gradual and fallible apprehension of the moral realm no more undermines the objective reality of that realm than our gradual, fallible perception of the physical world undermines the objectivity of that realm. The fact is that in moral experience, we do apprehend objective values. Actions like rape, torture, child abuse, and brutality are not just socially unacceptable behavior—they are moral abominations. As Ruse himself states, "The man who says that it is morally acceptable to rape little children is just as mistaken as the man who says, 2+2=5."[19] By the same token, love, generosity, equality, and self-sacrifice are really good. People who fail to see this are just morally handicapped, and there is no reason to allow their impaired vision to call into question what we see clearly. Thus, the existence of objective moral values serves to demonstrate the existence of God.

Objective Moral Duties

Or consider the nature of moral obligation. What I said of moral values goes for moral duties as well. Speaking on a Canadian university campus, I noticed a poster put up by the Sexual Assault & Information Center. It read: "Sexual Assault: No One Has the Right to Abuse a Child, Woman, or Man." Most of us recognize that that statement is evidently true. As Louise Antony remarked in our debate on the question "Is God Necessary for Morality?" any argument for moral skepticism will be based on premises that are less obvious than the reality of objective moral values and duties themselves.[20] But the atheist can make no sense of a person's right not to be sexually abused by another. The best answer to the question as to the source of moral obligation is that moral rightness or wrongness consists in agreement or disagreement with the will or commands of a holy, loving God.

Moral Accountability

Finally, take the problem of moral accountability. Here we find a powerful practical argument for believing in God. According to William James, practical arguments can be used only when theoretical arguments are insufficient to decide a question of urgent and pragmatic importance. But it seems obvious that a practical argument could also be used to *back up* or *motivate acceptance of* the conclusion of a sound theoretical argument. To believe, then, that God does not exist and that there is thus no moral accountability would be quite literally de-moralizing, for then we should have to believe that our moral choices are ultimately insignificant since both our fate and that of the universe will be the same regardless of what we do. By "de-moralization" I mean a deterioration of moral motivation. It is hard to do the right thing when that means sacrificing one's own self-interest and to resist temptation to do wrong when desire is strong, and the belief that ultimately it does not matter what you choose or do is apt to sap one's moral strength and so undermine one's moral life. As Robert Adams observes, "Having to regard it as very likely that the history of the universe will not be good on the whole, no matter what one does, seems apt to induce a cynical sense of futility about the moral life, undermining one's moral resolve and one's interest in moral considerations."[21] By contrast there is nothing so likely to strengthen the moral life as the beliefs that one will be held accountable for one's actions and that one's choices do make a difference in bringing about the good.

Theism is thus a morally advantageous belief, and this, in the absence of any theoretical argument establishing atheism to be the case, provides practical grounds to believe in God and motivation to accept the conclusions of the two theoretical arguments I just gave above.

CONCLUSION

In summary, theological meta-ethical foundations do seem to be necessary for morality. If God does not exist, then it is plausible to think that there are no objective moral values, that we have no objective moral duties, and that there is no moral accountability for how we live and act. The horror of such a morally neutral world is obvious. If, on the other hand, we hold, as it seems rational to do, that objective moral values and duties do exist, then we have good grounds for believing in the existence of God. In addition, we have powerful practical reasons for embracing theism in view of the morally bracing effects that belief in moral accountability produces. We cannot, then, truly be good without God; but if we can in some measure be good, then it follows that God exists.

NOTES

1. Fyodor Dostoyevsky, *The Brothers Karamazov*, translated by Constance Garnett (New York: Lowell Press, 2009), 665.

2. Minimally, we may say that theism provides a better explanation of the objectivity of moral values than atheism. Some theists content themselves with this more modest claim in justifying a theistic over an atheistic foundation for moral values and duties. In my mind, however, the stronger claim made here seems true as well.

3. Michael Ruse, "Evolutionary Theory and Christian Ethics," in *The Darwinian Paradigm* (London: Routledge, 1989), 262, 268–269.

4. Richard Taylor, *Ethics, Faith, and Reason* (Englewood Cliffs, N.J.: Prentice-Hall, 1985), 83–4.

5. Taylor, *Ethics, Faith, and Reason*, 2, 7.

6. Paul Kurtz, *Forbidden Fruit* (Buffalo, N.Y.: Prometheus Books, 1988), 65.

7. Kurtz, *Forbidden Fruit*, 73.

8. R. L. Rubenstein, Review of *Morality after Auschwitz: The Radical Challenge of the Nazi Ethic*, by Peter Haas, *Journal of the American Academy of Religion* 60 (1992): 158.

9. See, for example, Erik J. Wielenberg, *Robust Ethics: The Metaphysics and Epistemology of Godless Normative Realism* (Oxford: Oxford University Press, 2014), 36, 45–46.

10. See my critique of Wielenberg's Platonism in our debate "God and Morality: What Is the Best Account of Objective Moral Values and Duties?" YouTube, February 23, 2018, https://www.youtube.com/watch?v=6iVyVJAMiOY.

11. In Wielenberg's view, moral obligations are constituted by having decisive moral reasons for doing some action. For example, if I am trying to decide whether to steal someone's pocketbook, I examine the moral value of alternative actions and see that I have decisive moral reasons for not stealing the pocketbook. Therefore, I ought not to steal it.Unfortunately, Wielenberg's normative realism fails to ground unconditional moral obligations. Having decisive moral reasons to do an act implies at most that *if* you want to act morally, then that is the act you ought to do. In other words, the obligation to do the act is only conditional, not unconditional. But a divine command provides an unconditional obligation to perform some act. A

robust moral theory ought to provide a basis for unconditional moral obligations, which Wielenberg's view does not.

Moreover, Wielenberg's view has counterintuitive implications. For example, it follows from his view that if you have decisive moral reasons for doing something, then you are obligated to do it. That is incompatible with morally supererogatory acts, like sacrificing one's life for another, for even though such an act is supremely good, it is above and beyond the call of duty. Wielenberg's view also seems to imply that we are always obligated to do the best thing, whereas in some cases we are obligated at most to do a good thing, not the best thing. For example, even if it were morally better for you to become a doctor rather than an engineer, you are not morally obligated to become a doctor, for both careers represent good moral choices.

12. Wielenberg tries to avoid this coincidence by arguing that the same cognitive processes that produce our moral beliefs also cause the abstract moral properties to be instantiated. This claim depends crucially on a supposed causal connection between physical properties and moral properties, which is perhaps the most obscure point in Wielenberg's philosophy. In addition, his account seems to run afoul of Alvin Plantinga's evolutionary argument against naturalism. Plantinga's argument gives us reason to doubt whether our cognitive processes, which supposedly cause certain moral properties to be instantiated, will in fact trigger the appropriate moral beliefs, rather than beliefs that are merely conducive to survival. See discussion in our debate "God and Morality: What Is the Best Account of Objective Moral Values and Duties?".

13. Fyodor Dostoyevsky, *The Brothers Karamazov*, trans. C. Garnett (New York: Signet Classics, 1957), bk. II, chap. 6; bk. V, chap. 4; bk. XI, chap. 8.

14. Richard Wurmbrand, *Tortured for Christ* (London: Hodder & Stoughton, 1967), 34.

15. Kai Nielsen, "Why Should I Be Moral?" *American Philosophical Quarterly* 21 (1984): 90.

16. Stewart C. Easton, *The Western Heritage*, 2nd ed. (New York: Holt, Rinehart, & Winston, 1966), 878.

17. John Hick, *Arguments for the Existence of God* (New York: Herder & Herder, 1971), p. 63.

18. R. Z. Friedman, "Does the 'Death of God' Really Matter?" *International Philosophical Quarterly* 23 (1983): 322.

19. Michael Ruse, *Darwinism Defended* (London: Addison-Wesley, 1982), 275.

20. Louise Antony vs. William Lane Craig, "Is God Necessary for Morality?" YouTube, https://www.youtube.com/watch?v=6MhS8nU6ECM.

21. Robert Merrihew Adams, "Moral Arguments for Theistic Belief," in *Rationality and Religious Belief*, ed. C. F. Delaney (Notre Dame, Ind.: University of Notre Dame Press, 1979), 127.

REFERENCES

Adams, Robert Merrihew. "Moral Arguments for Theistic Belief." In *Rationality and Religious Belief*, ed. C. F. Delaney. Notre Dame, Ind.: University of Notre Dame Press, 1979.
Baggett, D., and J. Walls. *Good God: The Theistic Foundations of Morality*. Oxford: Oxford University Press, 2011.
Easton, S. E. *The Western Heritage*. 2nd ed. New York: Holt, Rinehart, & Winston, 1966.
Friedman, J. Z. "Does the 'Death of God' Really Matter?" *International Philosophical Quarterly* 23 (1983).
Hick, John. *Arguments for the Existence of God*. New York: Herder & Herder, 1971.
Kurtz, P. *Forbidden Fruit*. Buffalo, N.Y.: Prometheus Books, 1988.
Nielsen, Kai. "Why Should I Be Moral?" *American Philosophical Quarterly* 21 (1984): 90.
Rubenstein, R. L. Review of *Morality after Auschwitz: The Radical Challenge of the Nazi Ethic*, by Peter Haas. *Journal of the American Academy of Religion* 60 (1992): 158.
Ruse, Michael. *Darwinism Defended*. London: Addison-Wesley, 1982.
———. "Evolutionary Theory and Christian Ethics." In *The Darwinian Paradigm*. London: Routledge, 1989.

Taylor, R. *Ethics, Faith, and Reason*. Englewood Cliffs, N.J.: Prentice-Hall, 1985.
Wielenberg, Erik J. *Robust Ethics: The Metaphysics and Epistemology of Godless Normative Realism*. Oxford: Oxford University Press, 2014.
Wurmbrand, R. *Tortured for Christ*. London: Hodder & Stoughton, 1967.

Chapter Ten

Morality as Based on Natural Law

Richard Howe

Natural law is one of the oldest groundings of morality. While Plato is technically older than Aristotle, the latter articulated a version of natural law commonly accepted by the Greeks. Historically, natural law refers to the use of reason to analyze human nature in order to discover binding rules of moral conduct from nature or God's creation. It is one of the most universal forms of thinking about morality and can manifest itself in elegantly simple ways or in a decidedly complex fashion. The concept of natural law was documented in ancient Greek thought, especially by Aristotle, and was referred to in Roman philosophy by, among others, Cicero. References to natural law are also found in the Old and New Testaments of the Bible, later expounded upon in the medieval period by Christian philosophers such as Albert the Great and Thomas Aquinas. The School of Salamanca made notable contributions during the Renaissance. Modern natural law theories were greatly developed in the Age of Enlightenment, combining inspiration from Roman law with philosophies like social contract theory. Key proponents were Alberico Gentili, Francisco Suárez, Richard Hooker, Thomas Hobbes, Hugo Grotius, Samuel von Pufendorf, Matthew Hale, and John Locke. There is a powerful contemporary tradition in the Catholic church, but as Richard Howe demonstrates, it is by no means alien to the Reformed tradition, and its richness is increasingly appreciated by a wide variety of thinkers.

    Natural law is an extremely powerful line of thought, and it can be used for a wide variety of purposes. Early atheist thinkers like Denis Diderot has used it to attempt to indicate the superfluousness of God, and Romantics like Wordsworth and Shelley have appealed to it without formally formulating it. It is also a powerful weapon to those who wish to use it to prove the existence of God, as Richard Howe has indeed done on occasion—as has William Lane

Craig and John Lennox. It has also been used in more sinister circumstances. As Richard Howe shows, there are times when no other universally accepted notion of law seems to work, such as at the Nuremberg Trials. Here Howe presents a powerful argument for accepting that morality is ultimately immersed in and justified by a universally comprehensible natural law.

—*The Editors*

PROLEGOMENA

The question of God and His relationship to morality occupies a prominent place in contemporary Christian apologetics, largely in the form of the moral argument for God's existence.[1] Such an argument asks the question of whether or how there could be morality in any sense without God.[2] Specifically, the argument might focus on whether or how morality could be objective without God. This version will proceed: (1) If God does not exist, then objective morality does not exist. (2) Objective morality does exist. Therefore, God exists.[3]

Other questions, both philosophical and theological, also arise in an exploration of God and morality, including: what is it to be good, what is the distinction (if any) between good and moral good, what is sin, can we seek the good, and has God revealed any additional truths about morality besides what reason can discover.

In my attempt to answer some of these questions, it is important that I am transparent from the beginning about my own philosophical orientation. I will be exploring these issues from a Thomistic perspective, which is to say, from the philosophical commitments of Thomas Aquinas.[4] It is my position that the philosophical realism of Aquinas gives the most thoroughgoing accounting of goodness, morality, and their relation to God available to sound reason.[5]

In order to understand Aquinas on morality vis-à-vis the question of God, it is necessary to look at Aquinas's doctrine of Natural Law (together with the metaphysics that his Natural Law view presupposes) within which it is nested.[6] Once one sees how Aquinas's view parses out regarding such notions as good and moral good, one will begin to see that the question of God's relationship to morality is not as straightforward as the above syllogism might suggest.

WHY NATURAL LAW?

Natural law theory stands in contrast to other ethical theories in a number of ways. These various ethical theories can differ in how they regard the nature of morality. Generally, ethical theories define themselves in terms of the nature of human actions as such. They understand the nature of moral obligations in terms of the nature of acts. Deontological theories (mainly associated with Immanuel Kant) see moral obligations in terms of duty. The good ought to be done for its own sake. In contrast, utilitarian theories see moral obligations in terms of the consequence or *telos* of actions. For example, hedonistic theories see the goal of actions to be aimed toward pleasure. Aiming toward one's own pleasure is an egoistic hedonism. Utilitarianism would aim at pleasure (or utility) for the greatest number.

In contrast to those ethical theories that define moral obligations in terms of actions, natural law theory understands the goodness of actions in terms of the actor. The good is defined in terms of that which actualizes the perfection (or being) of the essence or nature of a thing. Moral obligations are defined in terms of what actions aim toward actualizing the perfection of the human being understood in terms of the nature of the human as human. Such theories run from secular, in terms of which the telos of the human is confined entirely to this life, without any prospect of a Creator or an afterlife (such was the thinking of Aristotle), to Christian, in terms of which the telos of the human is understood to include both this life and the life to come, considering throughout who we are as humans created by God and what our ultimate purpose is in knowing God.

Despite these obvious differences, there remains nonetheless quite a bit of common ground between many secular and Christian virtue theories. Though Christian virtue theories are further informed by Scripture, in the minds of many Christian thinkers in this regard, the notion of what constitutes virtue for a human being overlaps extensively with many secular theories. It is this common ground that can serve as the basis for an ethical theory that gives rise to a public morality for humans as such. Moral obligations can then be seen as binding on humans irrespective of whether they are Christians. Recognizing that morality can make its demands on human beings irrespective of one's personal religious (or philosophical or political) persuasion is characteristic of (though certainly not confined to) the natural law tradition. It comes even closer to a natural law perspective when it maintains that this morality (even if only vaguely considered) is something the public law is more or less obligated to track.

Philosopher Joseph Kosterski illustrates a key element here in his lectures on natural law theory. The ancient Greek playwright Sophocles, in his *Antigone*, tells the story of two brothers who were killed, one in noble defense of his country and the other in disgrace. Creon, King of Thebes, orders the celebrated burial of the noble brother while denying the other brother any burial at all—leaving his body also in disgrace to the mercy of the animals. Antigone, the sister to the brother, defies the king's orders and goes to bury her brother, arguing that her duty is to a higher law than the dictates of the human king. In WWII, the Nuremburg trials posed an interesting challenge. While the Allies had no doubt that the Nazis should be tried for the wrongdoings, it was not clear on exactly what basis such a trial could be conducted. The Allies—Russia, Great Britain, France, and the United States—could not legally try them on the basis of Allied law since the defendants were not citizens of any of those countries and thus could not be accused of breaking their laws. But neither could the Nazis be tried on the basis of German law since none of their war activities were illegal by German law. Hitler made sure of that. As such, the tribunal indicted the Nazis for "crimes against humanity." Martin Luther King Jr., when he suffered unjustly in jail for his efforts to extend civil and human rights beyond where there were being acknowledged in his day, appealed to the natural law as a moral code that transcended the law of men.

One concern arises over how the discourse on public morality is sometimes framed in the categories of "biblical" or "Christian" morality. While morality certainly is Christian in as much as it finds its grounding ultimately in the God of the Bible who created human beings, framing the discussion on public morality with unbelievers in these terms tacitly implies that, as long as one is not a Christian, one is under no obligation to accede to these "biblical" or "Christian" moral values. What is needed is a way to show our fellow human being that such public moral obligations apply to all irrespective of one's religious commitments. Thus, when calling ((for example) the prohibition against murder biblical or Christian, we do not merely mean that murder is wrong only in case you are a Christian or only in case you acknowledge biblical authority.

Consider this contrast. Christians do not require, or even expect, the unbeliever to be baptized or to partake of the Lord's Supper, both of which are certainly biblical and Christian values and actions. However, Christians certainly do expect unbelievers to be publicly moral, for example, in their obedience to the laws against murder. So then, what makes the difference? If the Bible teaches both that we should not murder and that we should, for example, observe the Lord's Supper (making them both biblical), why is the one obligatory for everyone and the other obligatory only for Christians? Upon what is this distinction based and how is it recognized and defended? One enduring answer to these questions is that the Natural Law pertains to such moral issues that apply to human beings as human beings and is knowable (to some degree or another) by human reason.[7]

COMMENTS ON NATURAL LAW THEORY

Let be begin to sneak up on the topic at hand by briefly summarizing Aquinas's natural law theory, touching on a few additional points in his metaphysics that are themselves presupposed in his natural law theory. It is only in this context that his understanding of morality can be understood. For Aquinas, natural law finds itself being one part of four aspects of law, working here with a somewhat loose understanding of law in terms of how God relates to the creation.

Eternal Law

Eternal law is God's providential working of the universe. It is the plan by which God
governs His creation. Though the universe is not eternal in itself, both the universe and God's law to govern it are eternally in the mind of God as the One who foresees and foreordains them, as Romans 4:17 hints.[8]

As the transcendent Creator by whose power the entire creation comes into and remains in existence, God superintends everything that comes to pass. Aquinas says, "It is evident, granted that the world is ruled by Divine Providence . . . that the whole community of the universe is governed by Divine Reason. Wherefore the very Idea of the government of things in God the Ruler of the universe, has the nature of a law. And since the Divine Reason's conception of things is not subject to time but is eternal, according to Prov. vii, 23, therefore it is that this kind of law must be called eternal."[9]

Not surprisingly, Christians have various understandings of the details of this superintendence. While there are interesting and profound and important questions surrounding this issue of how God superintends His creation, how natural law fits within the framework of the eternal law is (in some respects) indifferent to the answer to these specific questions. It is enough that one realizes that the eternal law is God's ultimate sovereignty and authority over His creation. Within this context, the natural law can be understood as the participation in eternal law by rational creatures by virtue of being rational. Aquinas explains:

> It is evident that all things partake somewhat of the eternal law, in so far as, namely, from its being imprinted on them, they derive their respective inclinations to their proper acts and ends. Now among all others, the rational creature is subject to Divine providence in the most excellent way, in so far as it partakes of a share of providence, by being provident both for itself and for others. Wherefore it has a share of the Eternal Reason, whereby it has a natural inclination to its proper act and end: and this participation of the eternal law in the rational creature is called the natural law.[10]

This term "natural" requires a closer analysis, which I will undertake in due course.[11] For the time being, let me make several observations. We see from Aquinas that the natural law is that aspect of the eternal law whereby the Creator governs and guides the actions of humans such that, when obeyed, it leads humans to their proper end. It remains to be seen exactly why such actions are regarded as moral. It also remains to be seen what it means to talk about proper ends of humans. The thing to note here is that the truths of the natural law are discoverable by reason irrespective of whether the human is in a saving relationship with God or, for that matter, whether the human even acknowledges the existence of God. Knowledge of these truths is a matter of creation not re-creation. The (perhaps to some) startling implication of this is that, inasmuch as such actions are moral, then morality is something in which, in some robust sense, even non-Christians can participate.

Human Law

More narrow still from the eternal law to the natural law is human law. For Aquinas, human law is a particular application of natural law to local communities. It seeks to implement regulations of human behavior stemming from truths knowable from the natural law.

> Just as, in the speculative reason, from indemonstrable principles, we draw the conclusions of the various sciences, the knowledge of which is not imparted to us by nature, but acquired by the efforts of reason, so too it is from the precepts of the Natural Law, as from general and indemonstrable principles, that the human reason needs to proceed to the more particular determinations of certain matters. These particular determinations, devised by human reason, are called human laws, provided the other essential conditions of law be observed.[12]

Aquinas observes that the human reason can only participate in that eternal law according to human reason's own mode—and then only imperfectly. The divine reason is infinite but human reason is finite. Thus, there is no pretense that this trickle down from eternal law to natural law to human law is infallible.

Divine Law

The narrowest of the four aspects of law is the divine law. It is the revelation of God's
law through Scripture to believers (if I may put a Protestant spin on this otherwise Catholic thinker). While the divine law certainly overlaps with the natural law, divine law will contain laws and prescripts that pertain only to those who are in a saving relationship with God.

But what need is there for the divine law? If the eternal law is grasped to the degree it can be by human reason (the natural law), which is then applied to particular situations (human law), what is left for the divine law to do for human beings? This trajectory from the eternal law through the natural law to the human law is toward the human being's end naturally speaking. But for Aquinas, the goal or telos of human life is not something that is merely natural.

There is a difference between mankind's "natural end" and what the Christian understands as mankind's ultimate end (purpose), which is knowledge of and communion with God or, as the Westminster Larger and Shorter Catechisms would have it, "to glorify God and enjoy Him forever." The latter, according to Aquinas, cannot be obtained naturally but only by supernatural grace.

WHAT IS NATURAL ABOUT THE NATURAL LAW?

I have been freely using the term "natural" and its cognates. The terms "nature" and "natural" have a number of usages. In more technical and philosophical contexts, "nature" refers to that metaphysical constituent of a thing by virtue of which it is the thing that it is. In this way, it is similar to the terms "essence" or "substance." David S. Oderberg defines essence as "an objective metaphysical principle determining [a thing's] definition and classification. Such principles are not mere creatures of language or convention; they belong to the very constitution of reality."[13]

To be sure, such metaphysical realism has fallen on increasingly hard times since the Middle Ages.[14] It remains, nevertheless, the philosophical backdrop within which the "natural" of "natural law" gets its meaning. As Edward Feser has observed, "It is widely assumed that the analysis and justification of fundamental moral claims can be conducted without reference to at least the more contentious issues of metaphysics. Nothing could be further from the spirit of Aquinas, for whom natural law . . . is 'natural' precisely because it derives from human nature, conceived of in Aristotelian essentialist terms."[15] Natural law is "natural" because, as a theory about morality, it defines morality largely (but not exclusively) in terms of human nature. As such, it has nothing to do with the idea that somehow we can discern morality by an examination of "nature" or from mere physical reality.

Several important metaphysical doctrines are tied up in Aquinas's understanding of nature in general and human nature in particular, much of which he adopted from Aristotle but with his own critical metaphysical additions and modifications.[16] For Aquinas (as with Aristotle), the nature of a thing not only is that metaphysical constituent of a thing that makes the thing what it is, but it also sets that thing on a trajectory of development.[17] As a living thing grows and matures, it does so, if unimpeded, toward its proper end or goal or telos. Aquinas understands this development to be the actualizations of perfections that exist potentially in the thing by virtue of its nature. This is easy to see in living things. An acorn grows into an oak tree. In so growing and developing, the potentialities within the acorn, by virtue of the nature it has, are actualized, aiming the plant toward it proper end, achieving greater and greater perfection. But (for reasons that are beyond the scope of this paper) for these potentials to be actualized is to say that they are made to be or to exist. The move toward a thing's proper end (i.e., the move toward a thing's perfection) is a move to the realization of being or existence itself. As the plant grows, it actualizes more and more of the perfections of being up to the limits of and according to the contours of its nature as an oak tree.

What about human beings? To be sure, just like the acorn to oak tree, a human aims at a telos as it grows from zygote to adult. But, for Aquinas, human perfection is more than just the human reaching his physical ends. Because of the difference between a human and an oak tree, the human contains a greater level of the perfections of being up to the limits of and according to the contours of human nature. The most important expression of human perfection is that which makes humans distinct from animals. It is that the human has a rational soul. Aquinas argues that a human's perfection pertains to this aspect of us most importantly. Why is this so? Again, following Aristotle, Aquinas maintains that that which determines what the proper end for the human is will have to do with that that is properly (i.e., uniquely) human. Because we have a rational soul, a human is able to be the "master of his actions" inasmuch as his actions "proceed from a deliberative will."[18] Aquinas explains:

> Of actions done by man those alone are properly called human, which are proper to man as man. Now man differs from irrational animals in this, that he is master of his actions. Wherefore those actions alone are properly called human, of which man is master. Now man is master of his actions through his reason and will; whence, too, the free-will is defined as the faculty and will of reason. Therefore, those actions are properly called human which proceed from a deliberate will.

More pointedly, humans have free will and thus have the capacity (again, unique among sensible creatures) to choose a course of action that either perfects or does violence to the nature and can choose toward or choose in opposition to advancing along this trajectory toward one's proper end.[19] This point is key. It is precisely because humans have this capacity of deliberation that we are moral creatures. Freedom of the will is a necessary condition for morality as such.

Another point that has been latent throughout is how Aquinas understands "good." I have not yet addressed the notion of "good" because it was necessary for me to get out the preceding points before Aquinas's understanding of "good" could make sense. Let me begin by noting that, in Aquinas, "moral good" is a subset of "good." We use the term "good" in a wide range of ways; we talk about a good meal, a good car, a good team, a good person.

While Aristotle himself seems to have disagreed, Aquinas maintained that there is something common among all these uses of the term "good."[20] A good x is, as George Klubertanz says, "that which is perfect according to its kind."[21] An x is a good x when it has all the perfections that an x ought to have by virtue of being an x. The good is that toward which all things aim. As I have said, as a thing actualizes its potentials toward its telos, those actualizations are the perfections of its being. Achieving its good is acquiring more being. This means that, for Aquinas, "being" and "good" are convertible. (This is why, by the way, that God is good. He is good because He is infinite being.)

Moral good is a narrower concept. Morality has to do with a human choosing an action that perfects the human toward what a human ought to be by virtue of the kind of thing a human is, in other words, because of his nature. What is morally good for a human to do is tethered explicitly to what it is to be a human. We can see, therefore, that not only is morality unique to humans among sensible creatures, but it also follows that God is not a moral being. This is so because God does not choose a course of action to perfect Himself as He aims at a telos. God does not have a telos and cannot be perfected because He already is infinite being itself—*ipsum esse subsistens*; substantial existence itself.

NO: MORALITY DOES NOT NEED GOD IN ORDER TO BE OBJECTIVE

Let me now directly address the issue before us. In what sense can morality be objective without God? First, both the Thomist and the standard apologetic views agree that God is not epistemologically necessary for morality. All agree that it is possible for an atheist to know that it is wrong to murder. This is so even when the atheist cannot fully understand why it is wrong.[22]

Second, because humanity's good is defined primarily in terms of the perfection of their nature, what is good for them will be good for them as a matter of fact. Now, to say this much still does not distinguish Aquinas's view from the standard apologetic view inasmuch as everyone would agree that being virtuous is good for a person's soul and will contribute to human flourishing collectively speaking. What I think the Thomist might resist is when the standard apologetic approach is worded in such a way as to suggest that these objective goods cannot be regarded as goods by the atheist. Along these lines, if someone remarked that this was a good knife because it had such a sharp blade, what sense would it make for another to say, "Who are you to say that a knife ought to have a sharp blade?" The question is nonsensical as a matter of principle. Whatever it is to be a knife, then to be a good knife is to possess all those perfections that a knife ought to have by virtue of being a knife. By analogy, certain questions like "Who are you to say that I (as a human) ought to do this certain action?" can be nonsensical as a matter of principle. (I am not suggesting that one could not come up with a question that makes perfect sense like "Who are you to say that I ought to listen only to country music?") But when it comes to many of the human virtues like honesty, fidelity, and courage, it is not as though we have not been having this conversation for more than 2,500 years as to what constitutes a good person. For Aquinas, I think it is fair to say that the oft-referenced sentiment in Dostoevsky's novel just is not true.[23] Consider how this might compare to our relationship to other aspects of reality. Gravity is a real thing. It affects the Christian and the atheist alike. As such, it is objective. It does not matter whether the atheist realizes why there is gravity or, for that matter, how it is that gravity affects us. It is enough that it does, and the atheist cannot help but know this. In a similar way, morality is real. It affects the Christian and the atheist alike. As such, it is objective. It does not matter whether the atheist realizes why there is morality (or, for that matter, how it is that morality affects us). It is enough that it does, and the atheist cannot help but know this. What is more, it is precisely because morality is objectively real that natural law theory can serve as a viable approach to issues of public morality in the midst of religious or philosophical diversity.

Last, if Aquinas is right that free will is a necessary condition for morality, then any philosophy of human action that includes a sufficiently rich notion of free will can have morality, at least in principle. It should be noted that Aristotle's god, despite the fact that his arguments for god's existence are picked up by Aquinas almost verbatim, bears little resemblance to the God of Christianity. Thus, for all intents and purposes regarding the current project, Aristotle's *Nicomachean Ethics* is an ethics without God, or at least without a god that any classical Christian would recognize.[24] To suggest that the *Nicomachean Ethics* is not an objective morality in any sense of the term seems, to me, to be clearly false.

YES: MORALITY DOES NEED GOD IN ORDER TO BE OBJECTIVE

One way in which morality would need God in order to be objective is the way anything would need God in order to have any attribute. It needs God before it can even exist. Morality has to do with human actions. Being a morally good person includes choosing those actions that perfect the human along the trajectory of and toward his proper telos. The human only has that telos because of his nature, and he only has that nature because it was created by God. Without God's creation, there would not exist any humans to be morally good. In so many words, a discussion about whether morality needs

God in order to be objective amounts to a discussion of cosmological argument, specifically Aquinas's *Secunda Via*—his Second Way.

Second, it is not only the case that God is the creator of all the elements that make

morality actual, but God is also the director of the teleology of all things in His creation. In Aquinas, God's relationship to the creation is that He has caused it to come into being and that He sustains the creation in existence at every instance of its existence. But none of this excludes the reality of secondary causes within creation. By the same token, even though the telos of all things is by virtue of the respective natures of those things (which is to say, they have inherent teleology), it is also the case for Aquinas that all things have an extrinsic teleology, being directed to their proper ends by God who superintends all of His creation. This is Aquinas's *Quinta Via*—his Fifth Way.[25]

Third, the precepts of morality take on their strongest obligatory aspect when they are understood to be the commands of God. Not only ought we act in certain ways because it perfects our being, but God, being the Creator and Superintendent of all his creation, has commanded us to act in such a way as to not only facilitate our own flourishing but also effect the flourishing of the human community and, by extension, fulfill our role in our relationship with the rest of His creation. These goals are what God has intended for us. Given the fact that He is our Creator and Sustainer, He has the authority to demand our obedience. This is the nature of law as "a rule and measure of acts whereby man is induced to act or is restrained from acting" as it manages certain behaviors such that, as these behaviors are repeated and become habits, they develop into the virtues. Aquinas goes on: "A private person cannot lead another to virtue efficaciously, for he can only advise, and if his advice be not taken, it has no coercive power, such as the law should have, in order to prove an efficacious inducement to virtue. . . . But this coercive power is vested in the whole people or in some public personage, to whom it belongs to inflict penalties."[26]

Fourth, it is sometimes not clear to us what some of our moral obligations might be.

While a great deal can be discerned from understanding our natures, God's Special Revelation supplements our moral data base. This is especially needed given the fact that we are fallen and can find ourselves often explaining away what otherwise might clearly be our moral duty.

Fifth, all of us have experienced the fact that merely knowing what is the right thing to do does not mean we have the power to live the right way. Romans 7 and 8 attest to the fact that, without God's Holy Spirit, we will find ourselves ultimately incapable of living right.[27] Last, we know from Special Revelation that our telos is not confined to the natural end within this life.

We also have a supernatural telos of eternal life in communion with God. But this ultimate purpose is only achievable because of God's grace.

CONCLUSION

In order to sufficiently address Aquinas's understanding of morality, it was necessary to show how this understanding relates to the broader question of his natural law theory. Further, it was necessary to discuss other metaphysical doctrines such as "nature," "teleology," "free will," "good," and "moral good." The sense in which morality did not need God had to do with the epistemology of morality, the objectivity of human good, and free will. The sense in which morality did need God had to do with the existence of morality, the teleology of morality, divine commands, moral knowledge, moral power, and man's supernatural end. Certainly there is much more that needs to be said regarding Aquinas's view of morality. Each one of the metaphysical points that give rise to his view needs itself to be more fully explained. It is hoped, however, that this brief summary will suffice to set the broader context in which those additional doctrines can be explored.

NOTES

An earlier version of this chapter (with the title "Does Morality Need God? The 'Yes' and 'No' Answer of Thomism") was presented at the Evangelical Philosophical Society in Atlanta, Georgia, on November 18, 2015.

1. I am indebted to Edward Feser for spurring on my interests in this topic with his "Does Morality Depend on God?" (http://edwardfeser.blogspot.com/2011/07/does-morality-depend-on-god.html, accessed November 13, 2015). I owe much of my thinking to his insights, but I do not want to necessarily implicate him in everything I have to say in this chapter.

2. One might argue that these are two issues are really the same since it would be difficult to distinguish morality without objectivity from abject moral relativism or even from moral nihilism.

3. For example, this is the form of the moral argument advanced by William Lane Craig. See http://www.reasonablefaith.org/the-moral-argument-for-god, accessed February 7, 2017. It should become clear that, while I do not repudiate this form of the moral argument, I contend that it collapses vital premises that show how it is that, in one sense, God is not necessary for morality (or morality's objectivity) and, in another sense, God is necessary for morality (or morality's objectivity).

4. Space constraints and purpose do not afford the opportunity to settle the debate over the viability of Aquinas's philosophy and its relevance to Christian thinking in general or to Evangelical Christian thinking in particular. The latter is especially noteworthy. No doubt Evangelical Christians will raise a number of objections stemming from the failings of Aquinas's theology vis-à-vis Evangelical theology. There is no doubt that Aquinas's theology (in certain places) differs significantly from Evangelical thinking and (in certain places) suffers because of it. The question, however, is whether those differences are essential to, are entailed by, or are the grounding for the philosophical doctrines that provide the contours of Aquinas's thinking on morality. In short, I think that they do not. Evacuating the distinctively Roman Catholic theological elements from Aquinas's thinking will not undercut the philosophical elements upon which his thinking on morality is built. For a treatment of how Thomistic philosophy can service Evangelical Christianity in general, see Norman L. Geisler, *Thomas*

Aquinas: An Evangelical Appraisal (Grand Rapids, Mich.: Baker, 1991). For a treatment of how Thomistic philosophy can service Reformed Evangelical Christianity in particular, see Arvin Vos, *Aquinas, Calvin, and Contemporary Protestant Thought: A Critique of Protestant Views on the Thought of Thomas Aquinas* (Washington, D.C.: Christian University Press, 1985).

5. To be fair, not all philosophers who would call themselves Thomists would subscribe to the school of Thomist thought to which I subscribe. Generally speaking, Aquinas's philosophy has variously been labeled as Classical Realism (which connects him with Plato and Aristotle), Moderate Realism (which connects him more specifically to Aristotle), Scholastic Realism (a term I learned from Edward Feser in his "Teleology: A Shopper's Guide," *Philosophia Christi* 12, no. 1 (2010): 142–159, republished *in Neo-Scholastic Essays* [South Bend, Ind.: St. Augustine's Press, 2015], which distinguishes his Christian philosophy from that of Aristotle's), Philosophical Realism, Thomistic Realism, and Thomism. Contemporary Thomism is characterized by several schools of interpretation differing over a number of issues. I would label myself as an existential Thomist (not to be confused with the philosophical movement known as Existentialism). Existential Thomism insists upon a certain understanding of existence (Latin *esse*) and how the primacy of *esse* is the key to understanding the entire metaphysics of Aquinas. The current popularity of existential Thomism in North America is due primarily to the influence of the founder of the Pontifical Institute of Mediaeval Studies, Etienne Gilson. For a look at the life, times, and works of Gilson, see Laurence K. Shook, *Etienne Gilson* (Toronto: Pontifical Institute of Mediaeval Studies, 1984). For a critical study of Gilson's interpretation of Thomas, see John M. Quinn, *The Thomism of Etienne Gilson: A Critical Study* (Villanova, Penn.: Villanova University Press, 1971). For a rejoinder to the responses to Quinn's work together with a defense of Quinn's position, see John D. Beach, "Another Look at the Thomism of Etienne Gilson," *New Scholasticism* 50 (1976): 522–528. For a more thorough examination of the range of interpretations among Thomists (to the end of defending existential Thomism), see John Knasas, *Being and Some Twentieth-Century Thomists* (New York: Fordham University Press, 2003).

6. My take on Aquinas's doctrine of natural law is a fairly common one but is not without its critics. What I have in mind are the current controversies like those generated by the thinking of John Finnis, Joseph Boyle, and Germain Grisze regarding whether and to what extent the metaphysics of Aristotle and Aquinas play into the theory or application of natural law. For example, John Finnis says, "It is simply not true that 'any form of a natural law theory of morals entails the belief that propositions about man's duties and obligations can be inferred from propositions about this nature.' Nor is it true that for Aquinas 'good and evil are concepts analysed and fixed in metaphysics before they are applied in morals'")John Finnis, *Natural Law and Natural Rights* [Oxford: Clarendon, 1980], 33). Here, Finnis is quoting D. J. O'Connor, *Aquinas and Natural Law* (London: Palgrave, 1967), 68 and O'Connor, op. cit., 19. With Robert George entering the discussion, there is now a controversy about the controversy in as much as George argues that their critics have misunderstood them when the critics accuse them of denying that these metaphysical doctrines are the grounding for Aquinas's view of morality and natural law. See Robert P. George, *In Defense of Natural Law*, rev. ed. (Oxford: Oxford University Press, 2001). For a treatment of a salient part of the history of natural law theory, see Pauline C. Westerman, *The Disintegration of Natural Law Theory: Aquinas to Finnis* (Leiden, Netherlands: Brill, 1998). While these controversies are not the topic of my paper, it should become evident on which side of the debates I come down.

7. In a podcast, William Lane Craig responded to me that it is not the case that we do not expect the unbeliever to be baptized (http://www.reasonablefaith.org/is-god-necessary-for-morality). He argued that since we do think that the unbeliever is obligated to believe the Gospel and, further, that anyone who believes the Gospel is obligated to be baptized, it follows that the unbeliever is obligated to be baptized. But Craig is missing a subtlety here. What I am getting at is there are moral obligations that obtain for the Christian as a Christian that do not obtain for the non-Christian as a non-Christian. Clearly there is an obligation for the Christian to be water baptized that does not obtain for the non-Christian in exactly the same way. One is direct (or immediate) and the other is indirect (or mediate). There is a direct moral obligation for the non-Christian to become a Christian and only in that case is there an obligation to be

water baptized. His moral obligation to be water baptized is mediated through his first becoming a Christian. Now contrast this with murder. The prohibition of murder (i.e., the obligation to not murder) obtains for both the Christian and the non-Christian in exactly the same way. It is not the case that the non-Christian is morally obligated to first become a Christian and only in that case is morally obligated not to murder. His obligation is immediate, just like the Christian's. What, then, is the difference between the obligation to be water baptized and the obligation to not murder? Why is the obligation to be water baptized different for the Christian and non-Christian and the obligation to not murder not? My point is that the contours of this difference tracks (in certain relevant ways) the contours of a natural law theory of morality.

8. "As it is written, 'I HAVE MADE YOU A FATHER OF MANY NATIONS' in the presence of Him whom he believed—God, who gives life to the dead and calls those things which do not exist as though they did" (Translation, New King James Version (Nashville: Thomas Nelson Publishers, 1982).

9. *Summa Theologica* (sometimes translated "Theologiae" and hereafter abbreviated as ST), I–II, Q 91, art. 1. Unless otherwise indicated, all translations are from St. Thomas Aquinas, *Summa Theologica: Complete English Edition in Five Volumes*, translated by Fathers of the English Dominican Province (Westminster, Md.: Christian Classics, 1981).

10. ST I–II, Q 91, art. 2.

11. See the section titled "What Is Natural about the Natural Law?" above.

12. ST I–II, Q91, art. 3.

13. David S. Oderberg, *Real Essentialism* (New York: Routledge, 2007), x.

14. Some realists might argue that there is cause for hope for philosophical realism in as much as certain contemporary philosophers are beginning to champion versions of it. In addition to the Oderberg text cited in note 14, one might consider these works as hopeful signs: Edward Feser, ed., *Aristotle and Method and Metaphysics* (Houndmills, U.K.: Palgrave Macmillan, 2013); John Peterson, *Introduction to Scholastic Realism* (New York: Peter Lang, 1999). In addition, many contemporary Thomists are celebrating the works of Edward Feser, including *Aquinas: A Beginner's Guide* (Oxford: Oneword, 2010); *Scholastic Metaphysics: A Contemporary Introduction* (Piscataway, N.J.: Transaction Publishers, 2014); and *Neo-Scholastic Essays* (South Bend, Ind.: St. Augustine's Press, 2015), as well as his prolific blogging at http://edwardfeser.blogspot.com. Historically, of course, there are numerous works championing Thomistic realism. See my bibliography at www.richardghowe.com/index_htm_files/BibliographyonClassicalPhilosophy.pdf.

15. Feser, *Aquinas*, 174.

16. The most important innovations are Aquinas's notion of existence (*esse*) and his notion of the essence/existence distinction. He deals with these in works such as *On Being and Essence*, trans. Armand Maurer (Toronto: Pontifical Institute of Medieval Studies, 1968), *Truth*, trans. Robert W. Mulligan, James V. McGlynn, and Robert W. Schmidt, 3 vols. (Indianapolis: Hackett, 1994), *On the Power of God*, trans. English Dominican Fathers (Eugene, Ore.: Wipf and Stock, 2004), and the *Summa Theologiae* (cited in note 10). For a summary of Aquinas's thinking on these notions, see my "Aquinas on Existence and the Essence/Existence Distinction," available at http://richardghowe.com/papers.htm. Important secondary sources include: Dominic Bañez, *The Primacy of Existence in Thomas Aquinas: A Commentary in Thomistic Metaphysics*, trans. by Benjamin S. Llamzon (Chicago: Henry Regnery, 1966); Maurice R. Holloway, *An Introduction to Natural Theology* (New York: Appleton-Century-Crofts, 1959); Gaven Kerr, *Aquinas's Way to God: The Proof in De Ente et Essentia* (Oxford: Oxford University Press, 2015); George P. Klubertanz, *Introduction to the Philosophy of Being* (New York: Appleton Century- Crofts, 1955); John Knasas, *Being and Some Twentieth-Century Thomists* (cited in note 6); Fran O'Rourke, *Pseudo-Dionysius and the Metaphysics of Aquinas* (Notre Dame, Ind.: University of Notre Dame Press, 2005); and Joseph Owens, *An Elementary Christian Metaphysics* (Houston, Texas: Center for Thomistic Studies, 1963) and his *An Interpretation of Existence* (Houston, Texas: Center for Thomistic Studies, 1968).

17. I am doing two things here in this unpacking: excluding artifacts and limiting myself to living things.

18. ST, I–II, Q1, art. 1.s.

19. In opting for free will, Aquinas is not taking sides in what we now recognize as the Calvinist/Arminian debate. In Aquinas, there are two ways for an agent to be causally related to an event or a thing. God is the primary cause of the existence (*esse*) of creation, and creatures are secondary causes of things existing in a certain way. It is the difference between causing something to be and causing it to be thus. As such, his notion of free will be somewhat more robust than the notion of free will one might find in that debate.

20. Aristotle says, "The good, therefore, is not some common element answering to one Idea" (*Nicomachean Ethics*, I, 6, 1096b25, trans. W. D. Ross, in Richard McKeon, ed. *The Basic Works of Aristotle* [New York: Random House, 1941], 940). As far as it goes, Aristotle could say nothing else given that he does not have a higher category than form in his metaphysics. Aristotle says, "So, too, there are many senses in which a thing is said to be, but all refer to one starting point" and then goes to connect all things that are said to be to substance. It will take Aquinas's notion of existence (*esse*) and his understanding of the convertibility of "being" and "good" to ultimately make sense of the common notion of the term 'good'. See Jan A. Aertsen, "The Convertibility of Being and Good in St. Thomas Aquinas," *New Scholasticism* 59 (1985): 449–470.

21. Klubertanz, *Introduction to the Philosophy of Being*, 199.

22. This point is continually missed by atheists and general audiences who listen to debates on God and morality. Michael Shermer, after having summarized the moral argument for God thus: "Humans are moral beings and animals are not. Where did we get this moral drive? Through the ultimate moral being—God," goes on to misunderstand the argument by concluding after his analysis, "Apparently you can be good without God." (Michael Shermer, *How We Believe: Science, Skepticism, and the Search for God*, 2nd ed. [New York: Holt Paperbacks, 2000], 98).

23. Fyodor Dostoevskii, *The Brothers Karamozov*, trans. Richard Pevear and Larissa Volokhonsky (San Francisco: North Point, 1990). The translation says, "'But,' I asked, 'how will man be after that? Without God and the future life? It means everything is permitted now, one can do anything?'" (http://infidels.org/library/modern/andrei_volkov/dostoevsky.html, accessed November 13, 2015).

24. Aristotle's god bears little resemblance to the classical Christian God in that he is not personal and not a creator.

25. "But just as A-T versions of the cosmological argument don't entail that natural objects don't have real causal power, so too the Fifth Way does not entail that natural objects don't have inherent teleology. To use the traditional metaphysical jargon, the reality of 'secondary causes' is perfectly compatible with the A-T idea that all natural causes must ultimately at every moment derive their causal power from God" (Feser, "Does Morality Depend on God?"). See also his "Teleology: A Shoppers Guide," in *Neo-Scholastic Essays* (South Bend: St. Augustine's Press, 2015), 28–48.

26. ST I–II, Q90, art. 3, ad. 3. This helps distinguish between what God commands and why God commands it and goes toward answering the false dilemma of *Euthyphro*. As Edward Feser observes, "We need to distinguish the issue of the content of moral obligations from the issue of what give them their obligatory force. Divine command is relevant to the second issue, but not the first" ("God, Obligation, and the Euthyphro Dilemma," http://edwardfeser.blogspot.com/2010/10/god-obligation-and-euthyphro-dilemma.html, accessed November 15, 2015).

27. It is interesting to notice how Aristotle comes up short in trying to explain how humans can still do what they know at one level to be the wrong action. It should remind the Christian of Romans 7. "It is plain, then, that incontinent people must be said to be in a similar condition to men asleep, mad, or drunk" (*Nicomachean Ethics*, VII, 3, 1147a17, 1041).

REFERENCES

Aertsen, J. A. "The Convertibility of Being and Good in St. Thomas Aquinas." *New Scholasticism* 59 (1985).

Aquinas, T. *Summa Theologica: Complete English Edition in Five Volumes*. Translated by Fathers of the English Dominican Province. Westminster, Md.: Christian Classics, 1981.

Aristotle. *Nicomachean Ethics*. In *The Basic Works of Aristotle*, translated by W. D. Ross and edited by Richard McKeon. New York: Random House, 1941.
Bañez, D. *The Primacy of Existence in Thomas Aquinas: A Commentary in Thomistic Metaphysics*. Translated by Benjamin S. Llamzon. Chicago: Henry Regnery, 1966.
Beach, J. D. "Another Look at the Thomism of Etienne Gilson." *New Scholasticism* 50 (1976).
Dostoevskii, F. *The Brothers Karamozov*. Translated by Richard Pevear and Larissa Volokhonsky. San Francisco: North Point, 1990.
Finnis, J. *Natural Law and Natural Rights*. Oxford: Clarendon, 1980.
Feser, E. *Aquinas: A Beginner's Guide*. Oxford: Oneword, 2010.
———, ed. *Aristotle and Method and Metaphysics*. Houndmills, U.K.: Palgrave Macmillan, 2013.
———. *Neo-Scholastic Essays*. South Bend, Ind.: St. Augustine's Press, 2015.
———. *Scholastic Metaphysics: A Contemporary Introduction*. Piscataway, N.J.: Transaction Publishers, 2014.
———. "Teleology: A Shopper's Guide." *Philosophia Christi* 12, no. 1 (2010).
Geisler, N. L. *Thomas Aquinas: An Evangelical Appraisal*. Grand Rapids, Mich.: Baker, 1991.
George, Robert P. *In Defense of Natural Law*, rev. ed. Oxford: Oxford University Press, 2001.
Knasas, J. *Being and Some Twentieth-Century Thomists*. New York: Fordham University Press, 2003.
O'Connor, D. J. *Aquinas and Natural Law*. London: Palgrave, 1967.
O'Rourke, F. *Pseudo-Dionysius and the Metaphysics of Aquinas*. Notre Dame, Ind.: University of Notre Dame Press, 2005.
Oderberg, D. *Real Essentialism*. New York: Routledge, 2007.
Owens, J. *An Elementary Christian Metaphysics*. Houston, Texas: Center for Thomistic Studies, 1963.
Quinn, J. M. *The Thomism of Etienne Gilson: A Critical Study*. Villanova, Penn.: Villanova University Press, 1971.
Shermer, Michael. *How We Believe: Science, Skepticism, and the Search for God*, 2nd ed. New York: Holt Paperbacks, 2000.
Shook, K. L. *Etienne Gilson*. Toronto: Pontifical Institute of Mediaeval Studies, 1984.
Vos, A. *Aquinas, Calvin, and Contemporary Protestant Thought: A Critique of Protestant Views on the Thought of Thomas Aquinas*. Washington, D.C.: Christian University Press, 1985.
Westerman, P. C. *The Disintegration of Natural Law Theory: Aquinas to Finnis*. Leiden, Netherlands: Brill, 1998.

Chapter Eleven

Ethics Needs God

Paul Copan

With the exception of William Lane Craig and John Lennox, Paul Copan is arguably the most active among our theistic contributors on the apologetics circuit. He is particularly well-versed in ethical matters, and his book on faith and morality, Is God a Moral Monster?, *gives straight answers to the questions that have been asked by Christians and non-Christians alike over the conduct of God as He appears in the Old Testament.*

Like William Lane Craig, he defends a version of divine command theory, which, as we have seen, holds that morality can only be valid if it is upheld by divine command. As such, Copan rejects naturalist accounts of morality, just as he rejects the presumption of atheism, that is, the notion that atheism should be the default position when evaluating arguments over the existence of God. He argues that there are good reasons for taking theism to be more "natural" than atheism.

When it comes to morality, like Craig, he defends moral values as objective, having value independently of human interpretation. In particular, like John Lennox, he believes that God has infused human life with intrinsic value, which renders homicide, for example, as much more than just a crime; it is a sin—a transgression against the ultimate authority. That means that moral values are given and are in principle discoverable by all humans who share a universal rational capacity. While he admits the theist's duty to acknowledge the intrinsic value of even the nontheist (and, like Craig, acknowledges that even the atheist can distinguish between right and wrong, as they form part of the same humanity endowed with a God-given capacity for right and wrong), he finds a natural explanation for morality ontologically flawed. (Ontology refers to the study of being, i.e., what is). It is possible to see Copan as responding to Nietzsche's challenge in Beyond Good *and* Evil: *"How could anything originate out of its opposite? For example, truth out of error? or the Will to Truth out of the will to deception? or the generous deed out of selfishness? or the pure sun-bright vision of the wise man out of covetousness? Such genesis is impossible."*[1] *Copan is not afraid of following the argument to its theistic conclusion: "Ontologically, however, a nontheistic metaphysic (that is, the actual ground or basis that makes moral knowledge possible) is inadequate: why think impersonal/physical, valueless processes will produce valuable, rights-bearing persons?"*

To some extent, Copan's argument aligns with Henk Stoker's in the sense that both find a distinct ontological difference between the world of matter and the reasons why humanity matters. For Copan, it is only theism that offers a comprehensive explanation as to the origins of the vocabulary that we normally associate with morality: rights, duties, and, above all, dignity and the priceless value of human life.

—The Editors

Let me briefly clarify what I do and do not defend in this essay. My argument will not advance the following points:

- Objective moral values exist. Both sides here represented assume this.
- Belief in God is required for recognizing moral truths. Properly functioning naturalists, Buddhists, Confucians, and theists know the right thing to do.
- Atheists/nontheists cannot live decently or be kind to others. Indeed, some may exhibit greater moral virtue than some professing theists.
- Atheists/nontheists cannot formulate ethical systems that overlap or mesh with theologically oriented ones.
- Certain Old Testament practices, actions, or regulations are historically and contextually confined and should not be taken as normative and universal. Frequently critiques of theism include inferior moral practices, laws, and actions in the Old Testament—and fall prey to many misunderstandings and misrepresentations. I thoroughly address this topic elsewhere.

What I am arguing is this:

- Theism offers a far more likely context than naturalism/nontheism for affirming objective moral values and duties. Naturalism does not lead us to expect the emergence of human rights and universal benevolence—a point equally applicable to other nontheistic worldviews.
- Many naturalists themselves observe that naturalism's context simply cannot lead us to human rights/dignity and moral duties.
- Theism offers a more plausible context than atheism/nontheism for affirming a cluster of features related to human dignity and moral duties.

- The convergence of contingent human dignity and worth and necessary moral truths makes much more sense in theism than in naturalism.
- *Euthyphro* objections leave theism unscathed and raise their own problems for the naturalistic/nontheistic moral realists.

In general, I shall argue that moral epistemology must be anchored in the metaphysical resources of theism to provide the most plausible context to account for objective moral values.

PRELIMINARIES ON NATURALISTIC MORAL REALISM

The leading atheist thinker, Louise Antony, repudiates as mercenary all ethical actions and attitudes motivated by fear of judgment or reward from God. God is morally superfluous. Antony's moral atheism is the "perfect piety."

In like manner, naturalist Erik Wielenberg claims that objective morality's ontological and epistemological foundation consists of certain brute ethical facts: they "have no explanation outside of themselves; no further facts make them true" (ontological), and we can know these brute ethical facts immediately without inferring them from other known facts (epistemological). Necessary moral truths didn't evolve with humanity but are "part of the furniture of the universe." They "constitute the ethical background of every possible universe," creating the framework for assessing the actions of any moral agent (whether human or divine). On Wielenberg's nontheistic, nonnatural moral realism, morality cannot be called "natural" since, like beauty, it supervenes on certain natural properties under certain conditions, though it is not reducible to these natural properties.

THEISM: THE MORE NATURAL SETTING FOR OBJECTIVE MORAL VALUES

Finding atheists who think God and objective morality stand or fall together is quite easy, and naturalistic moral realists should take note. Here's a sampling:

- Jean-Paul Sartre: "It [is] very distressing that God does not exist, because all possibility of finding values in a heaven of ideas disappears along with Him."[2]
- Bertrand Russell rejected moral realism and retained the depressing view that humanity with all its achievements is nothing but the outcome of accidental collocations of atoms; thus, he held, they must safely build their lives on the firm foundation of unyielding despair.

- J. L. Mackie: "Moral properties constitute so odd a cluster of properties and relations that they are most unlikely to have arisen in the ordinary course of events without an all-powerful god to create them."[3]
- Richard Dawkins concludes that a universe of "just electrons and selfish genes" would mean "there is, at bottom, no design, no purpose, no evil and no good, nothing but blind pitiless indifference."[4]

Moral values such as human dignity and worth make more sense on theism than naturalism. Why think that value would emerge from valuelessness? Wielenberg claims the "no value from valuelessness" maxim is question begging on the theist's part. (He favors the maxim, "From valuelessness, value sometimes comes.") Yet Wielenberg's maxim is itself terribly question begging. Just ask: what should we expect if naturalism is true? Russell, Sartre, Mackie, and Dawkins are just a few fish in the larger naturalistic pond who recognize naturalism's inability to generate objective values such as universal benevolence and human rights. Theism has no such problem.

As we shall see, the same applies to consciousness, rationality, and free will/personal responsibility. Naturalism itself leads us to question similar question-begging maxims such as "from nonconscious matter, consciousness sometimes comes," "from deterministic processes, free will sometimes comes," and "from nonrational matter, rationality sometimes comes." (In the spirit of Wielenberg, we could add yet another question-begging naturalistic maxim: "From nothing, something may sometimes come." Due to space limitations, however, I cannot elaborate here.)

The worldview favoring a robust moral world is theism, in which a good, rational, supremely aware Creator makes human beings in his image. God's existence secures the existence of genuine value and rights in the contingent world, easily accounting for human dignity, rights, moral responsibility (which includes rationality and free will), and duties. On naturalism, however, why think that morally responsible, valuable beings would be the product of mindless, nonrational, physical, valueless, nonconscious processes? Unlike theism, naturalism's context can't anticipate the emergence of value.

A personal Creator, who makes human persons in the Creator's image, serves as the ontological basis for the existence of objective moral values, moral obligation, human dignity, and rights. Consider: (1) Without the existence of a personal God, no persons would exist at all. God is the sufficient reason for the existence of anything (rather than nothing) at all. And (2) if no persons would exist, then no moral properties would be instantiated or realized in our world. Without this personal God and Creator of other persons, why think moral properties would be instantiated? Moral values—the instantiation of moral properties—and personhood are intertwined: moral properties are instantiated through personhood, which is ontologically rooted in God's personhood. Again, if naturalism is true and the universe is inherently meaningless, we simply should not expect human dignity and rights to emerge. Surely intellectual honesty forces us to admit that human rights and universal benevolence more naturally or fittingly flow from a theistic universe than a naturalistic one.

THEISM'S NATURALNESS VERSUS NATURALISM'S SHOCKING COSMIC COINCIDENCES

Even if such naturalists reject that humans are nothing more than accidental collocations of atoms or molecules in motion, the context problem still persists. Consider the following reasons.

First, a theistic context for human dignity and rights is far more natural and expected than a nontheistic one of valueless molecules producing value. To say that value "sometimes" may emerge from valuelessness (Wielenberg) reflects an ungrounded metaphysical optimism.

Second, the naturalistic moral scenario is indeed a shocking coincidence, unlike the natural connection between a personal, good God's existence and that of morally valuable creatures. Let's assume that moral facts are necessarily part of the universe's furniture and that the beings luckily evolved via a torturous, profoundly contingent series of unguided physical events to be morally constituted and thus obligated to those preexisting facts. It is strange in excelsis and staggeringly coincidental that these moral facts should (a) "just exist" and (b) perfectly correspond to intrinsically valuable beings that happen to emerge so late on the cosmic scene. These moral facts were, somehow, anticipating moral creatures that would evolve and be duty-bound to them! Theism, by contrast, does not lean on such a weak metaphysical reed; rather, it brings together unproblematically two otherwise unconnected features—moral facts (rooted in a divine necessary being's personhood) and moral creatures in whose image they have been made.

Third, objective moral values supervening upon naturalistically evolved, neurologically sophisticated organisms present a problem for the naturalist: why think that our moral awareness/development reflects those preexistent moral facts? After all, we could have developed a contrary morality that would have enhanced survival and reproduction. Michael Ruse offers this counterfactual: instead of evolving from "savannah-dwelling primates," we, like termites, could have evolved needing "to dwell in darkness, eat each other's faeces, and cannibalise the dead." If the latter were the case, we would "extol such acts as beautiful and moral" and "find it morally disgusting to live in the open air, dispose of body waste and bury the dead."[5]

Michael Shermer affirms that our remote ancestors have genetically passed on to us our sense of moral obligation within, and this is (epigenetically) reinforced by group pressure. Ultimately, to ask, "Why should we be moral?" is like asking, "Why should we be hungry or horny?" Yet C. S. Lewis earlier observed that, on naturalism, moral impulses are no more true (or false) "than a vomit or a yawn." Thinking "I ought" is on the same level of "I itch." Indeed, "my impulse to serve posterity is just the same sort of thing as my fondness for cheese" or preferring mild or bitter beer. Naturalism's inability to get beyond descriptions of human behavior and psychology ("is") does not inspire confidence for grounding moral obligation ("ought"). At best, the atheist/naturalist should remain tentative about it—though Antony and Wielenberg somehow confidently push past such moral tentativity.

Atheistic moral realists naively think they can escape Ruse's point that our "sense of right and wrong and a feeling of obligation to be thus governed" is of "biological worth," serves as "an aid to survival," and "has no being beyond this." What if our belief in moral duties is a "corporate illusion fobbed off on us by our genes to get us to cooperate"? The philosopher Elliot Sober rejects the purported claim that ethical beliefs can't be true if they're the product of naturalistic evolution, which commits both the genetic and naturalistic fallacies. That is, it's possible that even if one's beliefs are produced by nonrational mechanisms, this doesn't entail their falsity. Sober misses the bigger point: if our beliefs are accidentally true, being pumped into us by physical and social forces beyond our control, they still do not qualify as "knowledge" (warranted true belief). And we may hold many false beliefs that help us as a species to survive—for example, the belief in intrinsic human rights when we don't in fact possess them.

So naturalism's context doesn't inspire confidence in (a) the emergence of objective moral values; (b) the actual existence of human dignity, duty, and rights (however strongly we are wired to believe in their existence); or (c) the trustworthiness of our belief-forming structures since naturalistic evolution is interested in survival, not truth (more below).

THEISM AND THE REQUISITE FEATURES FOR MORAL BEINGS

Naturalistic moral realists will acknowledge that humans are "accidental, evolved, mortal, and relatively short-lived," but they claim that this, by itself, does not present the total (moral) picture. (This, incidentally, is precisely the point I've just made—namely, the emergence of human rights and moral values is non-question-beggingly anticipated by theism, not naturalism.) Such naturalistic thinkers commonly point to three key features or subvening properties on which human dignity and rights supervene: (1) freedom/free will, (2) the ability to reason and discern between right and wrong, and (3) and the capacity of self-awareness or self-consciousness.

A major criticism of naturalistic moral realists is the insouciant and gratuitous assumption that moral values just emerge via supervenience on natural nonmoral properties (such as a sufficiently developed brain and nervous system). The result? Morally valuable, duty-bound, rights-bearing human beings. Note atheist David Brink's parallel: "Assuming materialism is true, mental states supervene on physical states, yet few think that mental states are metaphysically queer." So if the mental supervenience on the physical is such a naturalistic "slam dunk," why not objective moral values? Many nontheists simply fail to take seriously just how gratuitous such assumptions are: why think matter and energy—which lack inherent meaning and purpose—could come close to producing rights-bearing, valuable beings? Theism has no such troubles—just the opposite, as we continue to note below.

Below we discuss a remarkable irony: these aforementioned naturalistic moral realists claim that one (or perhaps some combination) is sufficient to ground the three requisite features of human dignity and worth—the capacity for self-awareness/self-consciousness, reason, and free will. Yet other naturalists quite convincingly argue that naturalism cannot account for these very features on which the naturalistic moral realist hangs her hopes.

Self-Awareness/-Consciousness

Moral beings have the capacity of self-awareness, rising above genetics and environment to consider intentions, varying motivations, and prospective choices. Yet naturalistic philosophers of mind acknowledge that the emergence of (self-)consciousness from nonconscious matter is a huge problem:

- Colin McGinn: "We know that brains are the *de facto* causal basis of consciousness, but we have, it seems, no understanding of how this can be so. It strikes us as miraculous, eerie, even faintly comic."[6]
- Geoffrey Madell: "The emergence of consciousness, then is a mystery, and one to which materialism signally fails to provide an answer."[7]
- David Papineau: As to why consciousness emerges in certain cases, "to this question physicalists 'theories of consciousness' seem to provide no answer."[8]

In contrast to theism (which affirms a supremely self-aware being), naturalism's resources have no predictable room for (self-)consciousness. Strike one!

Reason

Moral beings have the capacity to take and reflect on alternative moral paths and make moral judgments. Now while the emergence of creaturely rationality in the context of a rational God makes sense, naturalistic evolution, in contrast, is interested in survival, not truth. That is, we may form many false survival-enhancing beliefs such as "humans are morally responsible" or "humans have dignity and rights"—a phenomenon that naturalists commonly acknowledge:

- Patricia Churchland: "Boiled down to its essentials, a nervous system enables the organism to succeed in the four F's: feeding, fleeing, fighting, and reproducing. . . . Truth, whatever that is, definitely takes the hindmost."[9]
- Richard Rorty: Truth is "un-Darwinian."[10]
- Michael Ruse: Morality is a "corporate" illusion that has been "fobbed off on us by our genes to get us to cooperate." That is, "we think it has an objective status."[11]

We are left wondering, "Why trust our minds, whose thoughts are the result of mindless molecules affecting other mindless molecules?" How has Ruse escaped this corporate illusionism to which all the rest of us are subject? As we have noted, Ruse's belief turns out to be accidental true belief (which does not qualify as knowledge)—not warranted true belief (which does). The same problem plagues the naturalistic moral realist as well.

The theist does not have to resort to such mental and moral gymnastics. If a trustworthy God has created our noetic structure (not to mention an ordered, biofriendly universe that our minds can study and understand), then we have all the more reason for generally trusting these faculties or capacities rather than constantly doubting their reliability—even if, here and there, we may get things wrong. Indeed, we have been designed to trust our faculties (moral, rational, perceptual), and constantly failing to trust them is a sign of cognitive malfunction. It would be wrongheaded to abandon them.

When it comes to naturalism, we should ask: why should Wielenberg and Antony adopt human dignity and rights over against the views of Ruse and Rorty, whose naturalistic evolutionism entails truth being incidental to survival? Naturalism doesn't inspire confidence here either. Strike two.

The Capacity of Free Will

Naturalistic moral realists commonly claim that humans possess moral responsibility/free will, having "risen above" the genetic determinism of our evolutionary predecessors. Again, this intuition of free will, however strong, is an illusion according to other naturalists:

- William Provine: "Free will as traditionally conceived—the freedom to make uncoerced and unpredictable choices among alternative courses of action—simply does not exist. There is no way the evolutionary process as

currently conceived can produce a being that is truly free to make choices."[12]
- Francis Crick: Our sense of identity and free will is "nothing more than the behavior of a vast assembly of nerve cells and their associated molecules."[13]
- Thomas Nagel: "There is no room for agency in a world of neural impulses, chemical reactions, and bone and muscle movements." Given naturalism, it's hard not to conclude that we're "helpless" and "not responsible" for our actions.
- John Searle: We believe "we could have done something else" and that human freedom is "just a fact of experience." However, "the scientific" approach to reality undermines the notion of a self that could potentially interfere with "the causal order of nature."[14]
- John Bishop: "Our scientific understanding of human behavior seems to be in tension with a presupposition of the ethical stance we adopt toward it."[15]

So the necessary metaphysical requirements for moral beings—(self-)consciousness, rationality, and free will/moral responsibility—are undermined by a naturalistic context of nonconscious matter directed by nonrational and deterministic processes. Value cannot emerge because self-consciousness, rationality, and free will cannot emerge in a naturalistic universe.

What's more, our natural history from the big bang to the bacterium is one without value and with no predictable hope for giving rise to valuable, rights-bearing beings. A universe of electrons and selfish genes has no metaphysical wherewithal to produce beings possessing intrinsic dignity and worth (and thus certain inviolable rights). Naturalistic moral realists Antony, Wielenberg, and Sinnott-Armstrong—wishful thinkers all—latch on to a theistically grounded human dignity and moral freedom, which is certainly understandable; after all, these atheists too have been made in the image of the God they deny. Yet their context leaves us with no metaphysical shred of confidence that value will or could be produced.

According to Ron Bontekoe, naturalism's morally bleak metaphysic undermines human dignity: "Human beings cannot be deserving of a special measure of respect by virtue of their having been created 'in God's image' when they have not been created at all (and there is no God). Thus the traditional conception of human dignity is also undermined in the wake of Darwin." In contrast, a good personal Creator proves to be the more robust, metaphysically rich, less surprising, and less ad hoc context for the emergence of intrinsic dignity and rights.

THE *EUTHYPHRO* QUESTION

Plato's *Euthyphro* dialogue raises the question: "Is what is holy *holy* because the gods approve it, or do they approve it because it is holy?" (10a). In theistic terms, either God's commands are arbitrary (something is good because God commands it—and he could have commanded the opposite) or there must be some autonomous moral standard (which God consults in order to command). Given the abundance of literature rebutting such a notion, it is no mild shock that Antony takes this as an "explicit and vivid" dilemma from which there is no escape.

The theist easily evades this false dilemma; there is a third way: goodness is nonarbitrarily rooted in God's necessarily good personhood (or character), not in divine commands. Antony's mistaken assumption that "good = commanded by God," and therefore God could issue entirely opposite commands, is strange *in excelsis*. Unlike humans, God does not have duties to follow, nor does he need them. Rather, God naturally does what is good because his character is good, loving, and just. Thus it would be strange that God would have duties or be obligated to his own divine commands—particularly when God's personhood is the very source of goodness. Antony incorrectly assumes that William of Ockham's version of the divine command theory is the only game of its kind in town—that God could command, say, torturing babies for fun, and this would become obligatory. Yet to say that there is no good or bad except what God commands (as Antony does) is a gross distortion. While God's commands are relevant to ethics, they do not define or constitute goodness. For instance, God may give commands (say, kosher or planting laws for national Israel) that are not permanently binding, nor is there any reason to think these are inherently good.

What's more, we've seen above that the horns of the *Euthyphro* "dilemma" are not exhaustive; moreover, instead of God's commanding something because it is good (or vice versa), we can speak of God's commanding because he loves us and because he is concerned about maximizing our ultimate well-being. Moreover, for God to command something like torture or rape goes against the very foundation of ethics—namely, God's necessarily good character. To ask, "What if God were to command rape or baby torture?" that would be like saying, "What if one could make a square circle or be a married bachelor?"

True, our moral intuitions are not infallible, even if we get the basics right; they may stand in need of correction. And a wise, all-good God may on rare occasions or in dire conditions command something jarring (e.g., for Abraham to offer up Isaac), which means he will have morally sufficient reasons for doing so (e.g., to test Abraham's faith that God will show himself trustworthy to fulfill his promise, even if it means raising Isaac from the dead). That being said, we do have certain unshakable intuitions that it is always wrong to rape or torture babies for fun, so it would be self-contradictory that a necessarily good God would command such things.

Strangely, Antony's writings do not address what seems a most obvious response to the *Euthyphro*. All human beings have been endowed with value by God (ontology) and thus have the capacity to know what is good (epistemology). God's commands—far from being arbitrary—are in accordance with God's necessarily good personhood. And when God acts, he simply does what is right. And we humans would not know goodness (epistemology) without God's granting us a moral constitution, including rights, reason, and free will (ontology).

More can be said about the *Euthyphro* here:

- If the naturalistic (or nontheistic) moral realist is correct about needing to have some standard external to God, then she herself cannot escape a similar dilemma, mutatis mutandis. We ask naturalistic moral realists like Antony: "Are these moral facts good simply because they are good, or is there an independent standard of goodness to which they conform?" Their argument offers them no actual advantage over theism. If two entities are sufficient to establish a relation (here, between God's personhood and human personhood), inserting yet a third entity—some moral standard independent of God to assess the connection between them—becomes superfluous. The skeptic's demand is unwarranted.

    For instance, atheist Michael Martin thinks that an ideal observer theory (IOT) renders a theistic grounding obsolete. ("Good" is what "an ideal observer would approve under ideal conditions.") Not so fast. For one thing, Roderick Firth, the IOT's founding father, was a theist who claimed that "an ideal observer will be a partial description of God, if God is conceived to be an infallible moral judge." Contra Martin, the theist can easily appropriate the IOT!

    Second, despite Martin's use of the *Euthyphro* against theists, he is hoisted with his own petard, exposing just how innocuous the *Euthyphro* objection really is: if torturing babies for fun is wrong because an ideal observer says so, then is torturing babies for fun wrong because the ideal observer says so, or does the ideal observer say so because torturing babies for fun is wrong? If we use Martin's (and Antony's) logic, we would still have a moral standard independent of the ideal observer—an IIOT!

- The naturalist's query becomes pointless: we must eventually arrive at some self-sufficient, self-explanatory stopping point beyond which the discussion cannot go. Why is this "independent moral standard" any less arbitrary a stopping point than God's own intrinsically good personhood? Why must we bow to the naturalist's insistence on some independent moral standard when God's moral goodness would suffice? Naturalist Wielenberg's invoking a nonnaturalistic realm (which resembles Platon-

ism) is already taking a transcendental step toward theism, conceding that something more than naturalism is required to ground moral realism.
- The necessity of moral truths does not diminish their need for grounding in a necessary personal God, who exists in all possible worlds. God, who necessarily exists in all possible worlds, is the source of all necessary moral truths that stand in asymmetrical relation to God's necessity. This can be compared to the necessary truth "consciousness necessarily exists"; this is precisely because God—a supremely self-aware being—exists in all possible worlds. God's existence also means that objective moral values are necessary—that is, they exist in all possible worlds precisely because a supremely good God exists all possible worlds. That is, God's existence is explanatorily prior to these moral values. The same can be said about logical or mathematical truths as well.
- God, who is essentially perfect, does not have obligations to some external moral standard; God simply acts, and naturally, it is good. An intrinsically good God is not duty-bound; rather than having moral obligations, he simply expresses the goodness of his personhood in his acts and commands. As H. O. Mounce suggests, "God cannot hold anything good unless he already values it. But then his valuing cannot depend on its being good." If the creator were evil, then we would not be obligated to obey or worship such a being since such a being would not be maximally excellent and thus worthy of worship ("worth-ship").
- Though God's personhood grounds his commands, they still play an important role. Divine commands may partially serve as guidance in particular instances where there would otherwise be no moral obligation (e.g., certain food, planting, or clothing laws to distinguish Old Testament Israel from surrounding nations). Furthermore, divine commands may strengthen or reinforce moral motivation. For example, sometimes we know what to do intellectually, but the gentle prodding or even strong rebuke of a caring friend may be just what we need to spur us into action. Beyond this, we know that commands often add greater weight or seriousness to moral obligations of which we are aware. We may be familiar with general ethical principles, but the command of a genuine moral authority often assists in our taking our duties more seriously than if we merely had a theoretical knowledge of general moral principles.
- The acceptance of objective values assumes a kind of ultimate goal or design plan for human beings. This would make little sense given naturalism (since we are the products of mindless, unguided processes), but it makes much sense given theism, which presumes a design plan or ideal standard for human beings.
- Even if there were some moral standard independent of God, it still would fail to account for how humans, given their valueless, unguided, deterministic, materialistic origins, came to be morally valuable, rights-bearing,

morally responsible beings. What's more, this transcendent moral standard assumed by Antony and Wielenberg still can't account for the human moral freedom required to submit to such a standard given a materialistic, deterministic world.

- The *Euthyphro* dilemma fails to distinguish between moral good (an axiological category) and moral right (a deontic category, denoting obligation/duty). For example, giving all one's possessions to the poor may be good, but this doesn't entail a universal obligation. This good–right distinction enables us to determine what good (supererogatory) actions rise above the obligatory. Again, what is good is not identical to what God commands, but what God commands will ultimately be good. And, as we've seen, God is necessarily good; so if he on rare occasion commands something jarring or morally difficult, he will do so with morally sufficient reason.

Not only does the *Euthyphro* dilemma pose no threat to a theistically rooted ethic, but a similarly configured argument (as in the first bullet point above) can be launched against the naturalistic moral realist who is convinced of the *Euthyphro*'s efficacy.

One final point: the naturalistically explicable impulse of self-sacrifice for one's own offspring or even species makes no rational sense—a sharp contrast to the theistic worldview. On naturalism, why should a person surrender his momentary existence—all the existence he will ever have—so that his offspring may survive? Or why endure lifelong imprisonment in a Communist jail for refusing to reveal the whereabouts of an innocent who is an "enemy of the state"? Accounting for self-sacrificial acts or virtuous acts that bring lifelong hardship and anguish or even death is problematic for naturalistic moral realists.

On the other hand, theism assures us that God does not demand of us more than we can bear and that God will guarantee that a morally virtuous life and even self-sacrifice are not in vain if one's trust is in God. In this case, God's existence guarantees that a moral life and happiness will ultimately come together. Naturalists must concede that, in their view, virtue will frequently go unrewarded and that the unjust and wicked will frequently "get away with murder." In contrast, the true believer is motivated by dedication to a personal being, not to mere abstract facts and duties. Ultimate happiness is not found in some crass material or hedonistic reward, as critics commonly charge, but in the enjoyment of the company of the God whom the believer has served and in whose personhood is the very standard of goodness. Thus the believer can and should be good for goodness' sake. That is, to pursue virtue for its own sake since God's personhood itself is the fount of goodness and God is also the guarantor that a life rightly lived will not, in the final day, be ignored. Atheism is not perfect piety.

NOTES

1. Friedrich Nietzsche, *Beyond Good and Evil*, edited and translated by Judith Norman (Cambridge: Cambridge University Press, 2002), section 2, 5.
2. J. P. Sartre, *Existentialism and Human Emotion*, translated by Bruno Ferchtman (New York: Citadel, 1985), 15.
3. J. L. Mackie, *The Miracle of Theism* (Oxford: Oxford University Press, 1983), 117.
4. Richard Dawkins, *River Out of Eden* (London: Weidenfeld and Nicholson, 2013), 5.
5. Michael Ruse and E. O. Wilson, "The Evolution of Ethics," in *Religion and the Natural Sciences: The Range of Engagement*, ed. James E. Huchingson (Orlando: Harcourt Brace, 1993), 311.
6. Colin McGinn, "Can We Solve the Mind-Body Problem?" *New Series* 98, no. 391 (July 1989).
7. Geoffrey Madell, *Mind and Materialism* (Edinburgh: Edinburgh University Press, 1988), 141
8. David Papineau, *Philosophical Naturalism* (Oxford: Blackwell, 1993), 119.
9. Patricia Churchland, "Epistemology in the Age of Neuroscience," *Journal of Philosophy* 84 (October 1987): 548–549.
10. Richard Rorty, "Untruth and Consequences," *New Republic* (July 31, 1995): 32–36.
11. Ruse and Wilson, "The Evolution of Ethics," 310–311.
12. W. Provine, "Evolution and the Foundation of Ethics," *Marine Biological Laboratory Science* 3 (1988): 27–28.
13. Francis Crick, *The Astonishing Hypothesis: The Scientific Search for the Soul* (New York: Charles Scribner's Sons, 1994), 3.
14. John Searle, *Minds, Brains, and Science* (Cambridge, Mass.: Harvard University Press, 1986 reprint), 87, 88, 92.
15. J. Bishop, *Natural Agency* (Cambridge: Cambridge University Press, 1989), 1.

REFERENCES

Baggett, D., and J. L. Walls. *Good God: The Theistic Foundations of Morality*. New York: Oxford University Press, 2011.
Copan, P. "God, Naturalism, and the Foundations of Morality." In *The Future of Atheism: Alister McGrath and Daniel Dennett in Dialogue*, edited by R. Stewart, 141–162. Minneapolis: Fortress Press, 2008.
Churchland, P. "Epistemology in the Age of Neuroscience." *Journal of Philosophy* 84 (October 1987): 548–549.
Crick, F. *The Astonishing Hypothesis: The Scientific Search for the Soul*. New York: Charles Scribner's Sons, 1994.
Hare, J. M. *God and Morality: A Philosophical History*. Oxford: Blackwell, 2007.
Linville, M. R. "The Moral Argument." In *The Blackwell Companion to Natural Theology*, edited by W. L. Craig and J. P. Moreland, 391–448. Oxford: Blackwell, 2009.
Mackie, J. L. *The Miracle of Theism*. Oxford: Oxford University Press, 1983.
Madell, G. *Mind and Materialism*. Edinburgh: Edinburgh University Press, 1988.
McGinn, C. "Can We Solve the Mind-Body Problem?" *New Series* 98, no. 391 (July 1989).
Papineau, D. *Philosophical Naturalism*. Oxford: Blackwell, 1993.
Ruse, M., and E. O. Wilson. "The Evolution of Ethics." In *Religion and the Natural Sciences: The Range of Engagement*, ed. James E. Huchingson. Orlando: Harcourt Brace, 1993.
Searle, J. *Minds, Brains, and Science*. Cambridge, Mass.: Harvard University Press, 1986 reprint.
Smith, C. "Does Naturalism Warrant a Moral Belief in Universal Benevolence and Human Rights?" In *The Believing Primate: Scientific, Philosophical, and Theological Reflections on the Origin of Religion*, edited by J. Schloss and M. J. Murray, 292–316. Oxford: Oxford University Press, 2009.

Chapter Twelve

Biologizing Ethics and the Destruction of Morality

John Lennox

Hitherto, we have mostly considered the question of morality as an abstract problem. This is the domain of thought that the Greeks called theoria, *from* theoros *(θεωρός), "spectator," from* thea *(θέα) "a view"* + horan *(ὁρᾶν) "to see"—the origin of our word* theory. *It expressed the state of being a spectator. Philosophy is usually considered to be a theoretical activity and is associated with assuming a position of critical distance from a phenomenon or situation, in order to think or speculate ("looking with the eyes of the mind"). However, the question of morality is an immediate and everyday problem with a decidedly practical dimension. The opposite of* theoria *is* praxis *(πρᾶξις), a Greek term for doing. While achieving wisdom is the aim of theoretical activity, the virtue applicable to the domain of life as it is lived is* phronesis, *Aristotle's notion of practical wisdom. Practical wisdom involves judgment and the ability to consider real-life problems.*

Questions like euthanasia, abortion, and capital punishment are real-life problems that demand the exercise of judgment. John Lennox's contribution considers the immediate question of the sanctity of life. He argues that a naturalistic ontology (especially in utilitarian form) has serious implications for what we consider to be the one unassailable foundation of morality: life itself. The sanctity-of-life principle is coming under increasing attack by utilitarian ethicists like Peter Singer and Jonathan Glover. In this text, he analyzes the internal logic of some of their arguments in an attempt to demonstrate that far from leading to a defensible ethical position, the basic stance of utilitarianism, together with the attempt to biologize ethics that is often associated with that utilitarianism, proves logically incoherent. This incoherence results from the fact that the naturalistic worldview shared by many utilitarians and sociobiologists leads inevitably to argumentation that depends on the move from "is" to "ought," whose illegitimacy was famously pointed out by Hume and Moore. He analyzes that "naturalistic fallacy" with special regard to utilitarian thinking. Lennox shows that, far from yielding a new and more robust ethic, the worldview behind the utilitarian stance leaves no basis for any defensible ethic whatsoever: more than that, it leaves no basis for the very rational thought that is the sine qua non of all ethical discourse.

The very influential evolutionary biologist E. O. Wilson begins and ends his famous book Sociobiology *with the claim that ethics must be "biologicized," that is, subsumed under biology: "What . . . made the hypothalamus and the limbic system? They evolved by natural selection. That simple biological statement must be pursued to explain ethics and ethical philosophers, if not epistemology and epistemologists, at all depths. . . . The time has come for ethics to be removed temporarily from the hands of philosophers and be biologicized."*[1]

Now in the hands of Wilson, Dawkins, and others, this attempt to biologicize ethics, in the sense of attempting an exhaustive explanation in biological terms of the existence of a moral dimension in human beings and in the sense of giving direction to morality itself, has considerable influence, and we must therefore investigate it in due course below.

—The Editors

REDUCTIONISM

In order to study something, especially if it is complex, scientists often divide it up into separate parts or aspects and, by doing so, "reduce" it to simpler components that are individually easier to investigate. This kind of reductionism, usually called "methodological" or "structural" reductionism, is part of the accepted process of science and has proved extremely effective. It is, however, very important to bear in mind that there may well be (and usually is) more to a given whole than simply what we obtain by adding up all that we have learned from the parts. Studying all the parts of a watch separately will not necessarily enable you to grasp how the complete watch works as an integrated whole (and certainly not enable you to tell the time), and there is more to water than we can readily deduce from a separate investigation of the hydrogen and oxygen of which it is composed. Even at this level, caution must be exercised, as Sir Karl Popper indicated: "There is almost always an unresolved residue left by even the most successful attempts at reduction."[2]

Besides methodological reductionism, there are two further important types of reductionism: "epistemological" and "ontological," which are of direct relevance to our argument here. Epistemological reductionism is the view that higher-level phenomena can be explained by processes at a lower level. The strong epistemological reductionist thesis is that such "bottom-up" explanations can always be achieved without remainder. That is, chemistry can ultimately be explained by physics, biochemistry by chemistry, biology by biochemistry, psychology by biology, sociology by brain science, and theology by sociology. As Francis Crick puts it: "The ultimate aim of the modern development in biology is, in fact, to explain all biology in terms of physics and chemistry."[3]

This view is shared by Richard Dawkins: "My task is to explain elephants and the world of complex things in terms of the simple things that physicists either understand or are working on."[4] Leaving aside for the moment the very questionable assertion that the subject matter of physics is simple (think of quantum electrodynamics or string theory), the ultimate goal of such reductionism is to reduce all human behavior, our likes and dislikes, the entire mental landscape of our lives, to physics. This materialistic viewpoint is often called "physicalism." But, like the "is to ought" argument, this kind of reductionism is in very serious trouble. Scientist and philosopher Michael Polanyi helps us see why it is intrinsically implausible to expect epistemological reductionism to work in every circumstance.[5] Think of the various levels of process involved in constructing an office building with bricks. First of all, there is the process of extracting the raw materials out of which the bricks have to be made. Then there are the successively higher levels of making the bricks—they do not make themselves; bricklaying—the bricks do not "self-assemble"; designing the building—it does not design itself; and planning the town in which the building is to be built—it does not organize itself.

Each level has its own rules. The laws of physics and chemistry govern the raw material of the bricks; technology prescribes the art of brickmaking; architecture teaches the builders; and the architects are controlled by the town planners. Each level is controlled by the level above. But the reverse is not true. The laws of a higher level cannot be derived from the laws of a lower level, although what can be done at a higher level will, of course, depend on the lower levels. For example, if the bricks are not strong, there will be a limit on the height of the building that can safely be built with them.

Or take another example, literally to hand. Consider the page you are reading just now. It consists of paper imprinted with ink. It is obvious that the physics and chemistry of ink and paper can never, even in principle, tell you anything about the significance of the shapes of the letters on the page; and this has nothing to do with the fact that physics and chemistry are not yet sufficiently advanced to deal with this question. Even if we allow these sciences another one thousand years of development, it will make no difference because the shapes of those letters demand a totally new and higher level of explanation than physics and chemistry are capable of. In fact, complete explanation can only be given in terms of the higher-level concepts of language and authorship, the communication of a message by a person. The ink and paper are carriers of the message, but the message certainly does not emerge automatically from them. Furthermore, when it comes to language itself, there is again a sequence of levels. You cannot derive a vocabulary from phonetics or the grammar of a language from its vocabulary and so forth.

The third type of reductionism is ontological reductionism, which is closely related to epistemological reductionism. A classic example of it is given by Richard Dawkins: "The universe is nothing but a collection of atoms in motion, human beings are simply machines for propagating DNA, and the propagation of DNA is a self-sustaining process. It is every living object's sole reason for living."[6]

The words "nothing but," "sole," or "simply" are the tell-tale signature of ontological reductionist thinking. If we remove these words, we are usually left with something unobjectionable. The universe certainly is a collection of atoms, and human beings do propagate DNA. Both of these statements are statements of science. But immediately after we add the words "nothing but," the statements go beyond science and become expressions of materialistic or naturalistic belief. The question is: do the statements remain true when we add those tell-tale words? Is there nothing more to the universe and life than that?

The late Nobel prize winner Francis Crick states: "You, your joys and your sorrows, your memories and ambitions, your sense of personal identity and free will, are in fact no more than the behavior of a vast assembly of nerve cells and their associated molecules."[7] If this is so, what shall we think, then, of human love and fear, of concepts like beauty, morality, and truth? Are they meaningless? On Crick's hypothesis, they are—and in that case, one further wonders by what means we would recognize it. But, as Fraser Watts has pointed out, even Crick seems to realize that there must be more to it than this, for he radically modifies his "astonishing" hypothesis by weakening it to the almost innocuous statement "You are largely the behavior of a vast population of neurons." Such a hypothesis ceases to astonish—except, perhaps, for the naïveté of its philosophical content.

Ontological reductionism, then, carried to its logical conclusion, would ask us to believe that a Rembrandt painting is nothing but molecules of paint scattered on canvas. John Polkinghorne comments on the hopeless inadequacy of this view:

> There is more to the world than physics can ever express. One of the fundamental experiences of the scientific life is that of wonder at the beautiful structure of the world. It is the pay-off for all the weary hours of labour

involved in the pursuit of research. Yet in the world described by science, where would that wonder find its lodging? or our experiences of beauty? of moral obligation? of the presence of God? These seem to me to be quite as fundamental as anything we could measure in the laboratory. A world-view which does not take that into account is woefully incomplete.[8]

By far and away the most devastating criticism of ontological reductionism is its self-destructive incoherence. John Polkinghorne describes its program as "ultimately suicidal." He continues:

> If Crick's thesis is true we could never know it. For not only does it relegate our experiences of beauty, moral obligation, and religious encounter to the epiphenomenal scrap-heap. It also destroys rationality. Thought is replaced by electro-chemical neural events.
> Two such events cannot confront each other in rational discourse. They are neither right nor wrong. They simply happen. . . . The very assertions of the reductionist himself are nothing but blips in the neural network of his brain. The world of rational discourse dissolves into the absurd chatter of firing synapses. Quite frankly, that cannot be right and none of us believes it to be so.[9]

Precisely. There is a patent self-contradiction running through all attempts, however sophisticated they may appear, to derive rationality and morality from irrationality. When stripped down to their bare bones, they all seem uncannily like attempts to lift oneself by one's bootstraps or, as suggested above, to construct a perpetual motion machine. After all, it is the use of the human mind that has led people to adopt ontological reductionism, which carries with it the corollary that there is no reason to trust our minds when they tell us anything at all; let alone that reductionism is true.

THE BIOLOGIZING OF ETHICS

The problem of reductionism often occurs in the context of utilitarian thinking, and it is particularly serious when utilitarianism is combined with Darwinism. Utilitarian thinkers like Peter Singer place great store on Darwinism, especially that aspect of it which, they feel, has demonstrated that nothing special attaches to human beings as a species—all species are part of a great continuum. Ironically, for Singer, this has an immediate ethical implication: humanity ought to reject speciesism. However, the contemporary reductionist theory of evolution by which Singer places such great store claims a great deal more than the mere continuity of biological life. It gives to us in the name of science a picture of life that, unfortunately for Singer's theory, is as inimical to the very concept of ethics as are the logical implications of his utilitarianism that we have already derived.

Holmes Rolston gently points out: "Science has made us increasingly competent in knowledge and power, but it has also left us decreasingly confident about right and wrong. The evolutionary past has not been easy to connect with the ethical future. There is no obvious route from biology to ethics—despite the fact that here we are. . . . The genesis of ethics is problematic."[10]

Indeed it is. Yet attempts have been made to try to construct a pathway from biology to ethics. Historically (that is, since Darwin) this has happened in essentially two waves. There was first of all the period of what has come to be thought of as traditional evolutionary ethics, or "Social Darwinism," as it became known. (It can, however, be traced to the work of social progressive Herbert Spencer from 1920 to 1930.) It forms part of the greater Victorian metanarrative of progress and is characterized by a distinct faith in the malleability of the human being through change in his physical circumstances. The second "sociobiological" wave started in the middle of the last century with the molecular biological revolution inaugurated by the discovery of DNA with all its implications for genetics and heredity. By contrast with the first wave, some at least of its major scientific promoters (though not all) insist that the new understanding of the mechanisms of inheritance leaves no room for any idea of progress in which to ground ethics. We shall discuss some of the implications of this below.

SOCIAL DARWINISM

Michael Ruse, who has been unremitting in his efforts to join ethics to biology, describes the essence of traditional evolutionary ethics succinctly as follows: "One ferrets out the nature of the evolutionary process—the mechanism or cause of evolution—and then one transfers it to the human realm, arguing that that which holds as a matter of fact among organisms holds as a matter of obligations among humans."[11] Ruse acknowledges that there is a problem with respect to the unproblematic acceptance by evolutionary ethicists of their doctrine: "Traditional evolutionary ethicists seem to be supremely untroubled by charges of fallacious reasoning. They are even inclined to agree that the move from is to ought is fallacious: save only in this once case!"[12] He is further troubled by their failure to acknowledge their commitment to a doctrine of progress.[13]

We see this attitude in Spencer, Haeckel, Fisher, and Julian Huxley. In that sense, they are humanists and regard human beings with their intellectual powers as evolution's supreme product so far. For them, human beings were very special and, because of their capacities, clearly superior to all nonhuman animals. Singer might well have accused them of speciesism! Ruse sums the position up: "Evolution leads to good and to things of great value. Hence it is the source of our moral obligations." Ruse is ambiguous toward the traditional view—much more needs to be said on this topic.

One of the reasons for the complexity of today's picture is that social Darwinism can hardly be said to have a stellar record, ethically or intellectually. Even G. E. Moore called Spencer's "is to ought" logic a prime example of the naturalistic fallacy.

But aside from logic, the idea of taking what happens in nature and applying it to human societies has had a rather unfortunate history. For example, Darwin himself drew some (very unfortunate) social and ethical implications from the twin principles of "the struggle for survival" and "the survival of the fittest" that he believed were responsible for the moral side of human nature. He and some of his contemporaries thought that they could not only satisfactorily explain the origin of species: they could safely predict the future development of the various races of mankind. It is easy to tell that even if he did not actively condone colonization, he accepted the broad Victorian motif of taking up the White Man's Burden: "At some future period, not very distant as measured by the centuries, the civilized races of man will almost certainly exterminate and replace the savage races throughout the world."[14] And even more politically explicit: "The more civilized so-called Caucasian races have beaten the Turkish hollow in the struggle for existence. Looking to the world at no very distant date, what an endless number of lower races will have been eliminated by the higher civilized races throughout the world."[15]

From a latter-day perspective, the inaccuracy of this view, to say nothing of its nonchalant paternalism, is astonishing. It is unlikely that the "Turkish," the "lower," and "the savage" races, as Darwin deems them, would find evolutionary ethics a solid base for establishing a good life.

The net result of this and other developments (for example, attempts at eugenics) was to discredit the social Darwinist approach so that by 1944 Richard Hofstadter could write: "Such biological ideas as 'the survival of the fittest' . . . are utterly useless in attempting to understand society. . . . The life of man in society . . . [is] not reducible to biology and must be explained in the distinctive terms of cultural analysis."[16]

The discovery of the double helix structure of DNA by Francis Crick and James Watson in Cambridge in 1953 has led a number of thinkers to raise questions about the moral status of the life upheld by DNA. Jacques Monod (the French biochemist, 1910–1953), for example, claims that evolutionary theory leaves us with a universe devoid of ultimate goals and moral duties so that it is impossible to jump from biology to ethics: "The universe is not pregnant with life nor the biosphere with man. . . . Man at last knows that he is alone in the unfeeling immensity of the universe, out of which he emerged only by chance. His destiny is nowhere."[17]

It is clear that if there is no personal Creator responsible for the universe, then the universe and human life are accidental products of impersonal, mindless, and therefore aimless natural processes—what other possibility is there? *Tertium non datur*. And human is no more or less than the ants so easily stepped upon.

The concept of meaning becomes self-contradictory, if not superfluous. One wonders why the truth of evolutionary theory would matter in such a universe. According to Peter Singer, "Life as a whole had no meaning. Life began, as the best available theories tell us, in a chance combination of molecules; it then evolved through random mutations and natural selection. All this just happened; it did not happen for any purpose."[18]

For Jacques Monod the implications for ethics are obvious. We cling to a moribund morality. "The liberal societies of the West still pay lip-service to, and present as a basis for morality a disgusting farrago of Judeo-Christian religiosity, scientific progressivism, belief in the natural rights of man and utilitarian pragmatism." Humanity should accept its status as a fluke of the universe. They "must at last awake out of his millenary dream and discover their total solitude, their fundamental isolation. They must realize that, like a gypsy, they live on the boundary of an alien world; a world that is deaf to their music and as indifferent to their hopes as it is to their suffering and their crimes."[19]

We are clearly dealing here with a punishing form of materialistic reductionism that views human beings as nothing but the sum total of their genes. The logical implication, then, is that morality must be based on the genes, though apparently, the prime, indeed the single, purpose of the genes is not to perpetuate but to reproduce themselves; a strategy is written into the genetic code in every cell in our bodies and brains. Generations of human beings are merely machines or vehicles for reproducing what Dawkins calls "selfish genes."

But if a person is nothing but his/her genes, and these genes control his/her moral behavior, how could he/she ever be blamed for doing wrong or praised for doing right? In any case, what sense would that make if the concept of morality is a genetically induced illusion? One cannot resist the temptation to say that it is a very strange kind of morality that is founded on such an immoral ploy as deception by an illusion to get our cooperation! That would be nothing but biological Machiavellianism. And why stop there: what reason is there then to think that this theory is not itself a genetically generated illusion?

Richard Dawkins nonetheless scrambles to rescue some semblance of a basis for morality (in this case altruism—see below) by saying that, even though humanity is nothing but its genes, we can somehow rebel against our genes when they would lead us astray. But astray from what? And whence this agency? "We are built as gene machines . . . but we have the power to turn against our creators. We, alone on earth, can rebel against the tyranny of the selfish replicators."[20] Dawkins at the beginning of his book says: "We are survival machines—robot vehicles blindly programmed to preserve the selfish molecules known as genes."[21] But then he appears to withdraw from this position in the final chapter of the book: "For an understanding of modern man, we must begin by throwing out the gene as the sole basis of our ideas on evolution."[22] Precisely! So his main message is to give permission to rebel again tyranny! But drawing upon which genetic material? And from where are we to draw this inspiration? The attempt to derive morality from genes is reminiscent of the attempts to derive morality from instinct—after all, on Dawkins's theory, instinct is presumably genetically determined—and it fails for the same reason. Consider the oft-quoted statement by Dawkins:

> In a universe of blind physical forces and genetic replication, some people are going to get hurt, other people are going to get lucky and you won't find any rhyme or reason in it, nor any justice. The universe we observe has precisely the properties we should expect if there is, at the bottom, no design, no purpose, no evil and no good. Nothing but blind, pitiless, indifference. DNA neither knows nor cares. DNA just is. And we dance to its music.[23]

If that is so, then we are left with no other option than to say that the architects of genocide in the killing fields of Cambodia, Rwanda, and Sudan were likewise simply carrying out their own built-in genetic programs. If it is so, then none of us can help being what some people misguidedly call morally evil; indeed, the very categories of good and evil becomes amorphous and disappear. This is pure nihilism. It is not easy to see what moral responsibility could mean in a population of biologically preprogrammed robot.[24]

Nor is it easy to deduce any kind of humanistic hope from such a view, a point which John Gray is at pains to make. He finds it ironic that Monod, in spite of his radical materialistic interpretation of life as written in the genes, also espouses the idea that humanity is a uniquely privileged species: "Like many others, Monod runs together two irreconcilable philosophies—humanism and naturalism. Darwin's theory shows the truth of naturalism: we are animals like any other; our fate and that of the rest of life on Earth are the same. Yet, in an irony all the more exquisite because no one has noticed it, Darwinism is now the central prop of the humanist faith that we can transcend our animal natures and rule the Earth."[25]

But then there is another delicate irony that Gray himself appears not to have noticed. His philosophy, he admits, undermines truth: "Modern humanism is the faith that through science humankind can know the truth—and so be free. But if Darwin's theory of natural selection is true [*sic!*] this is impossible. The human mind serves evolutionary success, not truth."[26]

But what about Gray's own mind when it leads him to write of philosophy over the past two hundred years that "it has not given up Christianity's cardinal error—the belief that humans are radically different from other animals"[27] ? One must suppose, according to Gray, that writing this sentence "serves evolutionary success." Well, it certainly would appear to serve the success of evolutionary theory, if it were true. But then Gray has undermined the very concept of the truth and so has removed all reason for us to take him seriously. Logical incoherence reigns once more. Monod's book is entitled *Chance and Necessity*. For Gray it is precisely that chance and necessity that proves that the idea that morality wins out in the end is a pretense. Indeed, for him, morality is very largely a branch of fiction and consists simply of "those prejudices which we inherit partly from Christianity and partly from classical Greek philosophy." What is really the case is: "At bottom we know that nothing can make us proof against fate and chance."[28]

A particular aspect of human social and moral behavior that evolutionary theory has always found difficult to account for is altruism. This is a problem since such behavior would seem to make it harder, not easier, for the race to survive on evolutionary terms. For the sake of the argument, we assume that, since evolution was always working to promote the survival of the species, it might somehow cause human beings to attach a moral significance to acts and practices that promoted the survival of the race. But then we would for the very same reason expect evolution to produce moral aversion to anything that made survival more difficult or less likely.

In light of this, it is very difficult to see how a mindless evolutionary process could explain the deep-seated, ubiquitous moral conviction that we have a duty to support those very people who in the nature of things are most liable to inhibit or even to threaten evolutionary "progress"—the weak, the handicapped, the ill, the aged. Should we support not only those of our own family, tribe, or race but people generally, even though supporting them will involve a serious drain on our resources and make the survival of the race more difficult? To argue that the instinctive desire to survive leads the healthy to support the weak and the ill in the hope that when the healthy themselves become weak and ill, others will support them, is not convincing. Such mutual compassion is highly commendable, but it is definitely not necessary for the survival of the race. If that survival were the sole aim of evolution, as the claim runs, evolution would never produce a sense of moral duty to spend resources on the handicapped, the weak, the ill, and the aged. We have already noted the confusion into which Dawkins is led when he tries to account for altruism by rebellion against the selfish genes.

Sociobiologists led by Wilson nevertheless think that they have found answers to this "the central theoretical problem for socio-biology"[29] by studying the social habits of nonhuman groups of animals and comparing them with the behavior patterns of humans. They start by observing that the idea that "nature is red in tooth and claw" is highly inaccurate and that there are in fact many examples of cooperation that have been noted in animal (and of course human) behavior. Cooperation of one organism with another to serve its own survival interests is called biological altruism, a technical meaning that does not carry moral overtones.

Thus biological altruism is not to be confused with genuine moral altruism. The key question then is: what is the relationship between biological altruism and genuine moral altruism? According to Michael Ruse, "Literal, moral altruism is a major way in which advantageous biological cooperation is achieved," and in order to achieve it, "evolution has filled us full of thoughts about right and wrong, about the need to help our fellows, and so forth."[30]

But this is not an explanation of what morality is or where it comes from. In fact, it would appear from this that Ruse is in essence admitting to failing to ground morality in evolution. Prominent evolutionary biologist Francisco Ayala points out in the same symposium that what Ruse (and Wilson) are saying is that it is "not that the norms of morality can be grounded in biological evolution, but that evolution predisposes us to accept certain moral norms, namely, those that are consistent with the 'objectives' of natural selection."[31]

And, let us not forget, all of this is subsumed under a morality that is an illusion fobbed off on us by our genes. The confusion seems almost complete. What resistance can the authors offer to our applying their own logic to themselves and concluding that their theories are a genetically induced illusion?

The effect of all this is that attempts to ground ethics in biology seem as doomed as the efforts to construct a perpetual motion machine. And yet, in spite of that, the drive to do so is as intense as ever. It is very natural to ask: why?

The answer lies with the nature of the worldview commitment of those making the attempt. A further investigation of the arguments would take us beyond our present remit, and the reader is referred to biologist Denis Alexander for a useful analysis of the empirical and philosophical inadequacies of these arguments from the perspective of a theist who holds to Darwinian theory at the biological level.[32]

We have seen that for much of the history of civilization, the universe and life were regarded as the productions of intelligent divine activity and so expressed purpose and mindfulness. Human beings were moral beings, and God was the norm and guarantee of ethical behavior. However, also since ancient times, there have been those who rejected any divinity and regarded the universe and life to be self-explanatory in purely materialistic terms. They hold that the universe is fundamentally mindless, purposeless, and material. This is, of course, a faith position, every bit as much as theism.

Now, of course, anyone is entitled to hold any faith position, but they may reasonably expect to be challenged to justify it by evidence. And it is just here that we have an irony as great as the one mentioned in the previous section. The discovery on which Crick, Monod, and Dawkins base their bleak materialistic philosophy of the meaninglessness and purposelessness of life is the discovery of DNA. And what is DNA? As is well known, it carries information. It can be thought of as a long tape on which there is an immense string of letters, more than three billion in a human, written in a four-letter chemical language. The sequence of letters contains coded instructions (information) that the cell uses to make proteins. Here is the irony. This information-rich structure together with its extremely complex and sophisticated microminiaturized protein machines and factories is precisely the kind of thing that in any other circumstance would cry out for explanation in terms of intelligent origin; that is, it is no more capable of being reduced to the interplay of chance and necessity operating on the physics and chemistry of matter than the writing that constitutes a letter can be reduced to the physics and chemistry of the paper and ink. Arthur Peacocke writes, "In no way can the concept of 'information,' the concept of conveying a message, be articulated in terms of the concepts of physics and chemistry, even though the latter can be shown to explain how the molecular machinery (DNA, RNA and protein) operates to carry information."[33]

Yet, notwithstanding the fact that both writing on paper and DNA have in common the fact that they encode a "message," those scientists committed to materialistic philosophy, like Crick, Monod, Dawkins, and Singer, insist that the information-carrying properties of DNA must have emerged automatically out of matter by a mindless process. The driving force behind their insistence is obvious. For if, as their materialism holds, matter and energy are all that exists, then it follows logically that matter and energy must possess the inherent potential to organize themselves in such a way that eventually all the complex molecules necessary for life, including DNA, will emerge: there is no other possibility. One is at a loss to see why religion is seen as such a problem: why select one "by-product" of evolution and deem it an obstacle to progress?

Their view is not new, and it is helpful to look at one of its important and powerful antecedents from the ancient world. Benjamin Wiker argues that, in order to understand contemporary materialism and its relationship to biology and ethics, we need to trace it back to the Latin poet Lucretius.[34] The Latin poem written by Lucretius and entitled *De Rerum Natura* ("On the nature of "things"—that is, "On the nature of the physical universe") is a brilliant description of Epicurean thought based on the atomic theory of Leucippus and Democritus. One of the most striking facts about Lucretius's work is that, starting from purely materialistic philosophical assumptions, he develops a theory of evolution that to some extent anticipates Darwin's work in most of its detail (apart from the transmutation of species) by many centuries.

Indeed, and this is the key point, if we only admit matter and energy (and perhaps also the laws of nature), then it is readily seen how Lucretius came to his conclusions—if materialism is true, then a moment's reflection will convince us, as readily as it did the ancient Greeks, that some kind of evolution by mindless processes is the only possibility. The universe and its constituent materials must of necessity have the power to produce life—and they are mindless. Does it really matter, then, which elements we favor in such a mindless universe?

It is difficult to find out why people like Crick, Dawkins, Singer, and Wilson *care* so much as to what their opponents think. They are convinced a priori materialists. Therefore, for them, the only admissible explanation of the origin of ethics is a materialistic one. As Holmes Rolston says: "If evolutionary theory is the only available explanatory category, then scientists can be expected to make a determined effort to cut all evidence to fit it, including ethical evidence."[35] Howard Kaye writes: "What thus makes it possible for biologists to deduce such far-ranging implications from their scientific work is neither the logic of facts nor the illogic of naturalistic and genetic fallacies, but the guiding presence of metaphysical, moral, and social assumptions embedded in their scientific work."[36]

Although we would then be justifiably asked what was responsible for those laws.

Of course, this does not of itself prove that their account of evolution is false, but it shows not only why their interpretation of it is loaded with materialistic philosophy but also why scientific challenges as to whether mindless processes can exhaustively account for the appearance of life on earth tend to be very unwelcome in an academic culture that is dominated by materialism (or its close sibling, naturalism). And not to be open to question because of philosophical prejudice is a very unhealthy intellectual state for any science to find itself in. There are interesting historical precedents for this kind of attitude in academic circles. For example, one of the great shifts in thinking that led to the rise of modern science came when Galileo challenged the Aristotelian methodology of arguing what the universe had to be like from philosophical principles, by actually going and looking at what it was like through his telescope. Aristotle had laid down that the earth was at the center of the universe and from the moon outward all was perfect. Galileo took a look and saw the "blemishes" on the moon formed by craters. It is strange that even today, the pressure of a particular philosophical view can hinder people following scientific evidence when that evidence appears to lead in a direction unacceptable to the philosophy. It is, indeed, more than interesting to observe that, after so many centuries, scientists still fall prey to the kind of thinking that they often ascribe, not always fairly, to those who believe in God. Perhaps one of the most striking contemporary illustrations of this is to be found in the writings of geneticist Richard Lewontin. In a review of Carl Sagan's last book, *The Demon Haunted World: Science as a Candle in the Dark*, the Harvard geneticist Richard Lewontin makes it abundantly clear not only that he is a materialist but that his materialism is held a priori.

Furthermore, not only is his materialism not derived from his science; it is the other way around—that materialism determines the nature of what he conceives science to be:

> Our willingness to accept scientific claims that are against common sense is the key to an understanding of the real struggle between science and the supernatural. We take the side of science in spite of the patent absurdity of some of its constructs . . . in spite of the tolerance of the scientific community for unsubstantiated just-so stories, because we have a prior commitment . . . to materialism. It is not that the methods and institutions of science somehow compel us to accept a material explanation of the phenomenal world but, on the contrary, that we are forced by our a priori adherence to material causes to create an apparatus of investigation and a set of concepts that produce material explanations, no matter how counterintuitive, no matter how mystifying to the uninitiated.[37]

This, ironically, is precisely the attitude that Galileo encountered when, on empirical grounds, he challenged the obscurantist Aristotelianism of his contemporaries. He accused them of being so blinded by their philosophical prejudice that they were not prepared to follow the evidence where it led. And in the parallel contemporary context of Darwinian theory, Holmes Rolston warns: "The ethical evidence might, in fact, be counterevidence to any extrapolation of the theory into this range of human behaviour. . . . There are precursor animal roots, but few will claim that morality is 'nothing but' genetically determined animal behavior."[38]

CONCLUSION

The twin-pronged attack on the sanctity of life doctrine in the name of the philosophy of utilitarianism on the one hand and the science of biology on the other is flawed in each of its prongs for essentially the same reasons: they both involve a (possibly a priori) commitment to materialism (or naturalism) and they fall foul of the naturalistic fallacy. And the problem is that the materialistic worldview not only undermines the sanctity of life doctrine, it also cuts the ground from all meaningful concepts of moral obligation (as distinct from mere prudence) and, what is even more damning, its reductionism is a corrosive acid that, in the end, does not stop before it destroys the very rationality on which those espousing the theory are dependent. In other words, it proves too much and ends up in the self-destruction of logical incoherence. We conclude, therefore, that the attack on the sanctity of life position has failed—that is, in the sense, that the logic of its arguments turn out to be self-contradictory and a self-contradictory argument cannot be a good one. It must therefore be rejected.

There is one final observation to make. If the naturalistic philosophy underlying the attack were true in some objective sense (as its adherents from Crick to Gray are obliged to think), then, setting aside the (apparently insuperable) problems that arise for the existence and nature of the rationality by which we might recognize that circumstance, the attack against the sanctity of life succeeds spectacularly. Not only is life not sacred, nothing is sacred. The category of the sacred has been abolished. Any attempt to impose "moral" limits on anything we undertake will be like trying to use our fingers to block a burst dike—it will be swept away on the incoming tide.

Dostoyevsky saw this long ago as the price we pay for rejecting God. G. E. M. Anscombe likewise argues that the concept of "morally ought" has "no reasonable sense outside a law concept of ethics."[39]

Now, as we have repeatedly seen, many who oppose the notion that life is inherently valuable are atheists. Helga Kuhse grounds her atheism as follows: "Since I believe, however, that G.E. Moore, R.M. Hare, and others have shown conclusively that appeal to authority—as a form of (super)naturalism—is not a defensible ethical position, I shall set aside any theistic accounts as to why it is wrong to end human life."[40] However, since her resultant naturalistic and utilitarian view not only does not lead to a defensible ethical position but leads, as Dostoyevsky indicates, to the effective abolition of ethics, we are tempted therefore to reverse the position to its polar opposite by parodying Kuhse and saying: "Since it has been conclusively demonstrated by Hume, C. S. Lewis, and others that an appeal to the authority of naturalism does not lead to a defensible ethical position, then we shall set aside any naturalistic accounts of why it is right to terminate human life and proceed to consider the more robust and logically coherent account given by the view that human beings are made in the image of God"! But that would require another essay.

NOTES

1. E. O. Wilson, *Sociobiology* (Cambridge, Mass.: Harvard University Press, 1975), 3, 562.
2. Karl S. Popper, "Scientific Reduction and the Essential Incompleteness of All Science," in *Studies in the Philosophy of Biology, Reduction and Related Problems*, edited by F. J. Ayala and T. Dobzhansky (London: MacMillan 1974), 260.
3. Francis Crick, *Of Molecules and Man* (Seattle: University of Washington Press, 1966), 110.
4. Richard Dawkins, *The Blind Watchmaker* (London: Longman, 1986), 15.
5. Michael Polyani, *The Tacit Dimension* (New York: Doubleday, 1966).
6. Richard Dawkins, *BBC Christmas Lectures Study Guide* (London: BBC, 1991).
7. Francis Crick, *The Astonishing Hypothesis—The Scientific Search for the Soul* (New York: Simon and Schuster, 1994), 3.

8. John Polkinghorne, *One World: The Interaction Between Science and Religion* (New York: Templeton Press, 2007), 72–73.

9. Polkinghorne, *One World*, 92.

10. Holmes Rolston, *Genes, Genesis and God* (Cambridge: Cambridge University Press, 1999), 215.

11. Michael Ruse, *Can a Darwinian Be a Christian?* (Cambridge: Cambridge University Press, 2001), 170.

12. Ruse, *Can a Darwinian Be a Christian?*, 182.

13. See chapter 3 in this book (Eds.).

14. Charles Darwin, *The Descent of Man*, 2nd ed. (New York: A. L. Burt, 1874), 319.

15. Charles Darwin, Letter to W. Graham, July 3, 1881, in *The Life and Letters of Charles Darwin*, vol. I (London: John Murray, 1887).

16. Richard Hofstadter, *Social Darwinism in American Thought*, rev. ed. (Boston: Beacon Press, 1955), 204.

17. Jacques Monod in Paul Davies, *The Eerie Silence* (Boston: Houghton Mifflin Harcourt, 2010), 25.

18. Peter Singer, *Practical Ethics*, 2nd edition (Cambridge: Cambridge University Press, 1993), 331.

19. Jacques Monod, *Chance and Necessity* (London: Collins, 1971), 168.

20. Richard Dawkins, *The Selfish Gene* (Oxford: Oxford University Press, 1976), x.

21. Dawkins, *The Selfish Gene*, ix.

22. Dawkins, *The Selfish Gene*, 20.

23. Richard Dawkins, *River Out of Eden* (New York: Basic Books, 1992), 133.

24. See C. S. Lewis, The *Abolition of Man* (London, Geoffrey Bles, 1940), 28. Steven Rose, who has no quarrel with Dawkins over evolution itself as a biological theory, argues strongly against the reductionism that lies at the heart of Dawkins's genetic determinism. He thinks that it is simply wrong: "I am distressed with the arrogance with which some biologists claim for their—our—discipline explanatory and interventionist powers which it certainly does not possess, and so cavalierly dismiss the counter-evidence" (1997, 276). He goes on to say: "The phenomena of life are always and inexorably simultaneously about nature and nurture, and the phenomena of human existence and experience are always simultaneously biological and social. Adequate explanations must involve both" (op. cit., 279).

25. John Gray, *Straw Dogs* (London: Granta, 2003), 26–31.

26. Gray, *Straw Dogs*, 26.

27. Gray, *Straw Dogs*, 37.

28. Gray, *Straw Dogs*, 107, 109.

29. Wilson, *Sociobiology*, 3.

30. Michael Ruse in Rolston, *Genes, Genesis and God*, 96.

31. Francisco Ayala in Rolston, *Genes, Genesis and God*, 127

32. Denis Alexander, *Rebuilding the Matrix: Science and Faith in the 21st Century* (Oxford: Lion, 2001). For a critique of sociobiology from an evolutionary perspective, see Langdon Gilkey's article in Rolston, *Genes, Genesis and God*, 163ff.

33. Arthur Peacocke, *The Experiment of Life* (Toronto: University of Toronto Press, 1983), 54.

34. Benjamin Wiker, *Moral Darwinism* (Downers Grove, Ill.: Inter-Varsity Press, 2002), 30.

35. Rolston, *Genes, Genesis and God*, 228.

36. Howard Kaye, *The Social Meaning of Modern Biology* (New Brunswick, N.J.: Transaction, 1997), 6.

37. Richard Lewontin, "Billions and Billions of Demons," *New York Review of Books*, January 9, 1997, p. 9.

38. Rolston, *Genes, Genesis and God*, 228.

39. G. E. M. Anscombe, "Modern Moral Philosophy," in *Ethics, Religion and Politics: Collected Philosophical Papers Volume III* (Oxford: Blackwell, 1981), 32.

40. Helga Kuhse, *The Sanctity of Life Doctrine in Medicine: A Critique* (New York: Oxford University Press, 1987), 11–12. Odd that the matter of appeal to biblical authority is settled for Kuhse by an appeal to the authority of some philosophers!

REFERENCES

Alexander, Denis. *Rebuilding the Matrix: Science and Faith in the 21st Century*. Oxford: Lion, 2001.
Anscombe, G. E. M. "Modern Moral Philosophy." In *Ethics, Religion and Politics: Collected Philosophical Papers Volume III*. Oxford: Blackwell, 1981.
Crick, Francis. *The Astonishing Hypothesis—The Scientific Search for the Soul*. New York: Simon and Schuster, 1994.
———. *Of Molecules and Man*. Seattle: University of Washington Press, 1966.
Darwin, Charles. *The Descent of Man*. 2nd ed. New York: A. L. Burt, 1874.
———. Letter to W. Graham, July 3, 1881. In *The Life and Letters of Charles Darwin*, vol. I. London: John Murray, 1887.
Davies, Paul. *The Eerie Silence*. Boston: Houghton Mifflin Harcourt, 2010.
Dawkins, Richard. *BBC Christmas Lectures Study Guide*. London: BBC, 1991.
———. *The Blind Watchmaker*. London: Longman, 1986.
———. *River Out of Eden*. New York: Basic Books, 1992.
———. *The Selfish Gene*. Oxford: Oxford University Press, 1976.
Gray, John. *Straw Dogs*. London: Granta, 2003.
Hofstadter, Richard. *Social Darwinism in American Thought*. Rev. ed. Boston: Beacon Press, 1955.
Kaye, Howard. *The Social Meaning of Modern Biology*. New Brunswick, N.J.: Transaction, 1997.
Kuhse, Helga. *The Sanctity of Life Doctrine in Medicine: A Critique*. New York: Oxford University Press, 1987.
Lewis, C. S. *The Abolition of Man*. London: Geoffrey Bles, 1940.
Lewontin, Richard. "Billions and Billions of Demons." *New York Review of Books*, January 9, 1997.
Monod, Jacques. *Chance and Necessity*. London: Collins, 1971.
Peacocke. Arthur. *The Experiment of Life*. Toronto: University of Toronto Press, 1983.
Polkinghorne, John. *One World: The Interaction Between Science and Religion*. New York: Templeton Press, 2007.
Polyani, M. *The Tacit Dimension*. New York: Doubleday, 1966.
Popper, Karl S. "Scientific Reduction and the Essential Incompleteness of All Science." In *Studies in the Philosophy of Biology, Reduction and Related Problems*, edited by F. J. Ayala and T. Dobzhansky. London: MacMillan, 1974.
Rolston, Holmes. *Genes, Genesis and God*. Cambridge: Cambridge University Press, 1999.
Ruse, Michael. *Can a Darwinian Be a Christian?* Cambridge: Cambridge University Press, 2001.
Singer, Peter. *Practical Ethics*. 2nd edition. Cambridge: Cambridge University Press, 1993.
Wiker, Benjamin. *Moral Darwinism*. Downers Grove, Ill.: Inter-Varsity Press, 2002.
Wilson, E. O. *Sociobiology: The New Synthesis*. Cambridge, Mass.: Harvard University Press, 1975.

Index

Abraham, 58, 59, 61, 63
Adam and Eve, 13
Adams, Robert, 143
Albania, 10
Algoe, Sara, 77
Albert the Great, 147
altruism, 33, 40, 46, 65, 74, 78, 81, 93, 94, 95, 99, 184, 186; basis for morality, 61, 97, 99; reciprocal, 37, 38
Amazon, 13
Anscombe, G. E. M., 189
Antigone, 149
apologetics, 155
Aristotle, 74, 148, 189; acorn-oak tree analogy, 153; *Nicomachean Ethics*, 156
Atran, Scott, 84
atheism, 33, 56, 59, 78, 105, 140; as crime, 60; atheist, 1, 4, 9, 33, 91, 104, 105, 107, 142, 143, 147, 156, 157, 163, 165, 168, 169, 173; new atheism, 83, 84, 105
Ayala, Francisco, 187

baptism, 150
Bentham, Jeremy, 9, 74, 103
Berkeley, Bishop George, 102
Bible, 58, 59, 63, 85, 124, 147, 150; as foundational text, 58; biblical morality, 20, 122, 150; Genesis, 123; and conscience, 128; and evil, 126
blindness, 12
Boehm, Christopher, 82

Brooks, Arthur, 87
Brown, Andrew, 1
Boyer, Pascal, 84
Byron, Lord George Gordon, 93

Categorical Imperative, 44, 46, 47, 55, 101; categorical obligations, 123, 131n5
Chamberlain, Neville, 85
Christianity, 1, 4, 5, 33, 45, 59, 91, 92, 96, 98, 113, 117, 120, 128, 129, 131, 133, 135, 136, 147, 148, 152, 156, 159n7, 160n8, 184; difference from Aristotelianism, 148; foundation of morality, 42
Cicero, 147
Cold War, 2
conscience, 2, 20, 60, 77, 113, 114, 116, 117, 119, 121, 122, 123, 124, 126, 130, 141; and consciousness, 115; and guilt, 115, 116
Copan, Paul, 6, 133
Craig, William Lane, 1, 5, 148
Crick, Francis, 182
Creon, King of Thebes, 149

Damasio, Antonio, 78
Darwin, 3, 21, 33, 34, 35, 50, 53, 54, 80, 81, 85, 91, 96, 106, 108, 171; relation to Kantian idealism, 44; social Darwinism, 35, 182, 183; view of life,

185
Dawkins, Richard, 2, 9, 33, 61, 81, 83, 93, 95, 96, 100, 108, 108n9, 166, 176n9, 178; on altruism, 97, 99; Dawkinites, 102; developing a movement for battle with believers, 84; group selection, 85; own religious orthodoxy, 84, 85; on pain, 92
Dembski, William, 33
Democritus, 188
deontics, 120
deontology, 35, 148
Descartes, René, 5, 22
de Sade, Marquis, 105
de Waal, Frans, 80
Diderot, Denis, 147
dignity, human, 58
double helix. *See* DNA
Dostoyevsky, Fyodor, 134, 140, 156, 189
DNA, 183, 185, 187, 188
Dennett, Daniel, 96, 102
Durkheim, Emile, 81

ego, 17, 18, 21, 22, 24, 41, 96
eternal law, 151
Eternal Reason, 151
ethics, 148; and psychoanalysis, 23. *See also* morality
evolution, 34, 35, 178, 182; evolutionary ethics, 182. *See also* natural selection
Euthyphro dilemma, 60

faith, religious, 1, 4, 11, 33, 57, 59, 62, 113, 133. *See also* Christianity
Feser, Edward, 160n15
flourishing, human, 15
Fukuyama, Francis, 6n2
Freud, Sigmund, 3, 19, 20, 22, 23, 25, 26, 29, 106, 126; *The Interpretation of Dreams*, 18, 19; relationship to Lacan, 17, 20, 22; *Totem and Taboo*, 19
Foucault, Michel, 30, 73

Galileo, Galilei, 189
Gentili, Alberico, 147
Graham, Jesse, 82
gravity, 155
Gray, John, 185
Greeks, 101

God, 1, 5, 11, 12, 34, 43, 44, 55, 75, 82, 84, 88, 108n9, 114, 118, 120, 121, 123, 125, 126, 130, 134, 135, 136, 138, 142, 144, 148, 149, 151, 152, 153, 155, 156, 158, 162, 163, 165, 166, 170, 172, 174, 175, 187, 190, 191; death of, 91; difference from divine and Kantian ethics, 58, 59; Euthyphro dilemma, 60; existence of, 83; fundamental moral laws, 60; unambiguous good, 113

Haeckel, Ernst, 182
Haidt, Joanthan, 4
Hale, Matthew, 147
Harris, Sam, 4, 9, 10, 17, 33, 73, 83, 85, 86, 92; falsification of argument, 105; *The Moral Landscape*, 11; and utilitarianism, 92, 94, 103, 105
Hauser Josh, 80
hedonism, 148
Heidegger, Martin, 92
Henrich, Joe, 82
Hitler, Adolf, 84, 149
Holy Spirit, 157
Homo sapiens, 97
Hooker, Richard, 147
Howe, Richard, 4
Hume, David, 35, 36, 50, 101, 102, 103
Huxley, Aldous, 74
Huxley, Julian, 182

idealism (German), 101
imaginary, Lacanian, 21, 24, 27
incest, 42
Irigaray, Luce, 25

James, William, 80, 143
Johnson, Samuel, 1
Joseph, Craig, 82

Kafkaesque, 130
Kant, Immanuel, 22, 44, 46, 47, 55, 101; caution, 101; grown-up idealist, 57; Kantian, 101, 113
Kay, Howard, 189
King, Martin Luther Jnr, 149
Klubertanz, George, 154
Kohlberg, Lawrence, 78
Kosterski, Joseph, 149

Kristeva, Julia, 26, 30n31
Kuhse, Helga, 189

Lacan, Jacques, 17, 20, 21, 23, 29; origin of ethical values, 23; relationship to Freud, 20, 22, 24; structure of language, 25, 26
Lennox, John, 1, 122, 163
Leowontin, Richard, 189
Leucippus, 188
Lewis, C.S., 117, 167, 191, 192n24
Locke, John, 5, 102
loyalty, 82
Lucetius, 187

Machiavelli, Nicolò, 184
Marx, 1, 74, 96, 99, 113
materialism, 184, 185, 188; material culture, 13
maternal, 27
Middle Ages, 153
Midgley, Mary, 93
Mill, John Stuart, 9, 78, 104, 107, 109n20
mnemotechnics, 97
Monod, Jacques, 183, 184
monotheism, 19, 59, 60, 61
Moore, G.E., 183
morality, psychological foundations of, 82, 83, 187; binding phenomena, 82; moral faculty, innate, 102; moral instinct, 2

natural law, 2, 5, 122, 147, 148, 150, 152, 156, 162; difference from other ethical theories, 148; "natural" in natural law, 151
natural selection, 34, 37, 38, 39
nature, 1, 4, 5, 10, 19, 34, 36, 40, 42, 48, 50, 55, 56, 62, 63, 65, 66, 67, 68, 79, 86, 92, 93, 96, 103, 108, 115, 120, 126, 133, 135, 148, 151, 152, 155, 156, 171, 188
Nazis, 28, 149
Neiman, Susan, 3, 59
Nietzsche, Friedrich, 2, 4, 5, 91, 101; criticism of the English, 101; goal of science, 105; on goals, 106; on morality, 96, 97, 98, 100, 105, 134
non-theist, 138, 164. *See also* atheist
Nosek, Brian, 82

Nuremberg Trials, 149

Oderber, David, 153
Oedipus Rex, 18
Olivier, Bert, 3, 17, 33

pain, 92, 96, 97
Parfit, Derek, 55
Pavlov experiment, 97
Peacocke, Arthur, 187
Pinker, Steven, 96
Plato, 24
providence, divine, 151
psychoanalysis, 18, 21
Putnam, Hilary, 34

real, Lacanian, 21, 23, 24
relativism, 11, 49, 55, 122, 158n2
repression, 18, 21, 23
Rockefeller, John D., 35
Rolston, Holmes, 188
Rose, Steven, 192n24
Ruse, Michael, 1, 3, 18, 95

sacrilege, 82
Sagan, Carl, 189
Salamanca, school of, 147
Sartre, Jean-Paul, 131n5
Saussure, Ferdinand, 23
science, 1, 3, 4, 10, 11, 12, 14, 15, 16, 17, 18, 20, 21, 33, 36, 40, 52n22, 60, 63, 73, 74, 76, 83, 84, 85, 88, 152, 161n22, 164, 178. *See also* nature
sexism, 82
Shelly, Percy Byssche, 93
Singer, Peter, 33, 184
Socrates, 60, 61
Sodom and Gomorrah, 58
Spencer, Herbert, 182
Sperber, Dan, 82
St. Anselm, 135
St. Thomas Aquinas, 147, 151, 152, 157; divine law, 152; goal of life, 152; goodness, 154, 155; natural law theory, 148, 150, 151; *Secunda Via*, 157; *Quinta Via*, 157. *See also* natural law
Stoker, H. G., 131n1, 132
Stoker, Henk, 5, 164
Stone Age, 13

Strauss, Claude-Levi, 23
Suarez, Francisco, 147
Superego, 17
symbolic, Lacanian, 20, 21, 23, 24, 25

taboo, 19, 23
tabula rasa, 102
Taliban, 11
teleology, 152, 153, 157
theism, 2, 19, 37, 121, 133, 135, 138, 140, 163, 164, 165; foundation for dignity, 5, 133; foundation for morality, 134, 136, 142, 143, 165, 166; pre-Darwinian, 37. *See also* Christianity; monotheism

unconscious, 17, 22, 23, 24, 25
utilitarianism, 9, 31, 44, 47, 74, 75, 76n1, 77, 91, 92, 103, 104, 105, 106, 107, 108, 181, 184; difference from deontology and virtue ethics, 148
utility, 148

veiling, compulsory, 12
von Pufendorf, Samuel, 147

Watson, James, 182
Weinberg, Steven, 36, 148
West as political concept, 92
Westminster Catechism, 153
White Man's Burden, 182
Wiker, Benjamin, 188
Williams, George, 85
Wilson, E. O., 74, 79
Wittgenstein, Ludgwig, 34
Wordsworth, William, 147

Zajonc, Robert, 78
Zizek, Slavoj, 24

About the Editors and Contributors

Paul Copan is professor at Palm Beach Atlantic University and holds the endowed Pledger Family Chair of Philosophy and Ethics. He has written and edited more than twenty-five books in the area of philosophy of religion, apologetics, theology, science and religion, and the historicity of Jesus Christ, including, among others, *Is God A Moral Monster?* (2011).

William Lane Craig is a theologian, analytical philosopher, and Christian apologist at Talbot School of Theology (Biola University) and Houston Baptist University. He is the author of more than a hundred publications and has updated the Kalam Cosmological Argument for the existence of God. He also argues for the historical plausibility of the resurrection of Jesus and has debated, among others, Christopher Hitchens, Lawrence Krauss, Louise Anthony, and his fellow contributor Sam Harris.

Jonathan Haidt is professor of ethical leadership at New York University's Stern School of Business, a social psychologist, and the author of *The Righteous Mind: Why Good People Are Divided by Politics and Religion* (2012). His most recent work (with Geoff Lukianoff) is *The Coddling of the American Mind: How Good Intentions and Bad Ideas Are Setting Up a Generation for Failure* (2018).

Sam Harris is the best-selling author of *Letter to a Christian Nation* (2006) and *The Moral Landscape* (2010). He is known (together with Richard Dawkins, Daniel Dennett, and the late Christopher Hitchens) as one of the Four Horsemen of the New Atheist movement.

Richard Howe is professor emeritus at the Southern Evangelical Seminary at Charlotte, North Carolina, with an MA in philosophy from the University of Mississippi and a PhD in philosophy from the University of Arkansas. He is past president of the International Society of Christian Apologetics (ISCA). He is the author of numerous publications on Aquinas, in particular the Second of the Five Ways, and has participated in a variety of debates.

John Lennox is professor of mathematics at Oxford and Fellow in Mathematics at Green Templeton College. He is the author of, among others, *God and Stephen Hawking* and *Gunning for God* (2011) and has debated Richard Dawkins as well as Christopher Hitchens. He has lectured at universities all over the world.

Louise Mabille is the author of *Nietzsche and the Anglo-Saxon Tradition* and *The Rage of Caliban: Nietzsche and Wilde Against Modernity* (2006) as well as numerous articles on Nietzsche and his fellow hermeneuticians of suspicion, Freud and Marx. Her current project focuses on Nietzsche in a secular world.

Susan Neiman is an American moral philosopher. She is the author of, among others, *Evil in Modern Thought: An Alternative History of Philosophy* (2002). She has reflected extensively on the Holocaust and is the director of the Einstein Forum in Potsdam.

Bert Olivier currently works at the Department of Philosophy, Nelson Mandela Metropolitan University and the University of the Free State. His fields of interest include psychoanalysis, poststructuralism, ecological philosophy, and the philosophy of technology, literature, and aesthetics. His current project involves understanding the subject in relation to the hegemony of neoliberalism. He is the author of, among other works, *Philosophy and Psychoanalytic Theory* (2009), and he is a regular contributor to Thought Leader in the *Mail and Guardian*.

Michael Ruse is a British-born philosopher of science who currently teaches at Florida State University. He is the author of more than twenty books on evolution and, among others, coeditor (with Richard J. Richard) of *The Cambridge Companion to Darwin's "The Origin of Species"* (2008). He is well-known for his concept of orthogenesis, presented in *Monad to Man: The Concept of Progress in Evolution* (1996). He is a noted opponent of creation science and intelligent design and the 2014 recipient of the Bertrand Russell award for his work in science and philosophy.

Henk Stoker is a professor of Christian apologetics and ethics at the North-West University's Faculty of Theology in Potchefstroom, South Africa. He is a widely recognized expert on cults and has written several books and articles on a variety of cults and religious groups, solo as well as in conjunction with his master's and PhD students. With postgraduate degrees in philosophy, psychology, and theology, he has also published on deontology and the foundation of ethics, especially Christian ethics.

Steven Weinberg holds the Josey Regenthal Chair in Science at the University of Texas at Austin. He is a Nobel Laureate in physics (together with Abdus Salam and Sheldon Glashow in 1979) for his work on the unification of the weak force and electromagnetic interaction between the elementary particles.